CITY ON
TWO RIVERS

Books by STEPHEN LONGSTREET

The General
Chicago 1860–1919
We All Went to Paris
Yoshiwara
War Cries on Horseback
Young Men of Paris
Canvas Falcons
The Pedlocks
Sporting House
A Treasury of the World's Great Prints
The Real Jazz, Old and New
The Burning Man
Man of Montmartre

CITY ON TWO RIVERS

Profiles of New York— Yesterday and Today

STEPHEN LONGSTREET

Illustrated with the author's drawings
and with old photographs

HAWTHORN BOOKS, INC.
Publishers/NEW YORK

This story of a city
we both love
is
dedicated
to
CHARLES N. HECKELMANN,
who helped so much

CITY ON TWO RIVERS

Copyright © 1975 by Stephen Longstreet. Copyright under International and Pan-American Copyright Conventions. All rights reserved, including the right to reproduce this book or portions thereof in any form, except for the inclusion of brief quotations in a review. All inquiries should be addressed to Hawthorn Books, Inc., 260 Madison Avenue, New York, New York 10016. This book was manufactured in the United States of America and published simultaneously in Canada by Prentice-Hall of Canada, Limited, 1870 Birchmount Road, Scarborough, Ontario.

Library of Congress Catalog Card Number: 74-15647

ISBN: 0-8015-1310-3

1   2   3   4   5   6   7   8   9   10

DESIGN BY S. S. DRATE

Contents

Contents

BOOK SEVEN
The World of Jimmy Walker

BOOK EIGHT
The Depression Thirties

BOOK NINE
The War Years

BOOK TEN
Into the Sixties and Seventies

Acknowledgments

This book has been a long-time project, and it would not have been possible without the family collection of letters and papers that I once borrowed, in addition to scrapbooks and unpublished memoirs of people I have asked to set down their early impressions of the city. Many of these writers have asked to be identified only by first name or initials. The B.R. manuscript of memoirs of a one-time Tammany figure remains, by family request, anonymous. Some of the material in chapter 25 is taken from the memoirs of W. W. Windstaff, to be published by the Southern Illinois University Press, and is included here with their permission.

Like most genre historians, I have been greatly assisted by material in the Library of Congress, The New York Public Library, and the available files of old newspapers. The Ross Collection has been most helpful, as have Rita Norton of the Los Angeles County Library; Helen Wurde-mann of the Los Angeles Art Association, so knowledgeable on the history of modes, manners, and social attitudes; Silvia Roth, who made sense of a much marked-over manuscript; and my friend and editor,

Acknowledgments

Charles N. Heckelmann, whose sharp sense of storytelling has kept the project on the right trail.

There are others, formal historians, who have vetted the material and pointed out historic gold, but who desire to remain mere initials: Thank you, H.K. and E.L. Drawings at the heads of chapters are from my sketchbooks and many are on loan from private collectors. Larger, water-color versions of some of them are at Yale and at Boston University.

Introduction

This tale of an ever-changing city is not meant to be a formal history but, rather, a dramatically highlighted narrative of the sounds and sights and tumult of a volatile metropolis in constant flux.

I was born in New York and had aunts and uncles living there at a time when Mark Twain—in conversation with my grandfather—could still be seen walking down Fifth Avenue in his white linen suit, his stogie lit, his hair in a halo of pale disorder. In the Hotel Chelsea, O. Henry often was to be seen stalling the editor of the *World*, to whom he owed a short story—although he was most likely too full of Tennessee sour mash to write it. Henry James had crossed the Atlantic for a finicky visit to New York, had walked past the genteel housefronts of Washington Square, and then had gone back to the teacups of London. Mabel Dodge, John Reed, Theodore Dreiser, and Sinclair Lewis were the avant-garde of the Village.

◈

As a small boy, riding in horsecars, I felt the first dawning of a hint that New York was not an absolute, not a city settled into one mold with permanent façades and habits.

My mother told me that J. P. Morgan, with a "nose like a ripe tomato," had been pointed out to her as he drove by, and that she had often glimpsed the three Rockefeller children in their knickerbockers going up the Avenue. And that Isadora Duncan, who came for dinner and drank it, and Emma Goldman, who advocated free love, had been visitors.

I do recall that at the tender age of four I was chased off the grass in some city park—where, with a cane made out of an umbrella handle and my father's derby over my ears, I had been imitating Charlie Chaplin, after seeing my first motion picture. I also remember an aunt of mine who awoke screaming the night newsboys yelled their extras about the sinking of the *Titanic*—and I couldn't forget the horror of the electric chair that executed the murderers of a gambler named Rosenthal.

❦

I was a teenager in the mid-1920s, studying art at the Parson's and reading T. S. Eliot's *Waste Land*. For me, a city kid, the twenties didn't roar, they purred by against a background of hilarious laughter: in images of Village studios, 52nd Street speakeasies, Theatre Guild plays, tabloids about Daddy Browning and Peaches, Jimmy Walker (usually described as "dapper"), the first popular glorification of jazz, the Harlem of "Bye Bye Blackbird," the excitement of the "modern" *Vanity Fair*, H. L. Mencken and George Jean Nathan in the green-covered *American Mercury*. I was drawing for *The New Yorker* (as "Henri") and for *Colliers* and the old *Life*.

The thirties were not pleasant, as depression breadlines formed and grown men sold apples on street corners. I was aware then—with a feeling of shock—that the theme of the city was always change—new heroes, new ideas, in everything a striving for the new. There was the Group Theatre, and a whole confusing period when being Marxist was the *in* thing and Union Square on 14th Street followed the Stalinist party line.

In the forties—the war years—New York changed again. I was an editor on *Time* and the first film critic of the *Saturday Review* (*of Literature*, then), under Harrison Smith, and my by-line was Thomas Burton. It was at this time that I decided I would some day write the story of this fascinating and unpredictable city.

❦

I moved to Hollywood in the forties to write the screenplay for the film *The Jolson Story*, then came back to write a play, *High Button Shoes*, which ran for a long time on Broadway.

And again, the city was a different place, a world now of John O'Hara characters and of the first Spanish-speaking families to come up from the Caribbean. There was change, always change, as I began to collect the material that was to go into this book.

❧

I hunted sun in the 1960s, and when I came back in the 1970s I was a stranger. I saw the blacks revolt, the gays escape from the closets, the women's lib leaders make fortunes in royalties and lecture fees. Accepted was the world of Allen Ginsberg, pot, and LSD. The new books I read were in the mood of *The Last Exit to Brooklyn* and *The Godfather*. So my theme of change remained valid.

A visiting British journalist, Peter Schrag, becoming aware of the quickening alterations in our cities, the loss of an identity that had been cherished as permanent, wrote:

> What kind of national identity is there, what sort of Americanism is possible, what sort of reconciliation, if any, is there with the chance that the future is limited, that life is finite, that tragedy and pain are ubiquitous, and that all frontiers are closing? . . . For a nation to exist, it is enough that it have a purpose for the future, even if the purpose remain unfulfilled . . . the problem to reinvent a future.

New York City is a unique personality, continually shifting and altering, becoming in each era a new and enchanting character, but often with agonizing and sinister undertones. It is a contradictory city, having its special virtues and certain personal aspects of social status-seeking, of crimes, glories, and political hanky-panky, which have always fascinated the rest of the nation.

❧

This is a detailed study of the city as it once existed, how it changed, and how its citizens lived and reacted, even during those days of the Draft Riots and the burning of New York, the year of Gettysburg; a city that was, for a short time under George Washington, the capital of a new nation; the city of the Dutch; the Astors in the fur trade; Fulton and his steamboat; the Vanderbilts in shipping; the Goulds and the Fisks in railroads; the Black Friday of the Gold Panic; Tiffany's, too; and the average New Yorker with his pleasures and his sports; Walt Whitman, who wrote odes to the Staten Island ferry; the Jews and the Irish; and always the slums and the crime that Charles Dickens found here.

I have tried to catch the color of the Four Hundred, who were once Society; the era of the Pulitzers, Hearst, Tammany, and the Tweed Gang; the hedonism of Stanford White and Harry Thaw; today's Spanish Harlem; the terrorized city of welfare and muggers—and Lincoln Center; Mike Gold's *Jews Without Money*; the city of F. Scott Fitzgerald and Milt Gross's *Nize Baby*; Babe Ruth, Joe Namath, and Norman Mailer—

with a backward glance at the age of John Held, Jr.'s flappers, Winchell's new journalism, and the beer baron era of Dutch Schultz.

Included, too, are the WPA Federal Theater Project, the rise of new voices, Odets and others; new art forms and new political scandals; the expanding Mafia; the city's many great newspapers, before they began to die; the turmoil of the bebop age of Dizzy and Yardbird, the first beatniks and the New Village; the New York School of Art; Jackson Pollock; the decline of Times Square; the night city and the day city of the "midnight cowboys."

I have told all this mostly through intimate vignettes of the seekers, dreamers, thieves, and sinners—not with dry charts and figures but by recalling the vibrant city of James Baldwin, Jimmy Breslin, and *The French Connection.*

I saw New York, like ancient Troy, being uncovered as not one but half a dozen cities—all with the same name, but all different as to habits, pleasures, costumes, and ideas—yet tied to the same island on two rivers. A great city, with its special images and myths, the dream of nearly every boy and girl west of the Hudson who hopes to conquer it. It is the only city since Balzac's Paris to become such a center of money, power, and pleasure; its facts are stranger than any fiction yet written about it.

❧

Wherever possible, I have gone back to original sources—to letters, memoirs, commission reports, court records, interviews, and to those yellowing pages of now-extinct New York newspapers and periodicals.

I am grateful to other workers in the field, and in the proper place I acknowledge my thanks. I hope I have avoided the traps of nostalgia and have sifted out the myths and legends.

STEPHEN LONGSTREET

BOOK ONE

A Great Place to Visit

1
It Began This Way

When I began to collect the material for this story of New York City, I found that most people had very vague ideas about its discovery and how it was actually settled. In fact, they seemed to know little beyond the schoolbook fact that the Dutch bought Manhattan from the Indians for twenty-four dollars' worth of beads and other trinkets.

Actually the first two European visitors to see the place never even got off their ships. In April 1524 an Italian, Giovanni da Verrazano, hunting the Northwest Passage—the Holy Grail of that era—in the service of Francis I, King of France, sailed his ship, the *Dauphine*, a hundred tonner, into the Lower Bay, below the point where the Verrazano Narrows Bridge was to be erected in the crowded twentieth century.

Gliding upon the waters, he soon encountered a dozen Indian canoes, paddled by feather-topped natives who "came towards us very cheerful . . . showing us where we might come to land most safely."

Verrazano ventured out in a little boat which he had lowered, but then, a storm coming in fast in thick black clouds over the Palisades, he went back aboard his ship, and stood out to deep water.

Like most seekers and greedy adventurers into the New World, Verrazano was affected by the period's Gold Lust Syndrome, and he could not help jotting down in his log that the place was not without "some riches . . . all the hills showing mineral matter in them."

Since the island was very thickly wooded at the time, and he never left the water to take one step on shore, one wonders how he figured out there were riches in minerals.

One of the pleasures of finding a new bit of land was the naming of it. Verrazano called the Upper Bay after the sister of Francis I: Santa Margherita. To please a French duke, he called the Hudson River the Vendôme. As for Manhattan itself, he honored that with the title the king held when heir presumptive: Angoulême.

‌⊷ⓢ⊶

The place was fast becoming popular, for just a year later, in 1525, a Negro, Esteban Gomez, working for King Charles of Spain, sailed westward, and by January 17, 1526, on a gray-green wintry day, he was off the coast of New York on the feast date of St. Anthony. So the ice-choked river, later to become the Hudson, he named San Antonio. Manhattan then had no year-round residents, for it was too cold for even Indian comfort in winter.

Esteban Gomez, seeing no natives and sighting no gold from his ship, also sailed away without going ashore.

It was a long time before any other European eyes saw the place. On September 2, 1609, a square-rigged galiot, commanded by Henry Hudson, came through the fog into the Lower Bay. The ship was the *Half Moon*, a two-masted eight-ton vessel with a slovenly crew of Dutch and English. (Later one of Hudson's crew set him adrift to die on an ice floe).

By the time the sun broke through the morning mist they were moving slowly north, and from the Upper Bay saw the island of Manhattan and a "great Stream," which is today named after Henry Hudson, a 315-mile-long river flowing south to the bay.

Hudson spent days exploring—the first European party to land in New York—greeting natives, who wore fine deerskin, smoked tobacco, and had décor of copper ornaments. The natives were willing to swap magnificent furs of beaver and otter for knives and trade beads.

Hudson tacked the *Half Moon* up the river, reaching a point of what was one day to be Albany. The Hudson in early fall was a magnificent sight. One of his boats proceeded two dozen miles more up the big river and reported it narrowing. Hudson realized this was no Northwest Passage, and hauled about and went down river and out to sea.

By 1610 Dutch seamen and traders were making the run across the Atlantic to Manhattan and some portions of the eastern seacoast, which they named New Netherland. Two live Indians were brought back by one enterprising captain with a load of furs. The exhibition of these bronze-colored natives in Holland excited interest. A business company was formed and ships were outfitted to sail for New Netherland in 1613.

How the island came to be called Manhattan by one of Hudson's sailors we don't know for sure. One theory is that the Indians who hunted there were called the Manhattans, but were members of the Algonquin tribes of the Wappinger branch. Their war cry was *"Woach Woch Ha Ha Hach Woach!"* There are counterclaims that the Dutch named the place —but for what? The red men of Staten Island and Long Island were actually connected with the Delawares, and one of their branches, in what is now called Brooklyn, was named the Canarsie. That name has survived in a stinking canal and as a district.

The Manhattan of these American Indians was about twenty-two square miles, very heavily wooded. It was a game paradise of wild turkeys, geese, ducks, deer, red and gray foxes, bears, wolves, mountain lions (!), chipmunks, weasels, and mink: found along trails that would one day be Park and Fifth avenues—where mink is still popular.

In 1621, to minimize confusion over trading rights, the Dutch West India Company was formed to exploit and regulate trade. Two years later the first true settlers came over in their version of the *Mayflower*—a ship twice as large called the *New Netherland.*

Actually, they were not Dutch, but French-speaking Protestants— people escaping from the Spanish Netherlands and its Holy Inquisition and murder of heretics. They had first gone into what is now Belgium, refugees seeking a place to be left alone. They were poor, and the Dutch West India Company would feed and clothe them in the New World— not for free, of course, but for repayment in product and furs. The settlers had signed on for six years, and could not engage in private trade.

Such were the first New Yorkers. They first settled on Governor's Island (Indian name, Pagganack—"Nut Tree Place") under the walnut and shellbark trees. Horses, cows, sheep, and hogs came in other vessels with more settlers and farm tools.

Manhattan was so wooded it took time to cut some of the timber and clear land. But soon there were actual buildings rising, not grand but practical, in what was to become New York City. Furs were the money-makers: In one year the Dutch Trading Company shipped 700 otter and 4,000 beaver pelts to Holland.

In 1626 Peter Minuit took over as director general of the colony to rule, make laws, and act as the judge in all its legal problems. It was he who bought the island from the Indians in that famous transaction on May 6, 1626. It is doubtful if they were the Indians who actually had the

5

hunting rights to the place, for other Indians lived on the island from time to time. However, there was an ornate legal document, all seals and penmanship. So the site was named New Amsterdam.

Broadway was originally a hunting trail (romantic historians say "war trail"). Its Dutch name was Heere Street (High Street). A farming section at the southern tip of twelve *bouweries* ("farms") was to be called the Bowery.

The company gave away vast tracts of land to those *patroons* ("patrons") who could produce at least fifty grown-up settlers, as civilization moved forward into the wilderness, ignoring the original natives. The average grant in the company's *peken-book* ("account ledger") was sixteen miles of river frontage to each estate. As to the size of land *away* from the river—it extended as far inland as the patron cared to go.

The patroons were usually directors of the trading company. Like Killiaen van Rensselaer, who never left Holland, yet acquired 700,000 acres, in addition to other land 24 by 48 miles on *both* banks of the Hudson. It was his son who came over the ocean to oversee these vast holdings when the old man died.

As values in land and furs skyrocketed and a need arose in Europe to send its poor out of sight, the New World became important. The English felt they had first rights to the place called New Amsterdam. The wisdom of Good Queen Bess made it a rule: Who was first to find a place didn't matter; it was *who* settled it. And Jamestown in Virginia had been settled early, so the eastern coast was all England's. And actually John Cabot had been there first in 1497.

The Dutch sent over a defense force with a new governor, 105 soldiers rimmed in iron, with pikes and muskets—the first military detachment to move into the town.

The soldiers were also sent with orders to stop the smuggling; the mother country didn't want gainful private trade or money-making among its servants and settlers. But smuggling was brisk and almost a proper trade with its own rules and procedures. Smuggling dealt in furs, guns for Indians (twenty beaver pelts a musket), black slaves for planters, and strong liquor by the hogshead and keg.

Occasionally the Dutch tried to tax the Indians and failed. At times there was trouble with the black slaves. The Dutch murdered 700 Indians, and in another massacre the toll was 500. The surviving Indians came asking for a peace treaty; it seemed better than being killed off. And all the time the tribes kept on losing their lands. Just twenty-eight years after the Dutch set up their first real-estate deal for Manhattan, the Canarsie Indian tribe, which held rights to what is now Brooklyn, sold it to the Dutch West India Company.

As for Coney Island, bought in May 1654, the document of sale is still kept in the Brooklyn Hall of Records. It lists the place and the cost as "A Neck of Land . . . an island called Conyne . . . for 15 fathoms of sewas [wampum], two guns, three pounds of [gun] powder." All worth $15 in the money of the time.

The Dutch businessmen, frugal stockholders, were practical people and the directors in Holland expected their shares in the New World to make money. The rule was if blacks or Indians made trouble, dealing with them was to be swift, practical, and—by the records—inhuman.

≈§§≈

The character most people remember from the Dutch hold on New Amsterdam is that legendary figure of fun, Peter Stuyvesant; he of the jolly, loud voice, the peg leg (and there are even some I have found who suspect he wrote "September Song"). The true and fully life-sized image of Stuyvesant is more that of an American Hitler—mean, arrogant, despotic, and with a touch of paranoia. He came out as director general of the colony in 1647, and he at once made it clear he planned to rule with an iron hand.

Stuyvesant, at fifty-five years of age, was a bit weather-beaten and no idealist. A tough soldier, dark of skin, with long, disordered hair when angry, the beak of a hawk for a nose. His left leg was missing, replaced by a wooden peg trimmed in silver. He had lost the limb in a military raid on St. Martins, an island in the Caribbean owned by the Portuguese. Stuyvesant had married a Huguenot blond, greedy as himself, who liked high living, blood-stirring music, and the fashions of the day. The couple were to stay seven years in New Amsterdam, and the director general's task was to make the place pay well.

The settlers didn't care for Peter's idea of how to rule them; they wanted some voice in how the colony was run. The town already had a solid prison and a poorhouse (on Beaver Street). The population of about 11,000 people and 120 houses wanted more, including some cheerful progress.

Privately people grumbled that Peter was stealing part of the tax money they paid. They were irked by his attempts to reform their habits. He was stern with those who got drunk in public, or stabbed or shot each other. Such passions did not produce furs, fish, or company income. It was a drinking town—rum, gin, brandy, and beer. At one time every fourth house was a groggery or rum shop.

Creeks and streams froze crystal-clear in winter, the sleighs were out, and young and old spun about on skates as if replaying scenes from an old Dutch painting. Hunting was good sport and fed the pot, for the

NEW AMSTERDAM'S FIRST DICTATOR
Peter Stuyvesant became director general of the city in 1647. His was a hard
and mean rule. He lined his pockets illegally, a habit of so many of the city's
bosses, even in modern times. (New York Historical Society)

Dutch were heavy eaters. They were also sensual and direct in their pleasuring, delighting in it.

The biggest commercial gift the Dutch passed on to later American industry and to holiday-exploiting merchants was the celebration of the birthday of St. Nicholas, which fell on December 6, usually a crisp snowy day. St. Nick wasn't much of a saint as to fame, or greatness, or even a particularly nasty martyrdom. But the Dutch made him an excuse for gift-giving, celebrating with bowl and plate, and showing the children the birch rods they'd be flogged with if they didn't toe the mark.

Christmas, which was then celebrated as a separate holiday, didn't get much of a play in New Amsterdam. Just how, over the years since then, St. Nicholas and the gift-giving and taking merged with our commercial Christmas season celebration of a sacred birth is not too clear. But every New York shopkeeper, doorman, and janitor and industry in general have been grateful for converting the two unconnected events into profit—when St. Nick became Santa Claus.

The Dutch also celebrated Thanksgiving, at odd dates, however, and not every year. Some official Dutch Thanksgiving fetes in the New World called for lots of wild dancing in the open by men and women. Weaving and gyrating around a huge fire, they drank free beer provided by the town's officials. The cost of beer for one such event was listed on the records as "58 guilders." The authorities felt it was worth it, since that event celebrated a Thanksgiving peace between England and Holland.

New York was destined to have the largest Jewish population in the world. The city's first Jewish settler was Jacob Barsimon, a Dutch Jew who arrived there in July 1654. A few weeks later, after a hard sea trip from Brazil, twenty-seven other Jews came to seek refuge in New Amsterdam. They were from the families of those Jews who went to South America after being expelled by their Catholic majesties from Spain and Portugal. The Church and the Inquisition followed them to Brazil, persecuting them without mercy and processing them by burning at the stake and the torture chamber. The Jews fled South America, leaving behind almost all their holdings. The ship's captain, another Christian, had auctioned off their few remaining belongings to pay for their passage.

The Dutch West India Company decided the Jews should be permitted to settle in New Amsterdam if they were able "to take care of their own poor." Peter Stuyvesant was irked by this and kept the Jews from most trades. They had to exist at first by the trade of slaughtering and butchering cattle. In time they were permitted to buy property, engage in wholesale trade, and enjoy most of the privileges of a citizen, but *not* the right to hold public office.

2
Englishmen in
the Noonday Sun

The Dutch West India Company was sprawled out all over the new world—too thinly, it turned out, with too many managers stealing private fortunes. It was doing so badly that by 1661 the company was bankrupt.

Charles II, meanwhile, had become king of England and was granting charters to Englishmen as owners of parts of America, including most generous rights to some holdings of the Dutch. Among the gifts he made in 1664 to his brother, the Duke of York, were Long Island and the new city of New Amsterdam.

To take possession, a British invasion force of four warships and 450 soldiers was dispatched to the New World. It sighted land and changed course to what is today Coney Island. Colonel Nicolls, commanding the British forces, asked Stuyvesant to surrender. The British sent in their mild terms: Give up and nothing changes except the flag. The citizens, hearing this, decided the terms should be accepted. Stuyvesant was infuriated. He tore up the British offer of fair terms and stomped on it with his wooden leg. He prepared for battle and ordered the city's guns, based at the Battery, to load and aim. Glowing matches were held ready.

A cleric told him, "It's madness. There is no help for us either to the north or to the south, nor in the east, nor in the west. What can our twenty guns do facing the sixty-two which are aimed at us from yonder frigates? Pray do not be the first to shed blood!" (This entire speech is suspect as quoted, but some such argument must have taken place.)

What helped Peter Stuyvesant to make up his wild-tempered mind was a petition drawn up by nearly a hundred of the most important citizens (one was his son) asking him to give up the forty-year-old town to prevent innocent bloodshed.

Peter read and pondered, and a sense of reality and balance returned. He motioned the gunners to put out their matches and the white flag was raised, whereupon Stuyvesant is said to have muttered, "I would rather I was being carried to my grave." The date was August 29, 1664.

The colony and town were at once renamed by its new master New York, in honor of the Duke of York. That Sunday Church of England services were held by the British chaplain. Colonel Richard Nicolls, forty years old, a popular bachelor, well-educated, handsome, appointed by the duke himself as the first British governor, became the city's new ruler.

He ruled over a sort of United Nations, for about 25 percent of the town's population consisted of Finns, Swedes, French, some English and Portuguese, plus blacks imported as slaves from Brazil. To take the people's minds off this sudden change in rule, the next year in New York was enlivened by two trials for witchcraft.

Robert Hall and wife were brought before the court of assizes, for the colony was now run by British rules of law. The couple was accused of bewitching and causing the death of one George Wood and infant child. The jury pondered, decided "there are some suspicions of the evidence of what the woman is charged with, but nothing considerable of value to take away her life." Nicolls wisely had the pair released, "there having been no direct proofs."

Peter Stuyvesant, shipped back to Holland, subsequently returned as a private citizen. In 1672 he died of old age on his Bowery farm, land facing what was later to be the Boston Post Road.

In 1673 the Dutch and British were at war again, and the Dutch, splendid sea fighters, recaptured the city of New York and gave it a new name, New Orange, after the Dutch prince, William of Orange.

But in 1674 there was another peace treaty and the Dutch gave back the town to the English for all time. Also, the town got its final name. Officially it became *New York City*.

◈

For over a hundred years the city of New York, its fine harbor and busy merchants prospered under British rule. It had its depressions and its crises of course. But, in the main, it was given to good living, took shares secretly in private ventures, and did much hard drinking.

The splendid forests were cleaned off Manhattan, windmills spun canvas-covered arms and ground meal. There were lots of windmills and horses and cattle. Tanneries made leather, and stank up the air until they were moved to the city limits. Cloth and furniture were in demand. The distillery was never at rest, consuming grains to turn into strong drink. The farms were producing abundantly, labor was cheap, and black slaves usually docile. The town really became the New York of the legends of Washington Irving; but only if one did not probe too deeply beneath the surface of things.

In 1683 the colony was divided into counties. Manhattan was New York, Brooklyn was Kings, other counties named were Richmond and Queens (for the king's spouse). The Bronx had to wait a long time (until 1914) to become a county. At the same time New York was cut up into wards, and if one was a free man and had property he got voting rights. Each ward could elect an alderman to help run the city and collect and spend money.

In 1689 rebellion and bigotry were responsible for a civil war in New York. The French and Indian conflict was on against the British colonies. The population of New York was 3,500, but only six companies of listless, indifferent militia were left to guard the place while the main military force was away protecting the settlement from the French and Indians.

As a result, a German captain of militia named Jacob Leisler saw a chance to take over New York for God. A sharp businessman, a deacon of the Dutch Church, a rum and gin importer, Leisler refused to pay customs to a Catholic tax collector, Matthew Plowman, as did other merchants.

"No Popery!" was the cry. According to respected historians, James II of England had made a secret deal with Pope Innocent XI "to force Catholicism on the American colonies." Rumor spread the ill-kept secret. Fearful Protestants in New York joined in forcing the governor to turn the forts over to them. Jacob Leisler, suspecting the governor of being loyal to the king and fearing a Catholic invasion of New York was in the offing, turned to a break with England to prevent it.

The colonies saw Catholics as we in our time saw Communists and Nazis—as enemies of freedom and tolerance. To prevent the French Catholics from seizing the colony, the militia captains decided to rule the city themselves.

Certainly Captain Leisler believed that—as a good Protestant—God was on his side, just as the Catholics felt that God—as the Pope's source of power and authority—was on their side.

For two years Captain Leisler was boss and ruler of New York. Spending his fortune (he had married a rich Dutch widow), he organized defenses against the French, who disappointed him by not invading down the Hudson River. (Historians have also wondered why they didn't come.) Leisler became unpopular; he was hissed in the street and things were thrown at him. Citizens wrote England's new rulers, William and Mary, about the bad times under the tyrannical Jacob Leisler.

In 1689 the king and queen sent an expedition to America to take over New York City and get rid of Leisler. The poor man, his mind now all aflame with Popery plots, decided the soldiers were Catholic conspirators sent by King James II in exile. He ordered his militia to fire on the British armed forces, which killed one soldier, and wounded others.

Leisler, defending the world against the Scarlet Woman, remained holed up in his fort and would not listen to reason. He sent his son-in-law out to state he would not give up the fort. The son-in-law, instead of being treated as an emissary, was clapped in irons. The British offered Leisler's soldiers freedom and a promise of no prosecution if they laid down their arms—which they were delighted to do.

Leisler and his close advisors were subsequently tried for treason, murder, firing on the king's armed forces, and destruction of life. After a week's pompous parody of a court of justice, Leisler and seven others were pronounced guilty and sentenced to be hanged.

Six of the convicted were pardoned as senses cooled. Leisler and his son-in-law might also have been freed, but the British commander, who had hesitated to sign their death order, was given a party, made drunk, and a pen put into his hand by Leisler's enemies. The execution order was soon signed.

3
Growing Pains

Early New Yorkers managed to live a full life. There was still plenty of wild country, fairly safe from Indian attack. There were taverns for drinking and feeding. It was a drinking age and a man could become famous as a guzzler. While the martini did not yet exist, mentions of rum, gin, and brandy and of a great intaking of beer in the smoke of grog shops and eating places fill many letters of those days.

It was a mixed population. By 1695 a count showed 175 families were of the Dutch Reform faith, 45 were Dutch Lutheran, 260 Huguenot, 90 Church of England, and 20 families were Jewish. A group outside the firm thumb of the Church of England were Protestants called Dissenters. It all added up to 1,366 families.

Catholic worship was outlawed, but there were a half dozen Catholic families in the city. As for Jesuits and other priests, they were all ordered out by 1700. A fine of 200 pounds could be assessed against anyone hiding a priest. As for divorce, it didn't exist. Only a special act of the legislature could legally separate a man and wife.

The law was as hard on Negro slaves as on Catholics and unsuccessful marriages. In 1711 New York had a thriving slave market on Wall

Street. Every affluent family felt it needed at least six slaves in an age of no plumbing, central heating, or dish washers.

However, all was not harmonious in master and slave relationships. A black woman and an Indian slave were burned at the stake for killing a whole family, including five children. In April 1712 twenty-three blacks began an armed revolt, issuing from an orchard in Maiden Lane fully armed with axes, knives, and guns. Their plan was simple: begin a reign of terror and show the town's thousands of slaves a way to rise up and massacre the white folk. The house of Peter van Tilburgh was set on fire. As the inhabitants rushed to escape from the burning building, nine were murdered, six wounded.

A cannon at the fort sounded the alarm of a slave uprising as the blacks killed two more whites, then fled into the wilderness. Roadblocks were set up to prevent escape from Manhattan, and at dawn soldiers and militia encircled and trapped the Negroes—all but a half dozen who decided to commit suicide rather than face Dutch justice and death.

The slaves were given a trial—a futile gesture. Two were burned alive, one was hanged alive in chains and permitted to starve to death. Others got solid floggings. One black woman was hanged, and a Negro rebel was tied to a wagon wheel and his limbs broken by a heavy hammer. In all, twenty-one black slaves died.

❧

The fashion in dress was from rags to very fine cloth. There were the tow shirts and breeches of the poor, in contrast to the young town dudes called "fribbles," with gold-headed canes, fancy waistcoats, curled wigs. Everyone among the gentry had his wigs, usually worn powdered and brought to a queue in back and tied off with ribbon, and, of course, knee breeches; a must were boots for riding or muddy weather, and silver buckles on one's shoes to show one had prospered, or acted as if one had. The beaver hat was usually still a tricorne. Only the poor farmer or forest hunter would think of wearing trousers.

The patrician woman relied on plenty of whalebone stiffening, and many petticoats worn under a hoop skirt, so she looked like a "frigate under full sail." The very wealthy showed their jewels, and the ability to clothe their women in velvet, silk, satin, lace, and brocade.

❧

William Bradford started the town's first newspaper, the *Gazette*, in 1725. This was two years after he told a seventeen-year-old boy, down from Boston, one Benjamin Franklin, to get out of New York. "My son at Philadelphia has lately lost his principal hand . . . if you go thither, I believe he may employ you." Thus New York lost Franklin.

15

By modern standards the *Gazette* wasn't much of a newspaper. It printed copies of items, already stale, from across the sea, advertising for runaway slaves, and catered to the businessmen by reporting customhouse figures and shipping items.

By 1731, with the population of New York at 9,000, the city's poor still had hardly bothered to learn to read. Even so, two years later Peter Zenger started another newspaper, *The New York Weekly Journal*, which printed such items as: "WHEREAS, the wife of Peter Smith has left his bed and board, the public is cautioned against trusting her, as he will pay no debts of her contracting."

Mr. Smith felt that buying this space could carry a bit more information, so he added: "The best of Garden Seeds sold by the said Peter Smith at the Sign of the Golden Hammer."

Zenger is remembered today—by journalists mostly—for going to jail for the freedom of the press. This was caused by his printing "two scurrilous ballads" about a governor turned rogue—"The accused was tried for printing these items, false, scandalous and seditious."

Newspapers that tried to expose political wrongdoers have never been popular in official circles. When it looked as if Zenger could get no lawyer to defend him, a stranger in town visiting the court stood up to speak. "I am concerned in this case on the part of Mr. Zenger, the defendant. . . . I am Andrew Hamilton."

He was a Philadelphian, the most famous lawyer in the colonies (and the first to be listed as "sharp as a Philadelphia lawyer"). Scottish born and no relative of the yet unborn Alexander Hamilton.

His defense of Zenger and his paper was simple, based on the freedom of the press. "It is not the bare printing and publishing of a paper that will make it libel. The words themself must be libelous . . . or else my client is not guilty."

At this cry for press liberty the chief justice frowned and, sticking to the common-law idea that the more truth told the bigger the libel, ruled, "The law is clear. You cannot justify a libel."

Hamilton knew how to heat up a courtroom, and went to work with a strong counterattack. "The practice of informations for libel is a sword in the hands of a wicked king, and an arrogant coward, to cut down and destroy the innocent." Early Americans without radio, films, or television delighted in oratory. Hamilton said he would leave it to the jury. "It is not the cause of a poor printer, nor of New York alone, which you are now trying. No! . . . the laws of our country have given us a right—the liberty of exposing an opposing arbitrary power . . . by speaking and writing *truth!*"

Hamilton finished with a bow and brought the courtroom to its feet cheering. The jury didn't bother to spend more than a few minutes to bring in the verdict: "Not guilty!"

No wonder Gouverneur Morris, a later statesman of the American Revolution, would write: "The trial of Zenger was the gleam of American freedom—the morning star of that liberty which subsequently revolutionized America."

◆§◈◈

By 1741 the city had no really isolated inhabitants. The population was 10,000, of which 2,000 were slaves under firm control of their masters and the officials. Three slaves found talking together in public could get forty lashes each.

No matter how harsh the rule, slaves still rebelled, and the problem of slave revolts plagued New York. In 1741 there were 154 blacks jailed, accused of trying to burn down New York. Fourteen Negroes were burned alive, eighteen died on the gallows, and seventy-one got shipped to the West Indies sugar cane fields.

But all was not such dramatic town entertainment. Education and higher learning was also coming to New York. In 1754 Kings College (for Hanoverian George II) got its charter, and for ten shillings the college was given land on Broadway near Church Street to erect its buildings. It was the sixth college in the colonies.

George II died and George III came to the throne. It would seem that he was determined to lose the colonies by his imperious actions. In 1765 New York heard of the Stamp Act, a tax on legal documents to support an army of 10,000 Englishmen in their red coats guarding the colonies against the French and Indians pressing in on the borders.

It wasn't that most of New York's 18,000 citizens couldn't afford the tax. The city was full of prosperous merchants and landowners. Their wives had diamonds in their ears, and all fashionable ladies at the many fetes and balls wore imported satins and laces. Books in well-tanned leather were being imported, as well as fine furniture. To have no snuff box in tortoise shell, gold, or mother-of-pearl was like walking hatless out-of-doors. Business was flourishing and smuggling was nearly the major industry, making a mockery of the English Navigation Acts.

In New York the Stamp Act was defied in mass meetings of merchants and the well-to-do to the cheers of the crowds, who preferred gin to tea and had no legal papers to stamp. It was decided British goods would be boycotted until the act was repealed. Americans loved slogans: an early bumper sticker read BETTER TO WEAR A HOMESPUN COAT THAN LOSE OUR LIBERTY. The mob took up the chant, and the underground Sons of Liberty infiltrated the crowds and led the shouting. The stamps were held back from sale, and the city was in rebellion.

The British armed forces in the city's forts waited as people gathered in a mob on the Commons. In the light of torches they hanged the governor in effigy. It seemed too early to go home, so the mob attacked the fort with battering rams. British gunners stood ready to fire their cannon into the massed Americans. But someone in the mob had the sense to see that a massacre was in the making, so all turned away from the cannon; it seemed better to wreck the homes of the Stamp Act officials. It is clear that firing on the mob would have brought on a civil war in New York. To ease pressure the stamps were turned over to city officials and locked up in City Hall.

The boycott of British goods continued, and it became the chic fashion to wear homespun, just as college students went into Levi's and blue denim as a mode in the 1970s. The boycott did great damage to British business as other towns of the American colonies joined in.

When New Yorkers got the news that the Stamp Act had been repealed, the city went into one of the riots of celebration so popular among its citizens.

Officially the party of celebration on the New York Commons was mostly given over to eating and drinking up great hogsheads and barrels of rum and beer. A whole oxen was roasted over charcoal.

The British didn't accept with any good grace the raising of a Liberty Pole (a pine tree) on the Commons. British soldiers kept chopping it down, while the Sons of Liberty always erected new ones.

George III called New York rebellious; the city was to be disciplined and with the rest of the colonies taught a lesson like a delinquent schoolboy. Taxes were put on imports of paper, lead, glass, and tea.

In 1770 the first American killed in the coming American Revolution was a citizen who died fighting British troops in what came to be called in New York the Battle of Golden Hill. It had begun with an officer facing a mob and ordering his sixty men: "Soldiers, draw your bayonets and cut your way through."

It was the wrong time for another event that same year. The gold-colored lead statue of King George III the city had ordered arrived, a rather plump, prancing bit of equestrian sculpture. It was placed on a pedestal on Bowling Green.

In April 1774, following the example of Boston, the New Yorkers dumped the cargo of the tea-ship *London* into the Hudson, not even taking time to paint themselves as Indians. Public meetings became louder on the Commons when news arrived of the closing of the port of Boston. It was a sign the colonies were thinking alike.

Lexington and Concord followed, despite King George's promise to serve the Americans "a few bloody noses to remind them of their duty."

Then came Bunker Hill (actually fought on another rise called Breed's Hill), and the First Continental Congress had already met.

New York City awaited the arrival of a general to command the revolutionary armies. He was a Virginia planter, a former major under Braddock in the French and Indian Wars, a land surveyor, plantation owner, married to the richest widow in the colonies. Now on April 4, 1776, after lifting the siege of Boston, George Washington, Commander in Chief of the rebel forces in the colonies, entered New York City.

He came to defend the city's 20,000 inhabitants, and to face an invasion of the British from across the sea. Washington believed New York was the key city that would hold the colonies together. In English hands it would end "the intercourse between the northern and southern colonies, upon which depends the safety of America."

Many Tories fled the city (at least 40 to 50 percent of the Americans, by most accounts, remained loyal to the king). Washington got his 200 cannon into place to defend the city, and dug defenses around the Battery. He had no cavalry, so trenches and redoubts would have to serve against whatever forces invaded New York.

It was a mixed bag that Washington commanded in New York. There were Virginians, green-shirted Marylanders, unsmiling New Englanders complete with Bible, who quoted Jeremiah: "and seek ye the peace of the city whither I have caused ye to be carried." There were riflemen from New Jersey and Rhode Island and some Pennsylvanians.

And the British attacked.

◈

New York City—always in a state of change—was not only a battlefield during the American Revolution but turned into as wide-open and sinful a place as any Western frontier town pictured in the most dramatic shoot-'em-up movie. Washington's army was entertained and overrun by whores, gamblers, sellers of rum and whisky.

Then the British landed on Long Island and Washington prepared to meet them on Brooklyn Heights. But the bawdy camp life in the city did not let up. One soldier wrote home: "The whores continue their employ . . . very lucrative . . . my guard . . . have broken up . . . men and women fighting, pulling caps, swearing, crying murder!"

There was also a plot to poison General Washington by "putting Paris Green in his peas." A member of Washington's bodyguard, a Thomas Hickey, was implicated, and he was hanged near Bowery Lane to the public pleasure of 2,000 citizens.

In June the British had landed 9,000 soldiers from among the more than 20,000 men they had on Long Island. Washington rushed 7,000 men to Brooklyn. To help him a mob in New York pulled down from its perch the lead statue of King George III. The tons of lead made nearly 50,000 rifle bullets for Washington's army.

The British eventually landed an army at Gravesend on Long Island, moving toward Washington's men stationed on Brooklyn Heights. Washington had made the military mistake of dividing his army. Half of his troops were in New York, the balance in Brooklyn. The British marched in three lobsterback columns, led by the fat Earl of Cornwallis. The American pickets were overrun and the Hessians came up, wielding bayonets, their cannonballs reaching deep into American ranks. After a brief period of resistance, the Americans began to break and run.

Then the rains came and Washington's men began to crowd Brooklyn Ferry, piling into leaky rowboats to get back to New York. Washington, seated on a white horse, rode back and forth among his beleaguered troops, supervising this disorderly retreat.

The British came ashore on Manhattan at Kips Bay—which later became East 34th Street—and the Americans fled again. Washington, still on his white horse, met his panicked soldiers at what is now Grand Central Station and in rage pulled his pistols and fired at his own fleeing men. The powder didn't go off, and so he took his whip to the panicked soldiers. He harried his men to the point where the Fifth Avenue Public Library now stands.

British bullets began to strike near him. He closed his eyes, and it appeared that he had decided to die facing the advancing British. An aide grabbed the bridle of Washington's horse.

"My God, general, you cannot stay here."

He was led away while the Americans tried to gather courage in the area of what was to become Central Park.

The British took a breather for tea time, deciding they could finish off the rebels *any* time they pleased. So General Howe and his staff dismounted at Mrs. Murray's house on 38th Street (now in the Murray Hill section) for wine and cakes. Mrs. Murray was charming, the staff officers witty London bucks. So Washington's demoralized men were not followed, and they began to gather on Harlem Heights on what was to become 125th Street, St. Nicholas Avenue, and 130th Street.

The battle began again with the furious popping of muskets at what was to be 116th Street—the site of Columbia University. For more than two hours the fray continued in the heavy New York summer heat. The British ranks finally broke and the Americans charged. During the fierce encounter England lost several cannon and 174 dead and wounded.

As for General Howe, he went into housekeeping with his mistress, Mrs. Loring, in Manhattan, and wrote to London that chasing Washington was "rather precarious" and that he needed more men. Yet he already commanded 20,000 men in New York, and sixty-six warships on the two

AFTERMATH OF BRITISH VICTORY
New York City in flames after Washington's defeat and retreat in 1776. This print was probably not made by an eyewitness. (Ross Collection)

rivers. Washington, on the other hand, had a thin force of 5,000 men who were despairing on Harlem Heights as they watched and listened to the revelry and tumult as the British took over the city.

The Americans were commanded by a general who had committed a serious military error in facing a British army that was reinforced by warships. Washington had lost control of his temper and had attacked his own panic-stricken, retreating forces. Many American soldiers deserted and fled to their homes. Some soldiers were caught stealing women's clothes, and Washington set up a whipping post: Thirty-nine lashes and a wash-down with salt water was the reward for looting or desertion.

Howe eventually attacked Harlem Heights and almost captured Washington. In his advance Howe got as far as New Rochelle. Washington settled in—he hoped—for a stay at White Plains.

For the rest of the war New York City was in English hands. But, as with Napoleon at Moscow, fire destroyed the best part of the city four days after the last battle on the island.

The fire began in the greasy interior of the Fighting Cock Tavern, and spread or was set in various places. The British said the Americans had set the fire and then cut holes in all the fire-fighting buckets kept handy for such events. Those accused of setting the fire were picked up by bayonets in some cases and tossed alive into the raging flames. Columns of smoke pluming skyward signaled to Washington that the city was burning around the British.

Enough remained of the city, however, to give the British shelter. Repairs were quickly made and new structures went up. General Howe set up house at East 51st Street and First Avenue.

In September the general had Nathan Hale hanged as a spy by the provost marshal, the event taking place at 45th Street and First Avenue. The famous line spoken by Hale, "I regret I have but one life to give for my country," was not original with him. He had read it in an old English play. But it served well enough to bring him into American history.

❧

Three thousand people still lived in New York, and it was soon a Tory center with 30,000 German and English soldiers in residence. New York became a jolly, high-living wartime city. Booze, women, and gambling were in steady supply. The gentry among the officers seduced virgins, dueled, read Caesar's *Wars* and Defoe, and went to the theater.

At war's end in November of 1783, 15,000 Tories fled New York as American soldiers recovered the city. Many took refuge in Canada. A few went underground in the city and when discovered were tarred and feathered. The homeward-bound British took to their ships under an agreement to leave peacefully.

Meanwhile, George Washington and his staff waited in Harlem for the words: *They are all embarked.* He was cheered as he rode down to the Cape's Tavern at Broadway and Thames Street.

On December 4, the raspy, wintry day turning New York noses red, there was a ceremony at Fraunces Tavern, at Pearl and Broad streets. Here Washington said farewell to his officers and staff over a buffet lunch. He was a serious man in a solemn moment, and he showed his emotion as he lifted his wine glass to respond to the glasses held up in tribute to him by the officers.

"With a heart full of love and gratitude I now take my leave of you. I most devoutly wish that your latter days may be prosperous and happy as your former have been glorious and honorable."

Washington broke down as he spoke and did not finish his speech. He added, "I cannot come to each of you, but I shall feel obliged if each of you . . . will come and take me by the hand."

After this simple, touching farewell, he went to Whitehall ship's slip to embark on a barge, the first step on his trip to Mount Vernon.

❧

The nation grew and New York grew with it. Its clipper ships, graceful as abstract carvings of birds, sailed to China around the Horn to bring back green tea from Canton at fancy prices. Duncan Phyfe came to New York to make furniture, and many of his few hundred pieces survive. Alexander Hamilton set up the Bank of New York. There were dangerous buildings of six stories on Queens Street (later Pearl Street).

Democracy had other rules then for the varying patterns of society. The rich did not want the workers and the poor to have voting rights. In 1804 the city charter relaxed a bit and granted any male paying $25 a year in rent the right to vote for an alderman. It took another twenty-five years for the average citizen to extend his rights to be able to cast his ballot for mayor.

On April 14, 1789, Washington was elected President of the United States. He had been offered the throne as George I by some. But he refused. He had great landholdings but no cash, and he had to borrow enough money to coach north for his inauguration in New York City, the capital of the new nation.

The city's White House—the natives called it "The Palace"—was located at 3 Cherry Street, now gone, its site part of the Brooklyn Bridge. The president later moved to a four-story place at 39 Broadway. Thomas Jefferson, a Southerner, insisted the capital should be on the Potomac, so he and Hamilton held a meeting to achieve some kind of understanding of each other's political position and the common weal. New York eventually lost out as the capital of the United States as Hamilton bowed to Jefferson's arguments.

❧

It is hard to think of New York City as some eighteenth- and nineteenth-century visitors saw it, lush with gardens, fruit trees, huge elms—a place the Dutch had called Bloemendaal ("Blooming Dale"), an area now mostly housing Lincoln Center for the Performing Arts. The rivers and the bay then produced huge lobsters, oysters, sturgeon, shad, and giant crabs. Over the trees great flights of passenger pigeons (now an extinct bird) could shut out the sun, and there were foxes, wolves, and bears prowling among the trees well into the nineteenth century.

RIVERSIDE DRIVE IN THE MID-NINETEENTH CENTURY
The new Riverside Drive along the Hudson River at 118th Street, looking
south. (*Frank Leslie's Illustrated Newspaper*)

Visitors who have roamed Tokyo, where there are no numbers on
houses and usually no street signs, or have become lost in Bel Air, California's exclusive deer paths, or hunted hidden alleys around Shepherd's
Market in London, are delighted at New York City's streets, numbered
as they go north while running east and west, and its avenues, also
numbered, running north to south.

It didn't just happen that way. It took four years, ending in 1807, to
bring order to the streets. The City Commission was made up of Gouverneur Morris (he had an oak leg that he once took off to hold back a
revolutionary French mob in Paris during the Terror), Simon de Witt,
and John Rutherford. They laid out the gridiron street slate or plat that
makes it much easier to locate oneself in the city.

As a constantly growing port, New York had depended on its
shipping. It was a great blow when President Thomas Jefferson ordered
an embargo on all American shipping in the nation's ports in order to
avoid war with the British. The English were fighting Napoleon and
needed sailors, so they were seizing American seamen on the high seas
and impressing them for service on their own men-of-war.

The embargo ruined New York. Weeds grew on wharfs, ships dismantled of masts rotted in the bay. Hundreds of New Yorkers were tossed into debtors' prison, many for owing less than $25 to some creditor. The Embargo Act failed in its purpose, for the War of 1812 did come to a city not prepared for it.

New Yorkers had their bumbling, hardly trained militia, some impractical forts and worn-out batteries. The Iron Greys merely looked warlike—a society regiment made up of smartly outfitted young men from the best families who didn't like to risk actual combat.

Washington, D.C., was invaded through Chesapeake Bay and many buildings, including the White House, were burned. But New York, with a population of 100,000 people that made it the largest city of the nation, was never menaced, and when the Treaty of Ghent was signed in December 1814, New York went wild with joy. One resident, John Jacob Astor, had paid a bribe to get news of the peace early, before it was official, and he unloaded his warehouse of hoarded supplies at wartime high prices.

As a money manipulator he had also made half a million dollars during the war by lending money to the government at loan-shark rates. Astor, who began as a fur trader, was either the richest or the second richest man in the United States.

Depressions follow wars, as New York was to learn again and again. By 1815 conditions were dismal in the city. Now, too, the first great wave of immigrants was surging in, and was to continue for more than a century, so that by the middle of the twentieth century 75 percent of all immigrants had come in through the Port of the City of New York.

Each generation of newcomers disliked the *next* generation of immigrants as "forrineers." Epidemics raised havoc among crowded slum dwellers; people newly landed were living in dreadful conditions. In 1822 yellow fever, called "Yellow Jack," took its toll.

By October the cold weather ended the epidemic. Life was restored to the city, business recovered, and people tried to forget. There were balls in New York, and women sported their new gowns. Thicker, larger safes were forged for the merchants—the dealers in land, furs, shipping.

The only fun the rest of the population had that year was the wry scheme of a butcher at the Central Market named John de Voe. He was a practical joker, and he said it was clear that the Battery section of Manhattan was getting too heavy, the city was in danger because it was so overbuilt there.

He insisted that a practical scheme was to saw off the sparsely settled northern end of Manhattan, then with huge sweeps, each 250 feet long, turn the island of Manhattan around so the northern end would become the southern end and the heavy southern end, of course, the northern. He hardly expected to be taken seriously.*

But human nature is credulous about any project if it's zany enough. What began as a jest was taken up as practical and a true crisis. John de Voe organized sawing teams to set up survey camps at the northern end, and men came forward offering to make the great oars and to man them for the island-turning.

The town became excited over the bold idea, and many thought it possible and practical. The first cuttings were to be made at Kingsbridge.

The authorities seem to have sat back in amazement—or befuddlement. After all, was it any crazier than the Erie Canal being dug at the time? However, John de Voe never did show up on the day the people gathered for the first cut to be made in sawing Manhattan in two.

The Erie Canal, with its locks and length, made New York, as a later historian put it, "the mouth of the continent." Certainly it provided a direct, cheap way to the west. Soon half of the country's imports were in the hands of New York dealers, and nearly that much of the exports. By 1825, 500 new merchants a year were opening up businesses in New York. There were twelve new banks—"marble, cast iron pillars and spittoons"—and a dozen marine insurance firms.

Also the average citizen no longer had to own property to be permitted to cast a vote in elections. There were so many immigrants (nearly 12 percent of the population was newly arrived aliens) that the gentry, the merchant class, feared that the people in the slums would fall under the political power of the ward heelers and of an expanding Tammany Hall.

In 1835 the home-grown bigots, the Native American Democratic Association, came into being. "We . . . will never consent to allow the government . . . to pass into the hands of foreigners." A year later some of the Irish foreigners organized The Ancient Order of Hibernians. Tammany as a power was on its way. One of the Harpers of Harper & Brothers ran for mayor on the slogan "No Popery," and was elected. In 1844 there were other super-Americans (presaging the America First group around Charles Lindbergh in New York in the 1930s), The Native Sons of America, The American Brotherhood, and The Native American Party. These patriots were all anti-Irish and anti-Catholic.

The pro-American, antiforeigner groups eventually banded together in 1849 to face the farewell performance of a great British actor, William Macready. The American actor Edwin Forrest was also playing New

---

* The whole idea may sound too incredible and absurd to believe today, but in 1972 I was assured by a group of people in Los Angeles that on a certain day the state of California would tilt and everything in it slide into the Pacific Ocean. I knew dozens of residents who left the state in a hurry because they believed it would really happen.

York and wasn't drawing as many customers as the Englishman. The American mastermind of the coming riots was a hack writer named E. Z. C. Jason, better known by collectors of dime novels as Ned Buntline, who later took a hard-drinking Western meat hunter named William Cody and turned him into the legend called Buffalo Bill.

Buntline was a rabble-rouser who used the American flag and preached the theme that all people from overseas were not as good as native-born stock. It is a quick way to mass popularity, as schemers from Huey Long to Joe McCarthy and some modern demagogues have found out. Cheer for the stars and stripes; call for direct action against those you don't like and label them un-American and therefore degenerate.

Macready wanted to cancel his appearance, fearing anti-British street violence, but nearly fifty New Yorkers signed a request he stay and act. Among the signers were Herman Melville and Washington Irving (who first called New York Gotham).

The bigots put up posters reading WORKINGMEN, SHALL AMERICANS OR ENGLISH RULE THE CITY? and gathered in saloons to plan action.

A force of 325 policemen was called out to guard the theater. To buttress the police a general and six companies of soldiers were held in readiness for trouble on Washington Parade Ground (later Washington Square). In addition, 300 fully armed soldiers marched downtown.

Every seat in the theater on Astor Place had been sold. The house was packed, and all the surrounding streets were jammed with people. It was clear the crowd knew "something was doing." The curtain went up on the English actor. *Macbeth.* There was hissing and the first fist fight. By the beginning of the second act the mob outside had burst inside and were being tossed out.

Vigorously clubbing as they went, the police charged the mob. Fire hoses were used, but the riot grew in volume. By reasonable estimates there were nearly 25,000 people in the mob, mostly the poor against anyone a step higher up. The workers were in fear of their underpaid jobs being taken by immigrants. The actor Macready went on with the play despite all the noise and smashing.

Ned Buntline was yelling to the mob outside, "Shall Americans or Englishmen rule? Shall the sons whose fathers drove the base-born miscreants from these shores stand by . . . ?"

The mob moved to seize the theater and set it on fire. Macready was smuggled out and rushed to New Rochelle and safety. Soldiers began to fire over the heads of the mob. Those in front thought the soldiers were using harmless blanks and began to toss rocks and bricks.

The order came to fire at the mob. The theater was finally set on fire and it burned briskly. Chaos reigned. Nearly two dozen people died in the rioting—shot or beaten to death—and 150 were injured. Among those

UNION NOMINATION

FOR PRESIDENT,

Abraham Lincoln

OF ILLINOIS.

FOR VICE PRESIDENT,

Andrew Johnson

OF TENNESSEE.

A LINCOLN ELECTION POSTER
One speech delivered at Cooper Union in New York City on a snowy evening in 1860 brought Lincoln to the attention of the nation. (Library of Congress)

tried for inciting and rioting was Ned Buntline, a mob hero. He was fined $250 and sentenced to a year on Blackwell's Island.

~§§~

Mobs in New York City were always alert and ready for rioting. In 1850 William Lloyd Garrison was heating up the issues of slavery and abolition at the meetings of the New England Anti-Slavery Society.

Two years later the first dramatic version of *Uncle Tom's Cabin* played the Bowery in Purdy's National Theatre. From 1852 to 1862 more than twenty-five ships out of New York Harbor were charged with being in the slave trade—"blackbirding" for Southern plantations. Blacks in New York were forbidden to ride the horse-drawn streetcars. Southern slaves provided New York cotton brokers with a fine product, and the brokers controlled the market with their great fortunes. A Yankee, Eli Whitney, had made it all possible with his cotton gin.

Out of the Middle West on Saturday, February 25, 1860, came a tall, rather odd-looking man who got off the Cortlandt Street ferry. There was six feet four of him without his stovepipe hat, and he was carrying a carpet bag. Practically unknown in the East, Abraham Lincoln was in town to make a speech, sponsored by the Young Men's Republican Union of New York, at Cooper Union.

Monday, the day of his speech, was blue-gray, cold and rainy. At the Astor Hotel Lincoln decided he needed a new hat for the event. He got one at Knox's at Broadway and Fulton. He also sat for Matthew Brady, the great photographer, in his studio on Broadway, exhibiting a brooding face, country boots, ill-cut black broadcloth, and a starched shirt.

Snow began to fall as Lincoln left Brady's salon, and walking became hazardous. Steam and vapor issued from the breathing Broadway crowd and the horse traffic. The snowfall turned into a storm. Lincoln's boots were too tight, and that night at Cooper Union he suffered as he faced 1,500 people who had paid twenty-five cents each to see the giant from the West whom some few were thinking of as a candidate for the new Republican Party to run for the presidency.

When Lincoln rose to speak his voice seemed weak, and there were cries of "louder!" He soon was into his speech with vigor. ". . . wrong as we think slavery is . . . let us have faith that right makes might, and in that faith let us to the end dare to do our duty as we understand it."

To many of us today, in the fury and climate of our own scandalous 1970s, what he said is no longer stirring. But in New York—where hundreds of Brady's photographs of him were to be sold—that night made Lincoln, as his words were reported in the American press.

Three months later Abraham Lincoln was, on the momentum of his New York speech, nominated by his party, and then elected. He was to admit, "Brady and the Cooper Union speech made me president."

BOOK TWO

The City Declares a War

4
The Fighting City

In the spring of 1863 the Southern Confederacy of rebel states began to plan its Battle of the Bulge. In April of that year President Abraham Lincoln, using the Conscription Act passed by Congress, demanded the drafting of 300,000 men, the conscription to begin on July 11 in New York City.

It was an unfair, dishonest act, for it contained a built-in escape hatch for the rich and affluent; any man whose number was called in the draft could buy himself out of serving as a soldier by a payment of $300.

This left hundreds of thousands who didn't have the $300, and many of these people generated a big-city rebellion against the president's proclamation that was to be called in New York City the Draft Riots.

The injustice exemplified by the act was responsible for troops on both sides going into battle singing "It's a poor man's fight, a rich man's war"; for in the South in most districts a man who owned six or more slaves was also exempt from service as a soldier.

New York during the years of the Civil War had a population of about 815,000, and 50 percent of these people were immigrants, born outside the borders of the United States and with no, or only fragmented, allegiance. The Potato Famine and crop failures had driven great numbers of Irish peasants to jam into the reeking holds of ships crossing the Atlantic. More than 203,000 of them were living in the poverty areas of the city, doing the meanest kind of rough work. Illiterate and barely eking out an existence, they were regarded by the rest of the populace with condescension and no pity. They would have to furnish the majority of the recruits at the draft drawings set for July 11.

They lived packed together in rookeries, in decaying tenements, in districts called Five Points and Mulberry Bend, and were given to high-pitched protest at their miserable plight.

Conditions in the nation were desperate. The Civil War, after three years of the most murderous battles the continent had ever endured, had reached a stalemate. Grant was besieging Vicksburg; in June Lee began moving north with 75,000 troops in a last desperate effort to break the deadlock. A Russian fleet rested at anchor someplace off New York harbor, ready to declare war on England *if* England declared war on the United States to break the cotton blockade—a blockade that was ruining the English mill owners by cutting off their supply of raw cotton.

Lincoln was still without a general in the East who had less of a proprietary affection for the Army of the Potomac—and who would fight. As a stopgap he appointed George Meade, and hoped Meade could find Lee's three columns, moving during the night of July 1 through the Pennsylvania countryside somewhere near a town where the rebels had heard there was a shoe factory. Many of the Southern soldiers were barefoot. On this warm July night a detachment of Lee's advance guard moved down the Cashtown road toward what was to be the three days' battle of Gettysburg.

Neither the battle nor the failure of Robert E. Lee to force a victory cheered the New Yorkers. Meade had permitted Lee and his forces to escape.

July 11 came as the city sweltered in the grip of typical sultry, damp summer weather. The drawing of numbers for those who would become conscripts was scheduled to begin. The various Provost Marshal's offices scattered around the city expected the usual grousing but no trouble.

No police guard was requested, and the city's 1,620 patrolmen had other duties. On call was the Invalid Corps, commanded by a Major Ruggles. The corps was made up of soldiers recovering from wounds, various malingerers, and walking cripples, and was used mostly to patrol and guard armories, arsenals, and places that produced munitions of war.

Rage against the bald unfairness of the draft and the savage exploitation of the poor, as well as resentment against the city's Negroes who worked for even cheaper wages than they did, combined with the heat rash in the reeking slums to fray tempers dangerously among the general populace. It was against the affluent and the blacks that the people's anger grew as the Provost Marshal's offices opened and clerks began to spin the drums containing the numbers from which the new recruits would be picked.

However, some of the newspapers in New York had been printing violent stories about the inequity of the Conscription Act. There was an organization, political in nature, called "Knights of the Golden Circle" that hinted it might use force and violence in the city to oppose the draft.

Just after dawn on Saturday, July 11, there were rumors that the Knights and their supporters were going to take over by force the U.S. Arsenal at Seventh Avenue and 35th Street. A police sergeant and fifteen men were sent to stand guard there, but the crowd was not large, nor did it appear to be in a mood for rioting. So the police made themselves comfortable inside and locked up the building.

The 9th District Draft Office had been set up at Third Avenue and 46th Street. The drum was spun and the crowd gathering outside muttered, shouted, and cursed but did not interfere with the drawing and listing of 1,236 names. The number demanded from the district would call for 264 more names. These would be selected on Monday.

Church bells broke the morning atmosphere of a not too quiet New York Sunday. Good Christians began to gather prayer books for the walk or carriage ride to church.

Street-corner groups of rough-dressed folk were debating and shouting at the news that a dozen or so well-known rich men whose names had been drawn for the draft had at once paid their $300 and freed themselves from living in the open in Virginia fields, in danger of damage to their bodies from rebel fire.

The slum districts—an American Hogarth's "Gin Lane"—were active all day with tippling and cursing, and a great sadness, too, among the women as they thought of their men going off to a war they hardly understood. They owned no slaves, and what was the Union to them? It was the Irish, who would bear the largest burden of the draft lists, who were most active in their debates about the injustice of it all. But were the Draft Riots a Roman Catholic insurrection "for the glory of the Pope," as they were to be called in the days that followed?

Actually it was a mixed rebellion; many of the poor and some criminals—people from all denominations—joined the mobs forming Monday morning. ("I went out to the streets, too hot in my rooming house, and ended running with a crowd" [from a letter of the times].) It was not, as so many historians have claimed, a planned looting of the city. And to call the mobs "gangsters and criminals," as has been done in popular recountings of the riots, is overlooking the truth—that before the burning and the looting got out of control, these were ordinary men, women, and children with no hope of getting their grievances heard.

A few fires had been set during the night, and people had gathered to watch the fire laddies do their work. No one made any effort to hinder them in their job. A hostile environment of physical violence had not yet shown itself. Superintendent of Police John A. Kennedy saw no reason for alarm, but did keep the guard on the arsenal, for thousands of rifles and pistols were stored there.

Sunday continued humid, as New York can be in July, and people seemed to be up early. Particularly at about six in the morning there had been movement on the West Side—groups that could be nothing else but a determined mob moving north along both Eighth and Ninth avenues. Scouts and wanderers were active in the side streets, shouting for people to join them. The mob, always growing, finally gathered on a lot just east of Central Park.

The householders in this fashionable district around the park looked out from their breakfast tables. What were these hooligans doing, with their cries and threats? There seemed a nervous instability in the shifting crowd on the weedy lot, and there was a distinct note of rage detectable in their mood. For in this residential section lived some of the men who had paid the price to have their names withdrawn from army service.

At about eight o'clock the mob began to stir, like some giant, ungainly creature, forming and reforming itself, turning south at last, breaking into segments like an earthworm dividing, one section going down Fifth Avenue, the other down Sixth Avenue. The columns merged at 47th Street, heading for the draft lottery drum at Third Avenue and 46th Street.

Other draft offices were attracting their own angry crowds. The Broadway and 29th Street office had a guard of about seventy policemen standing tense and worried under a captain and three sergeants; while sixty-nine men were rushing to the Third Avenue office. The cripples and battle-scarred men of the Invalid Corps took up their weapons and they, too, went to help hold back the mob at Third Avenue.

While the police force had about 2,200 men on its official lists, there were many slough-offs, easy jobs, desk cops, and just plain loafers, so that only about 1,500 or 1,600 officers were actually patrolmen on active duty.

The Third Avenue draft office was in serious trouble. For six blocks in all directions the mob held control. Carriages were stopped, horses frightened, a team unhitched. Passengers were pelted, top hats were dented or knocked off, and many were forced to flee.

The cry was "NO DRAFT!" Posters appeared crudely scrawled with the same message, NO DRAFT! By ten o'clock the mob, feeling its strength, was pressing the police hard against the draft office walls, and "the Black Joke gang" went into action. The Black Joke group was actually Volunteer Engine Company No. 33, which, like so many volunteer fire organizations of the day, was really a social club made up of tough males who gathered to gamble and tell tall stories and who enjoyed brawling in the neighborhood saloons. Sport was the bringing of a woman into the firehouse.

The Black Joke boys heard their fire chief's number had been picked in the draft, and they were determined to raid the office, smash the wheel, and burn the records.

A pistol was fired and the entire harum-scarum crew of Engine Company No. 33 rushed forward. The police clubbed all the attackers they could reach but fell back inside and barred the doors. The Black Joke boys eventually forced their way inside and smashed the wheel. However, the escaping police carried the records to safety. The mob set the building on fire, and other fire companies that arrived to douse the flames were held off by the mob.

Superintendent John A. Kennedy was still unaware that he had a civil war uprising in the city. He was a "mick" himself, he used to say, and he knew his fellow micks were given to a bit of temper and to the lark of breaking in when they could get hold of some whisky. Confident

THE DRAFT RIOTS OF NEW YORK CITY, 1863
The rebellion, begun as the poor man's draft protest, becomes a violent attack against all authority.

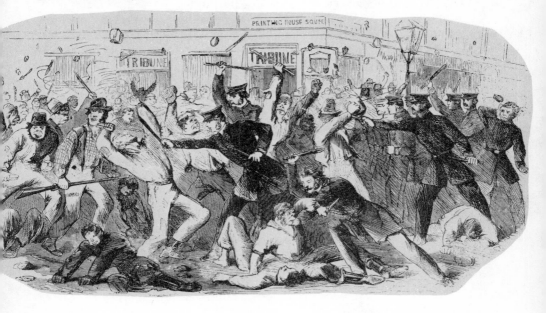

that he could handle the situation, he dressed in a civilian suit, ordered his open carriage, picked up a light bamboo cane, and, so armed, decided to see what was really happening.

Soon he saw the smoke and then the fire. He got out of his carriage and began to walk toward Third Avenue. The cries of those who knew him were menacing, "It's the Kennedy himself!"

Before he had a chance to retreat to his carriage, they rushed him, and a man in a worn army uniform (a discharged soldier, no doubt) knocked him down with a roundhouse punch. Kennedy sprang to his feet and struck his assailant across the face with his light cane, only to be knocked down again and this time was stomped upon; work shoes and boots began to kick viciously at his prone body. Struggling to his feet, he was seized and tossed over an embankment.

Kennedy, fearless and foolish, a bull-ring animal, still managed to get to his feet and head for Lexington Avenue. He was rescued by a solid citizen named John Wagan, for whom the mob still had some respect. Wagan told them the superintendent was already a dead man, and with cheers the mob turned back to the fire. Kennedy was covered with a sack, put in a wagon, and taken away for much-needed medical attention.

The Police Commissioners, much against their wishes, were forced to assume command. John C. Bergen was a stuffed-shirt politician. Thomas C. Acton was one of the founders of the Union League Club. James Bowen was a brigadier general of volunteers (in a time when officers were usually politically appointed), and General Bowen, it was discovered, had left weeks before to join his command.

So it was Bergen who took over and decided on repressive measures against the mobs in Brooklyn and Staten Island, while Thomas Acton had all of Manhattan Island to bring under control. Acton turned out to be a man who could function four days without much sleep (in that time never getting out of his clothes at Police Headquarters at 300 Mulberry Street). He became the commanding head of both the police and the army forces that were available.

Heavy fighting continued in the streets, and there were now bodies underfoot. The police, though badly mauled, were themselves wreaking fearful damage with their heavy hardwood clubs, crushing skulls when they could get in a good swing. Some police were wounded, and Sergeant McCredie was struck such a hefty blow that he fell backwards through a front door, shattering its panels.

McCredie was in dreadful shape, but he managed to stagger up the stairs, where he was hidden between mattresses by a woman when the mob came up in search of him. The woman told them the man had jumped out of the second-story window.

The mob was beating the police everyplace. The Invalid Corps was brought into action. Fifty limping convalescent soldiers, armed with sabers and muskets, marched up Third Avenue into a barrage of paving stones and bricks and a dead cat or two. When six of the soldiers had dropped to the street injured and one soldier lay dead, the officer in charge ordered a volley of blanks fired.

The mob came in shouting, and the next volley from the second rank fired ball-shot directly at them, killing and wounding a woman and six men. Infuriated, the mob closed in. As the soldiers tried to reload, they were clubbed down and some were shot with their own muskets. The Invalid Corps retreated, leaving nearly two dozen dead or wounded.

This was the turning point of the rebellion, which began as a poor man's draft protest and became a vicious assault against *all* authority.

5
Ordeal in Manhattan

The mob had its speakers and its section leaders, but it had no head, no leader to rally around. It was like any angry mass of infuriated people, moving in all directions but without a commander.

Meanwhile, on the side of law and order, companies of National Guardsmen and volunteer groups in the city were more or less organized or organizing. There were 700 soldiers, as well as sailors on warships anchored in the Hudson. There were garrisons in the Brooklyn Navy Yard, on Governor's Island, at Fort Hamilton, and at other installations rimming the city.

A thousand citizens were eventually sworn in, including many who had paid to get off the army lists. They would now be armed as Volunteer Special Police to go, not against Southern rebels, but against New Yorkers. And from the bloody battlefield around Gettysburg, where fighting had ended just a few days before, cavalry and infantry, dozens of batteries of artillery, and 10,000 soldiers would be used against the mob.

Most of the mob were unaware of just what was to be brought against them, yet they all knew official resistance to their holding the city captive was a matter of ultimate certainty. The brighter of the rebels realized (or so detectives and informers were to claim) that to loot the city and burn it they would have to destroy or face down the police. And that plan would require firearms. There were huge stacks of weapons in the State Armory at Second Avenue and 21st Street, as well as at the Union Steam Works farther north, which was an active munitions plant.

Alerted by detectives, the police rushed guard units to the armory and the steam works. Men were set at all windows, armed with pistols, skull-cracking nightsticks, and carbines. A mob attacked the armory with stones, bricks, pistols, and muskets.

By four o'clock they were battering powerfully at the main gates, one giant man swinging a heavy sledgehammer. As he beat in a panel, a man wriggled through the splintered opening. He was shot dead.

Infuriated, the mob attacked the gates with iron tools, tree trunks, and crowbars. Estimating that the situation was murderous, the police departed through a small opening in the back of the building, dropping eighteen feet to the ground. They retreated to the 18th Precinct Police Station at 22nd Street and Third Avenue. But the mob rushed it, captured it, and burned it. The police then fled to Mulberry Street headquarters.

At the armory the mob was in full control. While dozens of people began to loot the ground floor, others made their way to the third floor, where the carbines and cartridges were stored. Weapon racks were emptied and trouser pockets filled with ammunition. Fearing a sudden return of the police, the third-floor door to the drill room was locked and barred. This proved to be a fatal error.

The police did come back in force to retake the armory, moving four abreast, bashing any heads in the way, friend or foe, with their hardwood clubs. At the shattered entrance the police waited for the mob inside to rush out to attack them. As the rioters emerged, they were clubbed down. Meanwhile, those remaining inside set fire to the building.

The ancient building, constructed of timbers rather than brick or stone, became a great torch. Those escaping the raging fire with weapons were clubbed down. The fate of the people—men, women, and a few children—trapped in the barricaded third-floor drill room was horrible. Fruitlessly tearing and pulling at the locked door, they succumbed to the smoke and flames.

The third floor eventually collapsed with a roar and a shower of cinders, and the trapped people fell screaming into the roaring fire below.

The rest of the city was not at peace; it was also active in its fury of fire and violence. The major victims were Negroes. The rioters could hardly lay hands on the rich army evaders and the draft board officials fleeing to safety. The Negro, whom the desperate mobs regarded as the cause of the war and their rival for poorly paid work, became the low man in the pecking order.

From the Hudson to the East River, detachments of rioters looted, burned, and lynched. Street hangings averaged three a day as bodies swayed gruesomely from lampposts, trees, and gateways.

The Provost Marshal's office, located at Broadway and 9th Street, was set on fire, its official contents hacked to bits in the street. Weapons and portable loot now became the objects of the roaming mobs. Jewelry shops, specialty shops for taffetas, calico, silks, dimities, flannels were sacked. Hardware stores gave up nearly a thousand pistols, rifles, shot-guns—weapons then carried by such stores.

Mobs moved to burn out Mayor Opdyke on First Avenue, also the "goddamn Police Headquarters"—both points symbols of power to the mob. The headquarters became a kind of French Foreign Legion post under siege. Two hundred police and all the badly wounded patrolmen who could be rushed in past the mob, joined in holding it. Commissioner Acton, in command, set himself grimly not to surrender this Mulberry Street command post.

"We are going to put down a mob, and take no prisoners," said Inspector Daniel C. Carpenter, commander of the force positioned out-side the headquarters to bear the brunt of the first attack.

Carpenter moved his 125 men to Mulberry and Bleecker streets as the mob filled Broadway, both street and sidewalks from housefront to housefront, waving weapons and howling "like banshees."

It was too late to change or modify the draft orders of Mr. Lincoln. Besides, the mob was already past the point of no return. Yet any sensi-ble action on the first day of the draft drawings might have prevented this all-out explosion of despair, rage, and, now, unstoppable blood lust.

Inspector Carpenter moved his men forward in ranks of four, strik-ing the mob's advance line at Amity Street near the LaFarge house, whose Negro servants were being savagely beaten. One of the mob, carrying a big stick, rushed at the inspector as he moved briskly at the head of his men, his night club at the ready. The two men came together in a crush of limbs and flailing clubs. The inspector, an agile, powerful man, smashed in the skull of his attacker, killing him on the spot.

Shots and bricks showered down on the police; several were badly hurt. Still the crowd came on, "like some Roman legion," someone wrote later, taking its losses, but killing and disabling as it surged forward.

The fierce encounter lasted for fifteen minutes before the police finally turned back the rioters.

❧

And what of Mayor Opdyke? His neighbors had formed themselves into a guard force around his house. When the mob, wary of the strength

CIVILIANS VERSUS AUTHORITY

An old print showing mobs fighting the police on Fifth Avenue. (*Harper's Weekly*)

there, moved away, it turned its attention to the Colored Orphan Asylum. This was a four-story brick building on Fifth Avenue between 43rd and 44th streets. It was the home of about two hundred orphaned black children, all less than twelve years of age. A staff of about fifty adults, all fearfully agitated, was on hand. The superintendent bolted the front doors and hurried his charges out the back way to Madison Avenue, where they moved over to the 22nd Precinct Station House.

The mob shattered the doors of the asylum, while others began to break into houses around the place to loot and burn. The asylum furnishings were chopped to bits. Someone found a small Negro girl hiding under a bed, and she was murdered on the spot. Carrying off what they could, the rioters set fire to the place and some surrounding buildings.

Downtown, around the Battery and the waterfront, the Bowery and Five Points, mobs were in as ugly a mood as those above 21st Street. Negro families were beaten all over town.

Even the worst day must end. The mob held the damaged city as dusk descended. There was no doubt about that. A great city had been seized by its poor, its workers, the idle, the gangsters, and all those attracted by violence who had joined in "for the fun of it."

Harlem and the Upper West Side had their own mobs, and at West 86th Street Postmaster Abraham Wakeman's house was burned down. As the hours passed, the city still stirred, but not in sleep. At eight o'clock, the hot July night inflaming the rioters, police informers had reported a large mob moving down Fifth Avenue, intent on hanging Horace Greeley and seizing Printing House Square across from City Hall Park. Their aim was to burn down the Tribune building

Greeley had been printing stories in which he advocated using all the force needed, no matter how great, to suppress and punish the mob. His was not the only paper voicing that sentiment. There was no left-wing newspaper screaming "To the barricades!"

The New York *World* had at first spoken of the mobs as being "the laboring man of the city" (true for most of them), but as property and business places were destroyed and human lives taken, the *World*, too, changed over to the attitudes of the *Times* and the *Tribune*.

Horace Greeley was selected by the mob to be hanged as the symbol of indifferent respectability. A rather comic figure with his chin whiskers, often rustic garb, and with a mind soon to fail, he was, nevertheless, the most famous editor and publisher in New York City.

The excited mob, worked up to fury, entered Printing House Square. Only a single police sergeant was on guard, and he was clubbed to the ground by half a dozen rioters. Soon a series of fires was burning all over the structure. Horace Greeley and his staff had fled down a back staircase. The mob chased Greeley down Park Row. Here he ran into a restaurant, where a waiter hid him in a cloth under a table.

A detail of about a hundred police moved against the mob in front of the Tribune building, attacking from the rear. The rioters were driven from the building and attempts were made to put out the spreading fires. More police had been brought across the East River, and the frenzied mob found itself fighting its way to freedom, attacked front and rear.

The Tribune continued to be harassed during the night. Lanterns were placed in windows and the remaining employees of the paper were armed to aid the police. The building survived. In the morning detachments of marines and sailors appeared to take over guard duty.

Armed forces in solid numbers were moving into the city under military command. The police were no longer alone. Gatling guns—those primitive machine guns—were mounted in the Tribune windows, while the main lobby sprouted the dark snout of a field howitzer.

For a time the city seemed doomed to destruction by fire, but at eleven o'clock a sudden rainstorm moved in and the flames began to die out, steam and smoke replacing them as the downpour continued.

The police force had been beefed up, and at least 1,500 men fought the rioters through Monday night. Meanwhile, Mayor Opdyke had made early desperate calls for help to the commander of the National Guard, Major General Sandford, and to the Eastern Department of the Army under Major General John E. Wool. The Guard was notified to call up all men and officers, anyone with military service. All were directed to report to the arsenal on Seventh Avenue. Orders were sent out to pick up soldiers and sailors from the various forts around the bay and requests were made for artillery.

Governor Seymour had rushed down from Albany and met the mayor at the Nicholas Hotel. It was clear now that the mobs of citizens were in open rebellion and that Washington should be notified of the desperate situation. Urgent telegrams to the War Department asked that the New York regiments—men still recovering from Gettysburg—be sent to the city.

The 10th National Guard, about to move out to the bigger war, went into action at once against the mobs. Soldiers, marines, and sailors were deploying toward the city's spreading danger spots, and a battery of six-pounder guns was loaded and ready to fire.

Monday night found at least 2,000 army and National Guard troops on the alert. America was involved in its first major class war.

The Seventh Avenue arsenal commander reported he was in control there with a strong force and twelve-pounder mountain howitzers from Governor's Island; a detachment of 10th New York State Militia under Major Seeley; a detachment of 12th Regular U.S. Infantry from Fort Hamilton under Captain Franklin; the 3rd Regular U.S. Infantry from Governor's Island under Captain Wilkins; an Invalid Corps from Riker's Island; and some New York State Volunteers under Captain Lockwood.

꧁꧂

Tuesday, July 14, dawned with the city well washed by a rain that had now stopped. The smell from charred ruins filled the air, the smoke of smoldering timbers was evidence of the wounds the city itself had suffered. The sodden mob, few aware of the massive damage done, was out early. Its fury became desperate as it saw the growing masses of armed forces being marshaled against them.

By midmorning street barricades in the style of Paris uprisings were being erected at First and Ninth avenues in the form of piles of rubble, wagons, dismantled lampposts, street poles, boxes, barrels, kegs, and even the furniture from looted houses. On First Avenue the barricades snaked their way from 11th to 14th streets. Attacked head on, the barriers stood; it took till late in the day, after many savage attempts, before organized weapon fire drove the last living person from the barricades.

The Union Steam Works was still the goal of those seeking arms. The police marched off to protect it, moving along Second Avenue. Here they found that the rooftops had been supplied with rocks, bricks, and other heavy objects, which were immediately dumped upon them. The police maintained their orderly march and formed in ranks, swinging their clubs and killing many rioters.

Slowly the mob retreated and the police invaded the houses from which missiles were being tossed down on them. Many people who were trapped on the rooftops jumped to their death. Neither side had much use for prisoners. Finally, troops with cannon began to move in to help the hard-pressed police.

Colonel H. J. O'Brien, commanding one regiment of artillery, ran into the mob head on. His men fired volleys and he ordered his cannon to pour their loads of grapeshot into the massed insurgents. It was murder en masse at close range, as men and women were torn to pieces.

Well satisfied that he had given the mob "a whiff of grape," Colonel O'Brien marched his soldiers back to the arsenal. Colonel O'Brien is a puzzle for what he did next. He went back to the scene of slaughter on horseback and alone. While it is true he lived nearby and may have been worried about his family and property, why did he not take an armed escort with him? He found that his family, Mrs. O'Brien and the children, had gone off earlier to relatives in Brooklyn.

On Second Avenue someone pointed him out as the murdering colonel himself! A half dozen men leaped forward at the mounted officer and tried to pull him from his horse. He was also the target of brick throwers. Sensing his danger, O'Brien dismounted quickly and took refuge in a saloon at Second Avenue and 19th Street.

He still had no respect for the rioters nor did he fear them. An impatient man and obviously a brave one, he left the saloon to face the hate-filled men and women howling around him. With his sword and pistol at the ready he intended to reach his horse, across the street. Trying to shoulder past the mob, O'Brien was at once engulfed by cursing, battering, kicking men. Clubbed on the head, he was swept off his feet. Brutally punished by heavy boots and everything that could jab or swing at a prone body, he appeared doomed to a horrible death. A rope was tied across his ankles and the mob took turns dragging him over the cobblestones from curb to curb.

It is hard to believe that for the next three hours O'Brien survived the torture of knives and swords and the blows of stones hammered against his head and body. And all the time he was being dragged up and down the street like a trapped cat on a cord by cruel children.

Thinking O'Brien was at last dead, the mob left. The colonel lay in the street in the blazing heat of a July day; no one came forward to see if a spark of life remained or to offer him water. His ordeal was not over. As the sun sank over the Jersey Palisades, the mob returned for more sport. They dragged him into his own back garden, nearby, and seeing signs of life they worked him over with knives. Again they left him for dead. This time he was.

✦§✦

The bitter fight for control of the Union Steam Works was just as brutal. The police had not been able to remove the weapons piled up there, and the mob was aware it needed them if it hoped to stand off the official forces gathering against it. At first it had captured the works with ease. But two hundred policemen took the place back in some of the most desperate battling of the entire riots. Reports noted the piled-up dead and dying, people crawling like animated rag bundles all along the hallways of the factory and on the front walks.

With most available military arms and ammunition secure from the mob, the tide of battle gradually swung toward the growing forces of authority. Telegraph wires were down in some places but repairs were soon made.

All military posts were safe, the protection of arsenals and armories was firmed up, and public property stood under guard. The Sub-Treasury on Wall Street had not only war-hardened regular infantry encircling it but also a full battery of field guns, loaded and ready. The Brooklyn Navy Yard was under the guns of the gunboats *Gertrude, Unadilla, Granite City*, and *Tulip*, plus the training ship *North Carolina*. The Battery was under the ready guns of the ironclad *Passaic*.

✦§✦

Late Tuesday the governor with tardy wisdom at last issued a proclamation that New York City was in a full state of insurrection. A telegram from Secretary of War Edwin M. Stanton informed hard-pressed officials that five regiments of the Union Army in full war gear were being moved at all speed by steam cars and ferries to the city.

Wednesday morning the newspapers announced that the insurrection (I have found no notice of its being called a civil war) had passed its peak, that its back was shattered, and authority was again in control.

Such was the official notice in the city press. But the war in the city actually continued for three more days. Field guns and howitzers went into action against the rioting mobs. Saloons and groceries did a roaring business, or were looted of their contents with no payments made.

Refugees fleeing northward from the terror and the horrors were to be the prototypes of what happened later to big-city populations in subsequent, larger wars. Men, women, and children, hurrying toward Yonkers and White Plains, were observed carrying burdens, wheeling carts, or perched precariously on loaded carriages pulled by frightened horses. Railroad stations and depots became battlegrounds for those seeking places on the trains.

By nightfall, under swinging oil lamps, trained, battle-hardened Union troops were moving into the city by the thousands. Sweat-stained, in long-worn blue, they came—the 74th National Guard, 26th Michigan, 152nd New York Volunteers. And others.

The mayor issued a proclamation: all citizens of good intent to go about their business as usual, and all transportation to function once more. There was also put out a mysterious document—most likely by someone in the mayor's office or from the police—a proclamation that *the Conscription Act was now suspended in New York and would not be enforced.* Also that the Board of Aldermen at a specially called meeting had *voted $2.5 million for all poor men to buy their way out of army service.* So for a few hours it looked like a victory for the mob: NO DRAFT!

There is still a mystery about the identity of the person who ordered, printed, and issued this false proclamation. No matter; the mob was now beyond reason, and in most cases beyond hope. The last big fight, the dying agony of the rebellion, took place at Jackson's Foundry. Here cannon at very close range drove off those it didn't kill.

In a city accepting a state of siege, fires and shooting seemed almost normal. Friday still saw fighting, but it was slowing down. The mayor issued a new statement. The rioters, it read, had been fully dispersed and the military forces now in the city would control all illegal actions.

The military clout of General Harvey Brown, in command of the Regulars, was passed on to General E. R. S. Canby. By the end of the riots it was in the hands of General John A. Dix. Generals were replaced like pitchers in a hard-fought baseball game. The police seemed to spend most of their energies searching poor districts to recover stolen items.

Not so much interest seems to have been taken in the loss of life, or the plight of the wounded. No count a historian can accept as reliable seems to be on record. The rioters lost about 2,000 dead, and the number of wounded was in the neighborhood of 8,000 to 10,000. Many dead and wounded were carried off and hidden. Only a few police were listed officially as dead. Fifty to sixty soldiers were killed (no official listing by the War Department exists). Some 300 of the army men were wounded. The counting of Negro losses is most confusing. Some seventy-six were casually listed by someone as "missing." Eighteen were noted as being hanged. Five were certainly drowned in the Hudson and East rivers by pursuing mobs.

Property damage was more carefully documented. More than $5 million in actual damage was reported, but with no reckoning of loss caused by stoppage of business and a fleeing work force. Among important buildings the major loss included, besides the Colored Orphan Asylum, a Protestant Mission to civilize far-off savages, three Provost Marshal offices, three police stations, one armory, many factories and stores.

In a few days most prisoners arrested as rioters were released, either through some change of heart or, more likely, because of the political muscle of the Democrats. For the slums were rich in one thing: votes. Accordingly, under the control of ward heelers they were a powerful political force at election time. When the riots had simmered down, only twenty rioters were still in jail. Nineteen stood trial and were convicted, and some served as little as five years in prison.

Some people called the New York Draft Riots "the Roman Catholic Insurrection." No Catholic property was destroyed, and there were reports of mobs shouting "Honor to the Pope!" and carrying signs lettered DOWN WITH THE PROTESTANTS!. Certainly priests were not molested, and in several cases they held back the mob from some evil action.

Moralists and historians have pointed out that the riots cannot in any way be considered a Catholic–Protestant war. The issue was never religious. It was the violent cry of agony and rage of the poor against the unfair Conscription Act, a law that spared the upper middle class and the rich from being forced into the war's armed forces.

BOOK THREE

Tammany – A Tiger in the Streets

6

Tammany

The story of Tammany Hall is wreathed in the legendary cigar smoke of political gossip. A long time ago, according to an Indian myth, there was a great hunter, a mighty fighter, and a wise man in council. This was all before the white men came in their sail canoes. Chief Tammany—for he was a chief—lived in the forest west of the Allegheny Mountains. He beat the evil spirits in many battles, defeated their plans to harm his people. Chief Tammany did mighty deeds, such as burning up the plains to fire-kill or singe the evil spirits. He scooped out a river by hand to prevent the Great Lakes from flooding and destroying his tribe. A man known as one who always helped his people—such was Chief Tammany.

When George Washington had been inaugurated as the first president of the new nation in New York City, an organization was formed and given the name of The Tammany Society of the Columbian Order in honor of the great all-protecting warrior chief. However, at a still earlier date—1732—a Philadelphia social club had organized and observed a Saint Tammany day.

The New York Tammany Society became a power in the political world of both city and state. But it was not at first the despicable ward heelers' organization, intent on looting the city and depending on the dispossessed for its votes. Originally and well into the nineteenth century it was made up of bankers, merchants, men from good middle-class and upper-class New York dynasties.

The original Tammany had begun with a constitution dated August 1789 as a fraternal and patriotic organization. For the meetings all members dressed in beads, feathers, blankets, and marched in parade as Indians. In the nineteenth century the Indian gear and feathered headdress were dropped by the membership.

Mr. William Mooney, Tammany's first grand sachem, had been in George Washington's army, and ran an upholstery shop on Nassau Street.

Although the original Tammany was made up of entrenched families in banking, shipping, selling, and buying land, it did not remain that way any great length of time. By 1840 there were changes in Tammany, and its aim was restricted to that of controlling the masses.

From 1840 on, Tammany, now fallen into cruder, more cunning hands, became expert in attracting graft, gifts from those needing political help or wanting certain favors done in the way of permissive business laws and building codes.

The sign of things to come was clear when a public official embezzled $1,250,000 in city funds and left for parts unknown.

Tammany in the time of the Tweed Ring after the Civil War really became a massive political machine, housed in a brick building on 14th Street east of Irving Place.

The cornerstone was laid by Mayor John T. Hoffman (who owed his election to the Tammany gang) in the rising days of the Tweed Ring in July 1867 under a banner that read CIVIL LIBERTY, THE GLORY OF MAN.

Tammany Hall was the Democratic Party in the city, and from New York it controlled Albany, the state capital. It dominated the courts, owned judges.

It was a one-man rule, with William Marcy Tweed dominating the contract award committees, appointing ward bosses, and directing the election processes. Since he controlled jobs, patronage, and contracts, the city's various committees ran the administration in name only.

New York City, as *Harper's Weekly* saw it just past the mid-nineteenth century, was:

> a huge semi-barbarous metropolis . . . not well-governed nor ill-governed, but simply not governed at all—with filthy and unlighted streets—no practical or efficient security for either life or property—a police not worthy of the name—and expenses steadily and enormously increasing.

LOOKING DOWN FIFTH AVENUE WHERE IT CROSSES 36TH STREET
(MID-NINETEENTH CENTURY)
Count off three blocks and you are opposite the site of the present Empire
State Building. The Fifth Avenue coach shown in the foreground was, of
course, horsedrawn. (*Harper's Weekly*—author's collection)

But it could not deny the city was also the most bustling port in the nation and growing with amazing speed. After the Civil War it became the most dominant style setter, publishing center, theater-loving city in the nation. And, as it moved into a new phase in the 1870s, it had its amusing, exciting sides and its glories. Hotels such as the Metropolitan, Astor, and St. Nicholas were as splendid as any in Europe.

Of course the other extreme existed in the dens and slums of Hell's Kitchen, in the grog shops and thieves' dens where disease and crime bred. Brooklyn, Queens, and Richmond were not to be added to the city until 1898. The city was still only what is now called Manhattan and the Bronx.

But all visitors agreed it was a fine city of brownstone uptown ("uptown" was usually considered to end at the horsecar line of Seventh Avenue at Times Square). You had to take the Seventh Avenue line to reach Central Park. A hansom cab could cost up to $5 for a journey into the farthest reaches of the city at High Bridge.

Also, by 1868, there was baseball before a crowd of 2,000 at the Union Grounds—the Mutuals playing against the Eckford Club. Wall Street already was chalking up stock prices, but waiting for Edison to invent the stock ticker. Maiden Lane guaranteed its diamonds, Tiffany's engraved silver, and Lord & Taylor was more than a notion and button and pins bazaar.

Everywhere the horse was visible, and it fed the imported English sparrows into plumpness. There were no traffic lights, and so stages, coaches, carriages, and drays tangled wildly. A bit of the old city awaited the visitor to Trinity Church, "the biggest structure on the eastern seaboard," towering to the dazzling height of 248 feet.

The jam of shipping on two rivers and along the bay and Battery was proving the city was the nation's great greedy mouth, inhaling, exhaling products. Factory smoke smudged the skies, bank processing was growing, and land values could hardly keep up with the demand for footage on the best New York streets. People were being crowded into the island's limited space at an amazing rate.

In 1870 the city boasted close to a million in population. It was a city moving from rags and hand-me-downs to the cane-carrying, wing-collared sports in black suits with wide cravats set with stickpins. The older men wore top hats, the sports and dudes favored the derby cocked over one eye, hair roached up in bear grease or macassar oil.

The women moved encased in whalebone-ribbed corsets like the torture of the Iron Maiden, and floated about with a half dozen petticoats and wide, leg-hiding skirts. Shoes were calf-huggers, and the high-button shoe with mother-of-pearl buttons was chic.

A TORRID DAY IN NEW YORK CITY
The ambulance service of the public hospitals shown in action during a mad
dash through city streets. (*Frank Leslie's Illustrated Newspaper*)

Gas lit the city streets, which was romantic enough, but the yellow-green haloes given off by the lamps was not enough light to spoil the sinister games of footpads and holdup men. The city was dangerous in some sections, but not so dangerous as it was to become in the 1970s. Thomas Edison brought progress with his development in 1882 of the world's first electric light power plant, located on Pearl Street.

Overhead between cast-iron and tin cornices were strands of wires on street poles with spidery webbings of telegraph lines, soon to be joined by more poles, more lines of telephone and electric power.

It was the age of hair on head and face—not to be seen again until the 1960s and 1970s. The Tammany boys, the uptown sports and dudes, the laborer, the pimp and safeblower, all had their own ideas of hair—in pompadours with long sideburns (after General Burnside); the walrus moustache, thick, majestic, twirled and waxed to spikes at its ends; and the muttonchop, popular with Franz Josef of Austria-Hungary and all Wall Street brokers and bankers. The bartenders' special was a head of hair parted in the middle, larded, combed down over the ears.

Medical science in New York and elsewhere was notorious and a horror in its practice. The citizen of the city, like the nation, dosed him or herself with bitter-tasting and alcohol-drenched patent medicines. One washed with Pears soap, wore electric belts for joint pains, believed fresh air at night was a killer.

The German Jews invented ready-made clothing off the rack. But the seamstress and the fashionable lady's and gent's tailor remained. The harbor showed lumber unloading, New England ice packed in sawdust.

The Tweed Gang that was to dominate Tammany brought attention to the matter of trusts—the control of a needed commodity so as to raise its cost to the public. There were already trusts in coal (Mark Hanna),

BELLEVUE HOSPITAL IN THE SECOND HALF OF THE NINETEENTH CENTURY
The balcony on the left, moved here from Wall Street, is the one from which President George Washington made his first inaugural address. (Author's collection)

kindling wood, lamp oil (John D. Rockefeller), and ice, and, as a Senate investigation was to show, in steel (Andrew Carnegie, Henry Clay Frick), copper (Anaconda and the House of Morgan), railroads (James Hill, Jay Gould, Daniel Drew, Collis P. Huntington), and shipping (Cornelius Vanderbilt).

All the needs of the city and its administration could be milked and made to pay to any group that could control the voters, elect its own political muscle, and create and pass whatever laws it needed to put pressure on the trusts, which would then be forced to buy immunity from those laws with bribes, gifts, stocks, and "honest graft."

❦

The first seizure of a city and state by one man and his gang had to wait for the genius of William Marcy Tweed, and his bringing to political power that most corrupt municipal organization, Tammany Hall. The years of his power lasted from 1866 to 1871. The City of New York has never fully recovered.

Civic corruption on a major scale was created by Tweed and his general staff leaders, Peter Barr Sweeney, A. Oakey Hall, and Richard Connolly. Under Tweed they made corruption of democracy into a science that many other American cities have studied and followed. A system of control of patronage seemed perfect, and its hold on city and state lawmakers, the courts, the police, and the criminal element was often used to help get the voter in the proper mood. Certainly Tweed put together the first modern boss-run city and election machine, and even today it is a model to be studied.

Tweed was a modern executive, with the skill of those tycoons who run great corporations. Add to this an amazing talent for political organization and you have "The Boss." He was astute and knew how to pull together, manipulate, and consolidate as no one had yet done in city politics. He controlled the political clout, the vast majority of the city's poor, the derelict voters (often voting as repeaters).

Oddly enough he has come down to us as a New York legend, not as the true man. I polled a hundred people on Tweed. To most he was a tough, slum-raised, Irish stereotype, vulgar, rosary-kissing, and illiterate.

Nothing could be further from the real William Marcy Tweed. He was *not* a Catholic, *not* an Irishman. Not from some Five Points rookery of poverty and crime. He was actually a Protestant with three solid generations of Scots in America behind him. The family lived well on Cherry Hill. His father was a well-thought-of gentleman who had a fine business in the making of chairs and held shares in a firm of brush makers.

William Marcy Tweed was born into this respectability in New York City in 1829 and was spoiled by his mother. He entered business with the brush firm at nineteen, but it was dull to this sharp mind and in 1848 he

TAMMANY BOSS WILLIAM M. TWEED
He invented the modern big-city political machine, which has looted so
many American cities and made boss rule the greatest political power in the
land. (Ross Collection)

became a member of American Engine Company 6. It has as its painted
mascot a roaring tiger, which the cartoonist Thomas Nast eventually
turned into the notorious symbol the Tammany Tiger.

On election days the fire laddies were out supporting their party and
people in their ward with voting advice. And with blows if they had to.
The "Big Six," Tweed's company—seventy-five of them—got out the vote
for the Democrats and Tammany Hall. By 1850 Tweed was Alderman of
the 7th Ward. Now loot could be won in return for political favors.
Padded accounts, city contracts, and helping to lobby for the right bills
all meant cash on the line in return.

It was apprentice time for Tweed. He even went to Congress for two
years, but Washington, D.C., wasn't New York. Back home all he could
get was school commissioner. The Know-Nothings, the anti-Catholics,
super-American native bigots beat Tweed, and he even lost the 7th

Ward. He was thirty-one and a flop. He ran for sheriff and was beaten, but he came back to power by organizing the defeat of Fernando Wood for mayor.

Tammany had been badly split, and Tweed saw that he could be the healing surgeon. He sensed that power could come to whoever dominated the State Central Committee of the New York Democratic party.

Tweed had himself made chairman. He gave the impression of being fair, he had skill, and he knew how to line up followers to see things his way. It was just a step to the chairmanship of the General Committee of Tammany Hall. Tweed packed it with the men he was developing as his general staff. It was a time, Tweed saw, for getting rid of the old loyalists, the ancient sachems, the fat ward heelers, and aged graft hunters. He was out to stir things up and he wanted the honorary title of grand sachem. By skillfully maneuvering his followers Tweed became both chairman of the General Committee *and* the grand sachem.

With power he needed money, and he knew how to get it. The city used much printing and needed enormous amounts of office supplies. He bought control of a New York printing firm. Padding bills, creating false accounts, billing the city for excessive costs, the company did well.

Now Tweed did not only the city's printing but also the printing of permits and inspection forms for insurance companies, railroads, shipping lines, ferries. They had to use the Tweed printing plants to get favors done; all this besides the payoffs they made to remain untroubled by the city rulings.

Tweed depended on his ward bosses and made a science of developing them. The ward boss began his career with youth gangs, with the district's male population. He helped by giving aid to the poor in winter and running river picnic trips in summer.

A ward boss was actually of real service to the poor, the immigrant, the desperate in their poverty. Tammany was the only organization that offered massive aid. All it asked for in return was loyalty to the Tammany boss and the proper number of votes on election days.

7

... and the Irish

From the days when signs outside factories told them NO IRISH NEEDED to the officially approved St. Patrick's Day parade, the march of the Irish to political power in New York City has been part of the ingrained, often entertaining, history of the city.

The first record of a St. Pat's parade in New York goes back to March 17, 1779, when the Volunteers of Ireland, 400 strong and fairly sober, paraded behind, of all things, a British army band on Lower Broadway. They marched to a Bowery eating place to celebrate St. Patrick's Day, led by their colonel, Irish-born Lord Rawdon. It was all a scheme by the colonel to enlist them to fight against George Washington, "the damn rebel." But after all the "foine noble banquet of 500 covers," a lot of the marchers went over to Washington's side.

The true St. Patrick's Day parades didn't really amount to much until the middle of the nineteenth century, "when Irishmen were in plentiful supply in New York, driven from the Auld Sod by famine and flood, and British bayonets doing right by the landlords." (B.R. Memoirs).

The 1851 parade had to fight sleet and snow as the marchers followed Colonel Mike Phelan of the old 9th Regiment and the loud band.

The pipes and drums fought another storm the next year, but by now the St. Patrick's Day parade was a duty for every able-bodied son of Ireland in New York. The old route went up Third Avenue, crossed to Eighth Avenue and down via many turns to Park Row, and then up Prince Street to St. Patrick's Cathedral.

Usually in those days after a Mass the important members of The Friendly Sons of Saint Patrick ate heartily while drinking the potent brew at Keefe's Racket Clubhouse on Broadway.

⋯⸋⋯

After the Civil War the all-devouring Tammany Hall and William Marcy Tweed came to power. Tammany Hall was not at that time the only social order to rise to fame and membership in New York City. On February 16, 1868, in Military Hall at 193 Bowery, The Benevolent and Protective Order of Elks was born. Actually they had first come together as The Jolly Corks, being actors, singers, minstrels—all males who needed a Sunday place to drink beer, lark, josh, and sing. They began to gather in Mrs. Geisman's boardinghouse on Elm Street, just north of City Hall, to chase gloom from the usually stodgy Sunday of the city.

In 1867 an English music hall singer, Charlie Algernon Sidney Vivian, came to New York and became one of the gang at Mrs. Geisman's, joining The Jolly Corks at their simple, noisy beer-and-cheese feasts.

Charlie thought they should get a better name, and suggested the Buffalos. It was used by a splendid London group of sports, so why not use it here? But he was voted down eight to seven and the name Elks was voted in. (Today Elm Street is officially renamed Elk Street in honor of the Corks.) Why Elks, if not Buffalos? The story is that Phineas T. Barnum had a stuffed elk's head for sale at his Broadway and Ann Street museum, and it was bought cheap by the new club.

The original B.P.O.E. took in as members only actors and performers of the theater. But soon it was open to all males if "white" (black Elks had their own organization). First women broke the original rules; and then in 1973 there were threats against its tax-free status and the tax-deductible contributions of members.

In many places there was talk of withdrawal of liquor licenses. So the B.P.O.E. (often referred to by members as meaning Best People on Earth) voted out the word "white" as pertaining to its membership. What had begun as The Jolly Corks and the actor's need to enjoy gloomy Sundays in New York City grew in time to a membership of nearly two million in over 1,700 lodges, with 25,000 members in New York alone.

Early in the B.P.O.E.'s existence some spoke of it as a place where a man could get away from his wife and family, don a fez, feel like a sultan, and forget his own marriage vows. In fact, the city of New York issued no marriage licenses until 1908. Up to that year sea captains, magistrates, ministers of almost any faith could perform a ceremony to their liking—and, if they remembered, send a record of the wedding to the Health Department. No fee was demanded.

When marriage licenses became the law, a fee of $1 was voted, and an alderman could still marry a couple and pocket their offering. In 1916 the aldermen were disqualified from marrying couples, and a few years later the fee for licenses went to $2.

For outdoor sporting there was the ringtailed rooter, the New York bicycle fiend, one of those daring young men bent with grace over the handlebars, dressed in belted jacket, knickerbockers, Alpine hat, and perhaps a cape. Called a scorcher and a crackajack, he was a devil-may-care speed rider who performed much like today's drag-strip racers in their hopped-up cars.

The bike riders had taken up the two-wheeled dare-devil, chain-driven sports models with a whirling of pedals and a tinkling of bells that drove the more sedate and careful riders in Central Park and Riverside Drive to the side of the road. The primitive autocar was still a generation or two away, and for the less adventuresome a good team of horses and a striped rig was preferred for the Long Island roads and the pikes north to Yonkers and White Plains.

The wheel was a draisiana, draisina, drasienne, celerifère, or velocipede, all first names given the earliest bicycle. The first three from an inventor, Baron Carl von Drais of Baden, who made a vehicle as an aid to walking. By the middle of the nineteenth century New York City sportsmen were riding "bone shakers" over the cobbles, and the more daring ladies were taking up the sport. Soon there were guides to the wheels and how to tame them.

There were wheel-riding schools. Wrote one bicycle master, Charles Spencer, in *Bicycles & Tricycles, Past and Present*:

> I found it was almost indispensably necessary that everyone becoming possessed of a velocipede should be able to ride it before taking the machine away. In the spring of 1869 the fever was at its height. . . . Everyone possessed of a pair of legs seemed equally interested in the subject, and anxious to put them to a better use than the old-fashioned one of walking. . . . It was a droll sight to see eminent statesmen and wealthy merchants being wheeled helplessly along, one after the other, their whole attention concentrated on the effort of keeping their seats upon the machines . . . there would be a few who had already learned to balance themselves and who were now practicing vaulting on and off, greatly to the dread of those who were having their own first lesson.

Progress and some science came quickly. James K. Starley introduced the Ordinary, made of steel tubing, a suspension saddle, a high

THE WELL-DRESSED LADY AND GENT BIKE RIDERS
Fashion drawings of the great days of the two-wheel sport. The lady's bloomers are very daring. (Author's collection)

front wheel and smaller rear one. India rubber tires came in, reducing vibration and increasing power to propel.

Colonel Albert A. Pope, of Newton, Massachusetts, started the first successful bicycle manufacturing in this country. Pope sponsored a bicycle trip around the world by Thomas Stevens. He pedaled off in 1883 and returned in 1887.

Women and sports wanted a faster and safer bike, and in 1885 the chain rear-driven safety bicycle came in. It was easier to ride and less hazardous. The high front wheel was abandoned and the frame was redesigned so a lady could pedal without exposing too much leg.

H. G. Rouse wrote in 1890, advising women:

> Do not wear corsets, as you cannot jump nor climb hills with any comfort. . . . Wear a tight-fitting health band instead. . . . It is not advisable to wear a bustle. . . . Many ladies wear the outside skirt too short by three or four inches. The foot ought not to be exposed much more than when walking, and nothing could be more out of place or conspicuous than light-colored tennis shoes on a bicycle.

Actually, ladies' skirts, which trailed the ground, protected from the dust by a dust ruffle of mohair braid, rose immodestly above the ankle to the tops of their high-laced shoes for riding the newfangled bicycle. Eyebrows were raised when some wore bloomers, riding tandem "on a bicycle built for two." The costume was completed with striped cotton blouse with leg-o'-mutton sleeves and ribbons flying from straw sailors.

8
Society — Fisk and Gould

What of the people who stood above the Tweed Ring? The text of an 1872 book, *Lights and Shadows of New York Life*, by James D. McCabe, Jr., tells us how they lived—the Four Hundred and others:

> Extravagance is the besetting sin of New York society. Money is absolutely thrown away. Fortunes are spent every year in dress and in all sorts of follies. Houses are fitted up and furnished in the most sumptuous style, the building and its contents being sometimes worth a million of dollars. People live up to every cent of their incomes, and often beyond them. It is no uncommon occurrence for a fine mansion, its furniture, pictures, and even the jewels of its occupants, to be pledged to some usurer for the means with which to carry on this life of luxury.
>
> In no other city of the land is there to be seen such magnificent dressing on the part of the ladies as in New York. The amount of money and time expended here on dress is amazing. There are two objects in view in all this—the best dressed woman at a ball or party is not only sure to outshine her sisters there present, but is certain to have the satisfaction next day of seeing her magnificence celebrated in some of the city journals. Her vanity and love of distinction are both gratified in this way, and such a triumph is held to be worth any expense.

A writer reported in the New York *World*:

> Most women in society can afford to dress as it pleases them, since they have unlimited amounts of money at their disposal. Among females dress is the principal part of society. What would Madam Mountain be without her laces and diamonds, or Madam Blanche without her silks and satins? Simply commonplace old women, past their prime, destined to be wall-flowers. A fashionable woman has just as many new dresses as the different times she goes into society. . . .
>
> Walking dresses cost from $50 to $300; ball dresses are frequently imported from Paris at a cost of from $500 to $1,000; while wedding dresses may cost from $1,000 to $5,000. Nice white Llama jackets can be had for $60 to $200. Then there are travelling dresses in black silk, in pongee, velour, in piqué, which range in price from $75 to $175.
>
> Then there are evening robes in Swiss muslin, robes in linen for the garden and croquet playing, dresses for horse races and for yacht races, robes de nuit and robes de chambre, dresses for breakfast and for dinner, dresses for receptions and for parties, dresses for watering places.

No wonder all this glitter attracted once poor boys grown rich. Jim Fisk, Jr., who with Jay Gould was to try to corner all the gold in the United States outside of government vaults, was born the son of a Vermont wagon peddler of tin goods, dry goods, and notions. Jim, Jr., was a free-living youth, not all the proper New Englander, neither frugal, pious, nor given to Puritan guilt. He drank, he tumbled the farm girls off their feet in barns, he enjoyed the pleasures of having money and using it. And when he moved into New York society, his dress, jewels, uniforms were just a bit too garish.

During the Civil War he became an agent for the New York stock speculator Daniel Drew. Jim liked war and turmoil. He had enjoyed life as a wagon peddler, had even worked once feeding and caring for a traveling animal show. But war showed him how to make "real big money." He journeyed into danger, personally moving contraband cotton and handling sales of army blankets for contractors. He managed to outwit his partners until they bought him out for $60,000, a sum he immediately lost playing the market on Wall Street.

Large, florid, a gross feeder and drinker, his losses did not diminish his love of women and the good life. Banking with Drew and Jay Gould, soon Jim Fisk was head of a Wall Street brokerage firm, Fisk & Belden.

In just a couple of years, with a liberal doling out of cigars, whisky, and addresses of pretty women, he was a master of stock manipulation. His partner, Jay Gould, was small, razor-sharp. In his prime he sported a curly black beard, and his face was dominated by dark, brooding eyes and an eagle's beak (but he was not Jewish as bigoted legend has

NEW YORK DOCKS ON THE EVE OF THE CIVIL WAR
A busy scene of drays, horsecars, cargoes, ships, and ferryboats. Note family
of newcomers, with their packs and other belongings, in foreground. (*Harper's
Weekly*)

claimed). A quiet man most of the time, but a tiger in his business dealings. Facing a Congressional committee interviewing him about the evil of his kind of dealings, he could excuse his dishonesty and blurt out: "*We* made the country rich, *we* developed the country."

Gould was born in Roxbury, Delaware, of solid Yankee stock, and tended cows as a boy. Too small and frail to farm, he went to Hobart Academy and decided he wanted to become a surveyor. At sixteen Gould, in a real-estate turnover, made over $2,000, cheating his employer in the deal. Soon afterward he gave up the life of a wandering surveyor and came to New York.

Like so many of Balzac's characters, Gould hoped to conquer a city. He promoted a new kind of mouse trap, and this and other projects gave him by age twenty a nest egg of $5,000. He played the leather market—a good bet in an age of boots and horse harness—and got a partner who put up $120,000 to set up a big tannery in a place later to be named Gouldsboro. When the company failed to show any profits, the partner, an old man, moved in to take a closer look at the operation and discovered that Gould was an expert in crooked bookkeeping. In panic he sold out his investment to Gould for half of what he had put up.

Gould found a new partner named Charles Leupp, who soon discovered that he, too, had been cheated and ruined. He put a pistol to his head and killed himself. When his heirs tried to take over the tannery by force and a battle, they found a stubborn Gould holding the fort. In the end he was dislodged, but got away with much loot. In the Civil War Gould made new fortunes in railroad stocks and speculating in gold.

Gould subsequently married a woman with money, and with his father-in-law began to secure control of railroad lines. After ruining a road by contracts benefiting himself and stripping it of its assets, he usually bought the line back at bargain rates.

It was in his railroad adventures with Daniel Drew that he met Jim Fisk. They recognized each other; both regarded the public as dupes and fools in the area of speculation. Between them Gould and Fisk began to study the market in greater detail.

Fisk took a plump and strutting actress, Josie Mansfield, as a mistress. He left a wife to go to live with Josie, and spent money with reckless abandon on her. Gould, however, was a good husband and a puritan in the matter of the fleshly delights offered by New York. Both men were experts in the intricate secrets of stock dealing.

With Gould, Fisk and Drew took part in the wild chase for money by manipulating Erie Railroad stocks. And only their battle with the shell-hard old man, Cornelius Vanderbilt, "kept them from carrying off everything including the depot stove." Gould remained a careful, rather humorless man, but he liked boisterous Jim Fisk and they more or less trusted each other.

Gould was arrested for carrying a suitcase with half a million dollars in cash to Albany where it was used for bribing the legislators in the Erie control fight. The Erie was charged "legal expenses" of $1 million.

One man in whom he didn't "take much stock" got only $5,000. In court Gould faced judges he had bribed. He claimed what he had done was for the good of the railroad. He believed himself to be in friendly hands, since he had joined the Tweed Ring and had gotten some of the gang on the board of directors of the Erie. Gould became president of the Erie and Jim Fisk vice-president after Vanderbilt made his peace with them.

Fisk and Gould moved ahead, expanding into real estate. They owned the Opera House in New York on West 12th Street. Fisk took to managing the place and became a real theater dude. He displayed large diamonds, a crimson-lined silk cape. He lived behind the theater in a big house and enjoyed the high life of the stage. Josie lived nearby.

His was a flashy stage-door-Johnny front. But cunning as ever, with Gould he was moving into the control of coal mines, harbor leases, ferry-boats, and always rails. Once a ruined man broke into Gould's office and held a pistol to his head until Gould gave him a check for $25,000. Fisk would have tried to seize the weapon. Gould paid off.

The New York *Herald* wrote of Wall Street operations at this time:

> Within the past few days we have seen the most gigantic swindling operations carried on in Wall Street that have as yet disgraced our financial centre. A great railway, one of the two that connect the West with the Atlantic seaboard, has been tossed about like a football, its real stockholders have seen their property abused by men to whom they have entrusted its interests, and who, in the betrayal of that trust, have committed crimes which in parallel cases on a smaller scale would have deservedly sent them to Sing Sing. If these parties go unwhipped of justice, then are we doing injustice in confining criminals in our state prisons for smaller crimes.
>
> To such a disgusting degree of depravity do we see these stock operations carried, that members of the church of high standing offer, when "concerned," to betray their brother "pals," and, in their forgetfulness of the morality to which they sanctimoniously listen every Sunday, state that "all they care about is to look out for number one."
>
> A railroad treasurer boldly states that he has without authority over-issued stock of the company to a large amount. He offers it to a broker for sale, with the understanding that all received over a fixed value is to go into his (the treasurer's) pocket. From the fact that this man is not arrested for mal-administration of the company's property, we judge this to be a legitimate operation, and that this may hereafter serve as a model or standard of morals to all presidents, directors, treasurers and managers of railway and other great corporations.

Gould and Fisk remained silent. They had a bigger scheme hatching.

9

On a Black Friday

Gold, "that yellowy buttery stuff," has dominated the thinking of many. Columbus had the world thinking he had found the key to the treasures of China and India. Cortez murdered and tortured for it. Fisk and Gould saw the westward surge of the United States was as much a series of gold rushes, or rumors of gold finds, as the hunt of the homesteader for a clearing and the cattleman for range grass.

In New York during the summer of 1869 gold was on the minds of men like J. P. Morgan, Jay Gould, and Jim Fisk. Not just its scale of values as money, as credits in ledgers, but as images of the actual metal itself, the gold bars in the U.S. Treasury. The whole national economy rested in that gold reserve.

Jay Gould, having completed some strange and rewarding swindles in railroad stock, was studying the Gold Room of the New York Stock Exchange, an institution that controlled the dealings in the floating supply of gold. Gould envisioned himself cornering the nation's currency. The gold on the exchange could be controlled with his resources. However, the U.S. Treasury held about $80 million of the yellow metal. This *must* be kept out of the market if he and Fisk were to capture all free gold. If he could make sure the Treasury gold would not be thrown on the Gold Room of the Stock Exchange, he could manipulate upward the gold on the market and make a fortune by controlling the inflated price.

The major problem was to make certain President Ulysses S. Grant would not move the nation's gold from its vaults. And Grant, like some modern presidents, had greedy, demanding relatives, among them a son-in-law, Abel R. Corbin, a wobbly speculator, actually a front for some special interests, a lobbyist of sorts. Jay Gould gave Corbin "credits" of up to $15,000 of gold for himself. He didn't demand payment from Corbin, but, in return, Corbin felt he owed Gould a favor.

Gould's agents, meanwhile, were active in Washington explaining to the senators and congressmen that a rise in the value of gold on the open market would "help the farmer" and aid his grain sales in Europe. Trade, they promised, would leap forward. The Gould argument, a bit puzzling to many, was that gold prices must go up and the value of the paper dollar down. The result—national prosperity.

TWO OF THE MOST NOTORIOUS FINANCIERS IN AMERICA
James Fisk, Jr., (left) and Jay Gould (right) together made swindlers' history in New York City and schemed to take control of all the free gold on the market. (Author's collection)

But there was another Jay active on Wall Street—Jay Cooke & Co. This Jay was bearish on gold, out to lower the price of gold. Jay Cooke & Co. handled paper money, legal tender, government bonds. They were buying and selling millions of dollars' worth of paper, making fortunes from the inflated currency. Several large banking firms were allied with the Jay Cooke side, enjoying the business in the rise in paper money.

In June President Grant visited his son-in-law, Corbin, in New York City, and was entertained on Jim Fisk's yacht, the *Providence*. No actresses were present, but good whisky was available.

So yacht-borne, with bourbon glass in hand, cigar drawing well, Grant, the one-time business failure, army misfit, kindling wood peddler, was pleased to be so intimate with the kings of the railroad, stockbrokers, bankers—the nabobs that dealt in and made millions. Grant felt these people respected him for the wisdom, the skill (and butchery) with which he had managed to bring victory on so many battlefields.

Jay Gould had his ear, hovering over him and whispering as the yacht sailed on. Gould was explaining again and again that the free ride of gold on an open market, seeking its own level, not hindered by the metal in the U.S. Treasury, was good for the country.

Grant continued to sip his whisky and keep his cigar alight. There were journalists present and it was clearly evident that President Grant had not made any definite response to the gold crowd.

❦

Gold dropped to 125 in the Gold Room listing. Gould and Grant's son-in-law had a friendly connection in the person of the Subtreasurer of the United States in New York. He owed them favors. The gold lobbyists and what would today be called public-relations men were active—feeding, badgering, and hinting at the rewards for favors to be done that were there for all politicians within reach. (It was "honest" bribery—everybody could get a bone with some meat on it.) There was a fancy banquet set up for the Secretary of the Treasury, A. S. Boutwell. He made it clear in a speech that the Treasury would keep hands off.

Suddenly, then, gold rose to 133. Corbin, the president's son-in-law, was handed a check for $25,000 as "profits." In September Grant was again visiting the Corbins in their New York home. Things appeared to be going well, Corbin told the Goldbugs. The president had ordered Secretary Boutwell to keep the U.S. Treasury gold off the market "until the present struggle between bulls and bears is over."

Gold went to 137.

Did Grant actually give such an order? Did any conversation actually ever take place with the president? Corbin reported to Gould and his Goldbug pool that it had. It seemed to them the time was ripe for increased action. Subtreasurer Burrefield got a gift of $1,500,000 in a gold account opened in his name. Others also had gifts dangled before their eyes. Gould told Jim Fisk that even Mrs. Grant was involved in gold speculation.

The rumor about Mrs. Grant being "in gold" was spread by Fisk, and it did its work. Gold shot to 141. The Tammany bank (the Tenth National) gave the Goldbugs everything it had in resources, issuing certified checks to buy gold as if the checks were mere snowflakes. The only collateral asked for was the gold they were buying. Gould, Fisk, and the Goldbugs bought about $40 million in gold for delivery, which was actually about two times as much gold as was in existence on the free market.

The price of gold eventually rose to 144¼. Gould had produced a major coup so far. He had cornered all the gold, and he could demand payment in gold from those who had sold him gold, sold short, and didn't really have it. It was a squeeze play of genius. *If* Grant stood firm.

The gold shortage panic was on. The Goldbugs had all the gold, real and on call. For the nation to do business, produce, ship, import—that gold was needed. On September 15 the media (as at a later Watergate) began to suggest something was very wrong with the president and the people closest to him. Horace Greeley in the *Tribune* came out against the huge conspiracy to corner gold and demanded that the U.S. Treasury offer gold and gold bonds to ease the dangerous currency crisis. The other Jay, Jay Cooke, went to see Grant and Boutwell in Washington and lay the whole Gould-Fisk scheme on the line.

The Goldbugs at once put the screws to Grant's son-in-law, Corbin, to force him to earn his keep. They induced him to write a letter to the president in which he confessed to Grant that he was deeply involved and that the release of U.S. gold would ruin not only him but the president's daughter and their friends, too.

Grant was, for all his failings, a thoroughly honest man. A weakling and a fool in political affairs he may have been, but there was a rigid integrity in him not usually found in political affairs. The president was a public servant, not a power-seeking flouter of the Constitution. He never understood the dirty end of politics. Appointments to individuals, double dealing by railroads, dishonesty in the Indian agencies, the selling of public office and favors done by those around him—all this was to become the biggest betrayal of public trust until the events in Washington a century later.

The difference was Grant's integrity.

Once aware of the real facts of the Gould-Fisk gold scheme, Grant moved swiftly with the crisp alertness he had so often demonstrated on the battlefield. His daughter was informed in a personal letter to instruct her husband to sell all his gold stocks without delay. The president sternly rejected any idea that he was in any way connected with his son-in-law in relation to current events in the Gold Room. Corbin at once ran to Gould and blurted out the news—the president *wasn't* on their side. He would release Treasury gold for sale. Gould knew at once that his scheme had peaked and he was now in great trouble.

Friday, September 24, 1869, was to become Black Friday for Wall Street and the nation. Fisk had orders to keep buying gold, to try to lift the price to 200 before the news got out that the president wasn't playing ball. The brokers, Belden & Speyer, would do the buying in their own firm's name, taking all responsibility in the effort to boost gold to 200.

A close watch was kept on the telegraph ticker receiving messages direct from Washington so they would know the moment the U.S. Treasury made public its move to use the gold reserve.

The price of gold went to 150, 160, then to 165. Every large city witnessed the same riotous scenes, wild bidding, a frenzied mob of speculators, hopefuls and a few skeptics, none yet aware of Grant's reaction. Philadelphia, San Francisco, Boston, Chicago saw gold stocks become the most active in trading.

Secretary Boutwell began to fling millions in government gold onto the market. There was much publicity making clear what was being done against the Goldbugs. Less than fifteen minutes after this shocking turn of events, the gold bubble burst and the price of gold dropped. Rage, anger, fear, horror etched the faces of the gold brokers. In *Lights and Shadows of New York Life*, James D. McCabe, Jr., recorded:

> The end had come, and the exhausted operators streamed out of the stifling hall into the fresh air of the street. To them, however, came no peace. In some offices customers by dozens, whose margins were irrevocably burnt away in the smelting furnace of the Gold Board, confronted their dealers with taunts and threats of violence for their treachery.
>
> In others the nucleus of mobs began to form, and, as the day wore off, Broad Street had the aspect of a riot. Huge masses of men gathered before the doorway of Smith, Gould, Martin & Co., and Heath & Co. Fisk was assaulted, and his life threatened. Deputy sheriffs and police officers appeared on the scene. In Brooklyn a company of troops were held in readiness to march upon Wall Street. . . .
>
> At the Gold Exchange Bank the weary accountants were making ineffective efforts to complete Thursday's business. That toilful midnight, at the close of the last great passion-day of the bullion worshippers, will be ever memorable for its anxieties and unsatisfying anguish.
>
> Saturday brought no relief. The Gold Board met only to adjourn, as the Clearing House had been incapable of the task of settling its accounts, complicated as they were by ever fresh failures. The small brokers had gone under by scores. The rumors of the impending suspension of some of the largest houses of the street gave fresh grounds for fear.

The Stock Exchange was now the centre of attraction. If that yielded, all was lost. To sustain the market was vital. But whence was the saving power to come? All through yesterday shares had been falling headlong. New York Central careened to 148, and then recovered to 185¾. Hudson plunged from 173 to 145. Pittsburg fell to 68. Northwest reached 62½. The shrinkage throughout all securities had been not less than thirty millions.

Ruined men stood staring at chalked figures that had destroyed their lives. There were bankruptcies, rich men went insolvent, stripped right down to their high button shoes. The brokers were aware that gold buyers had pistols; and those firms that had touted gold heavily knew they were prime targets for murder by desperate men.

At the first news of disaster Gould had taken it on the run, leaving his offices by a back door. Fisk, claiming he hadn't been warned, gave Grant's son-in-law a bawling out, calling him a scoundrel. Actually Fisk had made a fortune. He had secretly been selling out his gold stocks. Some sources insist he made $11 million the morning before Grant released federal gold.

Jay Gould moved quickly to protect himself and his holdings. He owned several judges, and got out a dozen injunctions and court writs stopping enforcement by the Gold Room Board and the Stock Exchange of any contracts he would have to settle. The brokers, Belden & Speyer, paid out not a penny for gold bought; all their bids for gold stock were erased. One of the partners, Speyer, lost his mind for a time. Fisk, of course, had been too smart to sign any orders, so the brokers had taken all the risk upon themselves.

Not all brokers fared as well as did Gould and Fisk in escaping their responsibilities. It was recorded in the New York *Herald*:

> Failure to make good deliveries would have insured the instant selling out of defaulters "under the rule." As the majority of brokers were inextricably involved in the late difficulty, the only consequence would have been to throw them into bankruptcy, thus bringing some $60,000,000 under the hammer. The market could not have borne up under such an avalanche. It was decided that the Room should be kept open for borrowings and loans, but that all dealings should be suspended. One result of this complication was that gold had no fixed value. It could be bought at one house for 133 and at other offices sold for 139. . . .

President Grant's credibility was destroyed. He was smudged for being more than just indiscreet, and for being part of unlawful acts that led right "into the parlor of the President."

⊷§⊶

The investigations of Black Friday resulted in nothing being done for the public, nor was there any drastic reform of the stock market. Gould insisted that legally he had done no wrong. Appearing before the investigating committee, he represented himself as a pure and noble citizen. What he had done on the market was for that vast faceless mass "the people," and for the men with the hoes—the farmers.

Fisk was the clown of the hearings. He claimed to have been jobbed, led on by Grant's son-in-law and Mrs. Grant, told things that events would prove hadn't been so at all. He demanded that some of the Grant family—Mrs. Grant, the Grants' daughter—be brought to face a courtroom investigation.

The committee was extremely careful not to probe too deeply into this facet of the affair. The members' report was mealy-mouthed and concluded that the country's business had been paralyzed for a time, the foundations of money morality and big-business progress "rudely shaken."

Gould continued to play his games of shearing the public and debauching justice, carefully and with deliberation. But Jim Fisk was destined to face pistol fire, moving to a dramatic climax of his career.

There was something likable about the big bear of a man—even when his wickedness was being exposed to the public eye.

The journalist, James D. McCabe, Jr., wrote:

> His monogram was placed on everything he owned or was connected with, and he literally lived in the gaze of the public. He can scarcely be said to have had any private life, for the whole town was talking of his theatres, his dashing four in hand, his railway and steamboats, his regiment, his toilettes, his reckless generosity, and his love affairs.
>
> He had little regard for morality or public sentiment, and hesitated at nothing necessary to the success of his schemes. His great passion was for notoriety, and he cared not what he did so it made people talk about him.
>
> In some respects he was a strange compound of good and evil. He was utterly unprincipled, yet he was generous to a fault. No one ever came to him in distress without meeting with assistance, and it adds to the virtues of these good deeds that he never proclaimed them to the world.

In view of Fisk's interest and involvement in the theater, it is not surprising that he should encounter an actress who was to play a significant role in his life. She was Helen Josephine, "Josie," Mansfield who, at the time Fisk first met her late in 1867, had recently been divorced from her husband Frank Lawler. Fisk fell wildly in love with her and she became his mistress and lived with him for many years.

Of the theater world in the period of Josie's time on the stage, James D. McCabe, Jr., writes in *Places of Amusement*:

There are sixteen theatres in New York usually in full operation. Taking them in their order of location from south to north, they are the Stadt, the Bowery, Niblo's Theatre Comique, the Olympic, Lina Edwins, the Globe, Wallack's, Union Square, the Academy of Music, the Fourteenth Street, Booth's, the Grand Opera House, the Fifth Avenue, the St. James, and Wood's.

They are open throughout the fall and winter season, are well patronized, and with one or two exceptions, are successful in a pecuniary sense. There are usually from 50,000 to 100,000 strangers in the city, and the majority of these find the evenings dull without some amusement to enliven them. Many of them are persons who come for pleasure, and who regard the theatres as one of the most enjoyable of all the sights of the city; but a very large portion are merchants, who are wearied with buying stock, and who really need some pleasant relaxation after the fatigues of the day. To these must be added a large class of citizens who are fond of the drama, and who patronize the theatres liberally.

All these, it is stated, expend upon the various amusements of the place about $30,000 per night; and of this sum the larger part goes into the treasury of the theatres. The sum annually expended on amusements is said to be from $7,000,000 to $8,000,000.

It is said that the members of the dramatic profession and the various attachés of the theatres number 5,000 persons. They constitute a class, or rather a world of their own. The "stars" can make their own terms, but the rank and file of the profession have to take what they can get. The pay of these ranges from $15 to $50 per week. Some of the leading ladies and gentlemen receive from $100 to $200 per week, but these can be counted on the fingers of one hand.

Josie, by the time Fisk became enamored of her, was a bit on the battered side. Born in Boston she had known the hard edge of the West Coast in her girlhood. Her father was shot down and killed in public during some hotheaded disagreement in debate. Her mother took in boarders in San Francisco. On the Barbary coast Josie eloped with the actor Frank Lawler. But the marriage wasn't successful. She came east to take some theatrical assignments, got divorced, and went on to her lucrative liaison with Jim Fisk.

Josie was not a loyal mistress to Jim. She was greedy and sensual and she liked men—especially men with a great deal of wealth. Jim did business with all kinds of people, and one person he associated with on a deal in a Brooklyn oil refinery was the suave society figure of Edwin S. Stokes, whose moustache was as long as Jim's. However, his background was the silver spoon class of Philadelphia's Main Line. A real-life college athletic hero, Stokes was also a smart but not flashy member of the New York Stock Exchange, a lover of blooded horses, and had a rather dull family of a proper wife and children at home. He was ripe for Josie.

She met Stokes in 1870 at the Opera House. There was a dinner date, followed by a night of love. Stokes was like a being from another planet for Josie, and she decided to break with Jim and move away from the world of the theater. There would be an ornate nest for her, and Stokes's visits to keep her happy. But she was a girl with a sense of bookkeeping and insisted Fisk owed her $25,000 for, as one historian puts it, "past favors."

Fisk—as business associates knew—did not relinquish possessions with any ease, nor deal or dicker in soft reproaches. Josie and Jim had mean and nasty words to toss at each other. An exchange of letters, not very polite, took place. Josie did not get her $25,000 for body rent.

In 1871 Stokes sued Jim claiming he had $200,000 coming to him from their joint venture in oil refining. Fisk, like his friend Gould, had a way of leaving his partners well-clipped and lamenting their losses.

Stokes, for a Philadelphia gentleman, didn't act like one. He had Jim's letters to Josie, and these he claimed would prove that Fisk had been deeply, criminally involved in dishonest dealings in matters of railroad swindles and that, with Gould, the two pretty much owned a majority of New York's judges, courts, and politicians.

Jim boldly announced Stokes was a blackmailer with letters. Stokes and Josie sued Jim for libel. Lawyers moved in to handle the litigation for both parties. Stokes was still asking for $200,000 but Josie now sought $50,000 instead of the original $25,000 for going to bed with Fisk.

The city enjoyed the events leading up to the trial of the case in court, enjoyed Josie coming before the judge the first day, in black silk, violet gloves, and just *one* well-placed crimson feather.

After that day's court business was done, Fisk went back to his office in the Grand Opera House. Always helpful to politicians, he had a deal going to advance the New York Police Department its payroll of $250,000, which otherwise would have been delayed because reformers had, through a legal maneuver, temporarily locked up the city's money.

Stokes, while lunching at Delmonico's, was informed that he and Josie had been indicted by the grand jury for attempting blackmail.

It was 4:15 that afternoon, in the Broadway Central Hotel at Broadway close to Bleecker Street, that Edwin Stokes and Jim Fisk faced each other on what was called "the Ladies' Staircase" of the hotel. Both men were armed with pistols. Stokes shot first without hesitation. Jim went down, mortally wounded.

The dying Fisk, thirty-seven years old, had at his bedside both Jay Gould and Boss Tweed. Just before breath left him, he managed to say he had been paying a visit to a business associate's wife, nothing more, when he met Stokes on that restricted staircase.

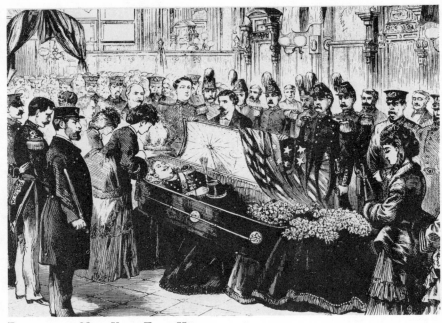

DEATH OF A NEW YORK FOLK HERO
Jim Fisk, shot to death by his mistress's new lover, lies in state in the Erie
Railroad Building. He is dressed in the uniform of his own private regiment.
(*Frank Leslie's Illustrated Newspaper*)

The funeral was fit for a monarch. He lay impressively large in a
coffin of rare wood with gold trim, the casket set up in his theater, and
for four days the curious could pass the catafalque and stare.

Josie bought mourning black but did not attend the rites for her late
lover. She fled to Europe. Edwin Stokes was tried three times for the
murder of Jim Fisk "by pistol shot." The third trial ended with a guilty
verdict of "third-degree murder," a rarely used grade of guilt in the
various classifications of homicide. His sentence was four years in prison.

Stokes, once out of prison, returned to New York City and bought a
big share of Broadway's Hoffman House.

Jay Gould, as Jim's partner, took over the running of the Grand
Opera House for the Fisk estate.

In time Josie Mansfield returned to the United States, but she did
not end her days in New York. She died, nearly twenty years after the
murder of Jim Fisk, in a small South Dakota town.

10

Reverend Beecher's Paroxysmal Kissing

One of history's great preachers, Henry Ward Beecher, enjoyed a great following among "the best people"—families that did not have Tammany Hall connections, that certainly were not living in the misery of the poor or involved in the struggles of the lower middle classes of the city.

In James D. McCabe, Jr.'s *Lights and Shadows of New York Life* we get a glimpse of high society among the best people:

> New York has long been celebrated for its magnificent social entertainments. Its balls, dinner parties, receptions, private theatricals, picnics, croquet parties, and similar gatherings are unsurpassed in respect to show in any city in the world. . . .
>
> Of late years it is becoming common not to give entertainments at one's residence, but to hire public rooms set apart for that purpose. There is a large house in the upper part of Fifth Avenue, which is fitted up exclusively for the use of persons giving balls, suppers or receptions.
>
> The proprietor of the establishment provides everything down to the minutest detail, the wishes and tastes of the giver of the entertainment being scrupulously respected in everything. The host and hostess, in consequence, have no trouble, but have simply to be on hand at the proper

time to receive their guests. This is a very expensive mode of entertaining, and costs from 5,000 to 15,000 dollars. . . .

About nine o'clock magnificent equipages, with drivers and footmen in livery, commence to arrive, and from these gorgeous vehicles richly dressed ladies and gentlemen alight, and pass up the carpeted steps to the entrance door. . . .

Every arrangement is made for dancing. A fine orchestra is provided. . . . About midnight the supper room is thrown open, and there is a rush for the tables, which are loaded with every delicacy . . .

After supper the dancing begins in earnest. If The German is danced, it generally consumes the greater part of the evening. . . . It is a dance in which the greatest freedom is permitted, and in which liberties are taken and encouraged, which would be resented under other circumstances.

This is a picture of a much freer society than has been represented by later writers. It gives us an understanding of the popularity of preachers like Henry Ward Beecher—and why even when scandal and public trial exposed their private morals, they lost little of their popularity.

In the 1870s Henry Ward Beecher (whose sister Harriet Beecher Stowe wrote *Uncle Tom's Cabin*) was the popular and fashionable pastor of the high-thinking Plymouth Church in Brooklyn. ("The greatest orator since St. Paul" [Abraham Lincoln].)

Hundreds crossed the East River on weekends in what were called "Beecher's Boats" to hear him preach against sin, slavery, pride, vanity, and spending one's capital. He was neither young nor handsome. A man with a growing family, he was approaching sixty. Physically, he was short and fat, and he wore his hair long.

He was also what one letter writer of the times called "lickerish" (equivalent in meaning to today's "randy" or "horny"). He seduced two respectable married women in his parish—Elizabeth Tilton and Lucy Bowen—and taught them (it was later testified) the games of "nest-hiding" and "paroxysmal kissing."

Elizabeth Richards Tilton, called "Lib" by friends, was hardly the vamp type to lure Beecher, the stud lion, into open scandal. A small, dainty woman with big dark eyes, she had been a fan—there is no other word for it—of Henry Ward Beecher since she was ten, and a friend of one of his daughters. He had read the marriage service over her and Samuel Tilton, a member of his church, in 1855, and sent them off to the marriage bed with praise—"One of the finest pairs I ever married." He also got Mr. Tilton a job as editor of a religious magazine. Then one night in July 1870 Lib confessed to her husband that she and the great Christian preacher had sinned, and had been sinning for some time.

Why had she confessed? She claimed she hated the "necessary deceit of concealment." It was all over now, and she got her husband to promise

Fourth of July procession passing Brougham's Lyceum on Broadway in the 1850s. (*Gleason's Pictorial Drawing Room Companion*)

to take no legal action against a great man, but one as weak in a moral sense as he was strong in his loins.

What brought Beecher's sexual adventures out into the open, after much private gossip, were attacks on the preacher by a remarkable woman, Victoria Woodhull, who was the first female ever to be nominated (by the 1872 convention of the National Woman Suffrage Association) as a candidate for the presidency of the United States.

Victoria and her sister, Tennessee Claflin, had been the darlings of the declining promiscuous years of old Commodore Vanderbilt. Victoria had begun her career as an advocate of women's rights, first as an actress, but mostly as a part-time prostitute and blackmailer. Also as a spiritualist seer with second sight, giving séances on the future and the past. As a Wall Street stock operator she is reported to have made $500,000. All her life she was an advocate of a nonmarriage sexual relationship, written up by the press as "free love."

At the time Victoria put Beecher's sexual straying into the limelight, she was a journalist, publishing a magazine called *Woodhull & Claflin's*

Weekly, and it was in its pages that she accused Beecher of adultery. She
declared he was a closet fornicator, instead of coming out in the open
and advocating free love, and physical intimacy, while also acknowledg-
ing that the sex needs of women were equal to the needs of their male
counterparts. To all intents and purposes she was one of the first women's
libbers.

Beecher, his lechery exposed, still retained the faith of his followers.
Though attributions were made about his immense physical potency, he
made it clear to the pious that Mrs. Tilton had made the first passes—
"She thrust her affections on me unsought."

In January 1875, despite his promise to his wife, Mr. Tilton sued
Henry Ward Beecher, the minister of his church, for the "alienation of
Mrs. Tilton's affections." It was a shocker that "convulsed New York" and
then the nation.

It was not an era of free sexual discussion. The puritanical religious
atmosphere of the nation in the late 1800s is difficult to imagine in these
days of loss of faith and ideals, of almost complete sexual license, of the
deteriorating institution of marriage.

The trial eventually ended in a hung jury, and the members of the Plymouth Church regarded the outcome as completely clearing their preacher. Beecher, more popular than ever, drew thousands to hear him preach, and when he traveled across the land to face packed lecture audiences, he pocketed the huge fee of $1,000 a night.

Arguments about whether he was a sexual monster, a seducer of married women, or had been betrayed and falsely branded by addled females went on in thousands of homes. It was settled for some people three years after the trial when Mrs. Tilton wrote a letter, reproduced in nearly every newspaper in America, in which she confessed that "the charge of adultery . . . was true." She and Beecher had, indeed, copulated and betrayed their marriage beds.

11
The Tweed Gang

When, in 1871, the William M. Tweed Club of the 7th Ward "gussied up its new headquarters at 105 East Beward, William M. Tweed himself and not 'an erl painting' laid out $20,000 for pictures, rosewood furniture, wallpaper, a grand piano, mirrored walls and a sumptuous carpet" (B.R. Memoirs). For the pleasures of the thirsty male, as a club member, there were a long bar and a billiards room, usually called a pool parlor.

To keep the voters' families happy, the 8th Ward rented the steamboat *Sleepy Hollow* to pull two barges carrying 700 persons and its ward leader, elected State Senator Mike Morton, to a grand time. Out of the public eye back at the club on Hudson Street, a really grand guzzling and feeding took place. The records for a typical year reveal that 50 cases of champagne, 100 kegs of beer—bottled brew was for uptown—50 gallons of turtle soup, 200 gallons of New England clam chowder (no tomatoes), and 4,000 pounds of corned bef were consumed.

It was George Orwell who wrote that in his *Animal Farm* society, "All are equal, only some are more equal than others." Tammany, too, had a group more equal than others—members who formed themselves into a special class as the Americus Club. Membership was limited to just one hundred Tweed organization men—officials, judges, bankers, and merchants. They had private acres, a luxury clubhouse at Indian Harbor, Connecticut, while Tammany rank and file simmered in the deadly summer heat of New York, many sleeping on fire escapes or in parks.

Patronage kept Tweed in power. Hire the right men—true blue party men. Control the mayor's office. Mayor Oakey Hall was not a man given much to office work, still he had a staff of six marshals, five clerks, a record clerk, a copying clerk, two messengers, and a sergeant-at-arms.

The City Permits Department was a gold mine for private graft. Before Tweed exploited it, it collected about $100,000 a year. With the Ring in control taking payoffs, its books showed a little over $11,000 in good years. Where six men had once run the department, there were now twenty-two. Some accountant once figured out that to collect $194 in 1871 cost nearly $3,000.

With the police serving as collectors, and given orders about whom to arrest and whom *not* to arrest, crime spread. New York City had more crime with its one million population than London had with its three million. A police captain figured out the city had 30,000 professional criminals and 2,000 illegal gambling houses, most of them paying protection money to the police and Tammany.

Even a murderer, if properly connected with the Tweed Ring, was fairly safe from the hangman's rope. One sample. Pat Duffy was the brother of Alderman Pete Duffy. One night, while drunk, he casually killed a Negro for no known reason. Tammany bailed him out, a judge spoke up: case dismissed.

For assault and attempted murder of a steamer captain, Pat Duffy was fined six cents. During the period from 1867 to 1870, he murdered a man in front of a police station, a Negro barber and the owner of a restaurant. The wife of the last murdered man "could not be located as a witness." Pat was freed on bail and the case was dropped.

In 1870 Pete Duffy, while serving on the General Committee of Tammany Hall, stabbed a police officer to death and pleaded guilty. Sentenced to Sing Sing for nine years, six months, he only served a year after William Marcy Tweed got Governor John Hoffman to sign a full pardon for Pete Duffy.

Doing good service for Tammany clients was the shady and brilliant law team of shysters, Howe and Hummel. They successfully defended criminals of all types—madames, pimps, box men (safe robbers), dips (pickpockets), boosters (shoplifters)—and political figures caught with their fists in the City Hall till.

The partners were theater lovers and handled legal problems for John

Drew, Lillie Langtry, Edwin Booth, and other actors and actresses, besides a whole range of Tammany crimes by regulars.

In court William Howe could convince a jury that a woman-killer had pulled the trigger of the death weapon six times *by accident*. Howe was the large-sized partner who modeled himself on the clothing style of Tammany Mayor Oakey Hall. He robed his bulk in violet-colored waistcoat, checked pants, a scattering of diamonds, and gold watch chains.

Howe was a great courtroom weeper, and from a simple shoplifting case to dropping a dead body into the harbor, he could bring up a steady flow of tears as part of his legal maneuvering for the defense.

Abe Hummel, in contrast to his partner, was a shrimp of a man. "Under five feet, not much body with little meat on the small bones. His bald pate nearly always balancing a Derby hat. No diamonds for Abe" (B.R. Memoirs). An ivory skull on his watch chain was show enough.

Howe was an expert in the blackmailing of New York men who had gotten involved in breach of promise suits. And no wise girl ever permitted herself to be unbuttoned, unlaced, seduced by a rich man without afterwards rushing down to see Abe.

It was clear to the uptown reform elements that a change was needed. But the problem of the opposition was how to bring the Tweed gang down. William Marcy Tweed controlled enough of the city workers to be always certain of a majority. The police and the courts were in his pocket. There had been reform committees. There were official upstate investigations. But there was no true uprising against the Tammany Ring by New York citizens.

What finally aroused the people to attack Tweed was just a set of ink drawings, work done over a period of time by a popular cartoonist, Thomas Nast. These gross images of Nast's "Tweed" appeared to shock Tweed out of his confidence. But were these drawings capable of bringing down the entire nest of Tammany supermen?

Actually, Thomas Nast was the first great political cartoonist of the nation. Tammany Hall labeled him the "Nast-y artist of *Harper's Weekly*, a Journal of Devilization."

The *Times Literary Supplement*'s picture of Thomas Nast shows him to have been a man of his times.

Thomas Nast was born in "the German Palatinate" and was brought to America as a boy by his father. The elder Nast had been a musician in the Bavarian army, a Protestant serving in the army of a Catholic state, and he may have suffered from the Catholic prejudices of the Wittelsbachs. In any event, his son developed somewhere a hatred of Rome. Like *Harper's Weekly*, for which he drew, he was a rather belated convert to the cause of the Negro, and he usually attacked the causes his publisher supported.

Thomas Nast, Image Maker

Boss Tweed, drawn (above left) as a grafting moneybag, is said to have offered the artist $500,000 to stop drawing him. Nast, who invented the Democratic donkey and the GOP elephant as political symbols, also had his own impression (right) of the Irish as political bosses. (*Harper's Weekly*—author's collection)

It is possible, although the evidence is not compelling, that Nast was a genuinely devoted believer in freedom for the Negro and genuinely "liberal" in the modern American sense. Grant is supposed to have said of Nast, "He did as much as any man to preserve the Union and to bring the war to an end."

Nast, in any event, is most remembered for his attack on the Tweed Ring. In the course of his campaign he invented the celebrated symbol of the "Tammany Tiger." He also invented the Democratic Donkey and the Republican Elephant.

Tweed was actually more complex than Nast's cartoons made him out to be. He had done some little reading in law, and a pal, Judge George Barnard, admitted him to the bar. As a lawyer Tweed got such fees as $100,000 from Jay Gould's racket-run Erie Railroad, to see that it didn't encounter any political problems in its looting of the stockholders.

He and his family moved to fashionable Murray Hill, into a very splendid mansion in what was called "the best part of town." He liked to have people tip their hats to him. As Deputy Street Commissioner he controlled thousands of jobs and saw to it that deserving Democratic voters filled them, and tipped their hats to "The Boss." He held the position from 1863 to 1870. When he came to the office, the department had a budget of $650,000. Tweed soon raised it to over $2½ million.

It was the beginning, the blueprint of the Tweed Ring in power. Greater looting of the city was ahead, and more sinecures for the faithful and greedy would be created. Like a general of genius, Tweed surrounded himself with "a staff as greedy as Ali Baba, cunning as Machiavelli, and as daring as Jesse James" (Arthur Train).

The most presentable of the gang was the Tammany-elected Mayor, "Elegant Oakey"—Abraham Oakey Hall. From 1868 to 1872 Tweed kept him to head the city and used him as a kind of Tammany court jester.

Oakey had many talents. He wrote plays, he was a fine lecturer in an age of great platform speakers—Mark Twain, Bill Nye, Henry Ward Beecher, and others. He was a journalist, a member of the bar, a well-known theater first-nighter, a clubman.

James Gordon Bennett, a strange, wild playboy (he wanted to be buried in a giant stone owl on Columbia Heights) and owner of the New York *Herald*, greeted Oakey as "a refreshing novelty to have for Mayor of New York, a strictly honorable, capable man . . . able to sing a good song."

It would be hard to ask anything more of a Tammany mayor. Tweed saw Oakey as a much-needed ally. A front man who could change color and direction—"spin around to any situation on a dime." Oakey had been a Presbyterian Swedenborgian but ended up as a Roman Catholic. In politics he had at times dipped into support (in return for rewards) of the Whigs, Know-Nothings, and Republicans and had been both a rebel and a Tammany Democrat.

Oakey had served as District Attorney for a time and made a fortune with his law firm, much of it stemming from the Tweed Ring "stealing the city blind" (a phrase coined during the Tweed Ring era). As District Attorney Oakey had brought 12,000 criminal cases before the bar, but it was common knowledge that he had buried 10,000 others out of sight.

He kept his legal hands off the 10,000 saloon keepers who never paid their excise whisky tax. In 1870 his law firm collected $204,500 in fees for "legal services to the city."

For all Oakey's grace and skills, Tweed needed a roughneck at his side to balance the elegant mayor, and he found him in Peter Barr Sweeney. The most sinister-looking of the Ring's staff officers, he was short and wide, with a big head dominated by thick blue-black hair that grew everyplace it could find roots except for chin and cheeks. A huge walrus moustache, small, shiny eyes, and a quiet, catlike stance completed the picture. Pete, or "Sly," Sweeney never spoke much, and dressed at all times in a high black silk topper and thick black clothes.

Pete was the Tweed mole, turning up in secret rooms, hallways, discreet lobbies, back rooms off saloons, caucuses, and wherever skullduggery, schemes, plottings, political careers were being made or ruined. He recemented friendships and healed wounds.

He took his rewards in solid, not heavenly things. He was a director on the boards of railroads, banks, gas companies, docks—wherever it was possible to squeeze out some graft, a kickback, to be paid off for favors done, or wrongdoings done and paid for.

At least he was Irish—in the popular pattern of Nast's pictures of the city looters. He was born poor in 1824 to a mother and father who both ran saloons. As a young man growing up, Pete worked as a waiter and joined the poor man's social club to power—the fire department. He was pious, as so many thieves are. He took his godhead seriously at St. Xavier's on 16th Street. Squire Pete built his political clout in the 6th Ward by running a show-time saloon that featured entertainers, a ten-cent admission price, and a three-cent shot of whisky.

Pete was a tough in-fighter; he beat back the Silk Stocking districts of New York who supported the Republicans. He paid for the job as City Chamberlain, the route to much "honest graft," as O. Henry once labeled it. The gimmick Pete used was the fact that all city monies secured from taxes and other sources were placed under the Chamberlain's care—and he was permitted to put this money on deposit and *keep* the bank interest paid on it for himself.

Another wheel of the Tweed machine, who seemed at first to be a minor figure, not too bright, lacking charisma and showmanship, was Richard Connolly, known as "Slippery Dick," boss of the important 21st Ward. Other names one finds for Connolly, in journals and letters, are "Slimy Dick," and when on the bench, "Big Judge." He became a top man in Tammany and Comptroller of the City of New York. In appearance, the Irish-born Connolly (Banta, Ireland, the only immigrant on the top Tweed staff) was "a big buster of a feller," with an impressive hinge of a nose, well-shaved in an age of mighty moustaches and beards. His eyes actively followed events behind gold-rimmed glasses. Paunch and jowl were fit for a prosperous ward boss. Dick had been, before becoming Comptroller, Cashier and General Manager of the Central National Bank.

◈

I have spent considerable time and space on these men because they set up the original political patterns, fostering and promulgating ideas that are still alive and functioning in New York and other big cities.

There they were in Nast's cartoons—a powerful combination of thieves, rogues, politicians, and lawyers ("Let us begin by hanging all lawyers" [Oakey Hall quoting Shakespeare later in life]). They were practical men, aware that every person has his price, and so creating the most powerful corrupt system of city and state government that this nation had seen to date. Theirs was a tight, well-built organization so that, while reformers could from time to time dent it, retire it for a short period, it has returned to power in New York again and again, and has been imitated successfully from Newark to Chicago to Los Angeles.

William Marcy Tweed was aware of one cardinal rule that he passed on to Oakey, Pete, and Dick: You had to run a wide-open city if you wanted to plunder it. Vice paid its share of the take.

"Honest graft," also known as boodle, the swag, the juice, was a common and easy way for public officials and underlings to become rich. Vice flourished, well protected, along the Bowery in whorehouses and dance halls, saloons and beer gardens. In the district between Seventh and Eleventh avenues from 14th Street to 42nd Street, were nests of criminals protected by the police and the ward bosses. ("Hell's Kitchen, no less," said one policeman, and so the district was named.)

The area between Fifth and Sixth avenues, from 23rd to 30th streets, was called by the moniker of Satan's Circus. Here all kinds of erotic games were offered as "the sins of depraved France." Fences openly bought the results of last night's crime from thieves, second-story men, pickpockets, and safecrackers. There were strange hotels, honkytonks, and more saloons. The most notorious place was the Haymarket. The city, at the time, had 10,000 legally licensed saloons, but blind pigs and groggeries (the first speakeasies) without official permit also existed.

Satan's Circus soon was called "The Tenderloin," named after a remark of Police Captain Alexander Williams, also known as "The Clubber." ("There's more law at the end of my nightstick than in all the law books ever written.") Legend says he named the district unknowingly when he was sent to command the 29th Police Precinct where the graft and payoff to the police and politicians was the richest.

"I've had nothing but chuck for a long time, and now I'm going to get a little of the tenderloin."

⋙⋘

The city needed protection, but it did little to clean up the sore spots. Affluent citizens felt poverty was the fault of the poor because they had "no git up an' go." When it was suggested that the city's working population was underpaid, exploited, and should form unions, one rich man said, "The rich were put on earth by God to see to the poor, and unionizing was going against God's will."

The *New Metropolis Magazine*, in fact, published the following classification of the city's population:

> On the island of Manhattan the people may be divided into seven classes: the very rich, the rich, the prosperous, the well-to-do comfortable, the well-to-do uncomfortable, the comfortable or contented poor, and the . . . uncomfortable poor. . . .

So there was Hell's Kitchen, Rotten Row, Bummers Retreat, Mulligan's Alley, Rag Pickers Row to fester in the city and breed crime and misery. The comfortable or contented poor existed only in fiction.

During the Tweed regime the poor of the city numbered about a half million people. Nearly 20,000 of them lived in holes and cellars, usually windowless, below the street level. A twelve-story rotting tenement held 1,000 humans. There were 15,000 professional beggars; one could rent a baby (genuine sores and deformed limbs cost extra) to carry around and beg from passersby. One survey estimated that at least 30,000 children lived most of their formative years in the reek and mud of alleys—smoking, gambling, stealing, foul-mouthed, erotic Huck Finns of Cockroach Row and Dead Cat Alley.

Under a sign that read PUNCHES AND JULEPS, COBBLERS AND SMASHES TO MAKE THE TONGUE WAGGLE WITH WIT'S MERRY FLASHES the cream of sporting life gathered at Harry Hill's concert saloon on West Houston (pronounced "House-tin") Street, where alderman and muscle man, politician and bet-taker mixed. There one could see heavyweight champion John L. Sullivan, John Morrissey the gambler, and the Tweed Tammany twins—Sweeney and Connolly—plus a whore, Sadie the Goat. New York name-droppers adored (the way late film stars were worshiped) Big Nose Bunker, Sheeny Mike, Dutch Heinrich.*

Harry Hill's concert saloon had an admission charge of twenty cents for men, but women were admitted free. The prostitutes and their sports liked to dance, and visitors came to watch their gyrations.

All of this fast or hard living, poor times or good, existed elbow to elbow in the city, where the ward heelers controlled the voters and delivered the elections to Tammany and William Tweed. The original charter for the city, in 1686, had set up the ward system, a pattern that was to be very helpful to takers of graft and makers of corruption. Originally there were six wards, and each ward permitted its citizens to elect one alderman and an assistant alderman. At first, aldermen were kept in their places by the affluent members of society appointing the mayor and recorder. But when these and other positions became elected officials, the wards got to vote, to elect or defeat. Boss rule was the result.

In 1867 more offices were added to the city government to drain off surplus and provide extra graft. Boards of Charities and Corrections, Education, and Immigration and Taxes were established.

The power of the Tammany Ring consisted in full control of the

---

* "It's a blazing shame the era of nicknames is gone. No kid anymore is called Fatso, Four Eyes, Gimpy, or Jug Ears—the bloody world's become just buggering punch holes in an IBM card, not people" (Brendan Behan in a Third Avenue bar).

ward clubs. The leader of each ward was forced to organize a good rowdy club in his district, to keep an eye on the voters. He handed out free coal to the chilly, food to the hungry.

"Sure now, it's the Hall's doin', comin' from Tammany the mother and father of us all" (B.R. Memoirs). If a girl was pregnant, well, a little muscle from some club members could find an unwilling but ready bridegroom. If a playful lad was sent to reform school for a bit of smash and grab, or a man to Sing Sing for looting a warehouse, one could appeal to a Tammany lawyer and Tammany judge, even to upstate Albany.

❧

City advertising in heavy doses succeeded in keeping most of the New York newspapers from attacking the Tweed Ring. Except for the *Times* and *Harper's Weekly*, the rest of the press took the advertising and looked the other way when reformers came to them demanding exposure of political crimes. Only when it was clear that the hounds of justice were nipping at the Ring's heels did the newspapers discover corruption.

Renting space in the city markets called for a secret payment of between $500 and $5,000, "which sums it was never thought proper to pay into the City Treasury." Even to put up a sign or a sidewalk display could call for a $10 graft payment.

The Tweed Ring sold 20,000 water meters to merchants at a cost of $60 each, which made Tammany a profit of nearly a million dollars. The Tweed Ring also made other millions in graft in the completing of the new Court House. The Ring's plastering contractors ran up a bill of nearly $3 million for work that the reformers figured out could have been done for $20,000.

In 1870 the Tweed Ring passed a new city charter with which it began to reorganize the city government so that Tammany's control of all city printing and contacts became airtight.

Meanwhile, the rich personal life of William Marcy Tweed could not be hidden away from the poor. There is no doubt his wife and family enjoyed living on Fifth Avenue in a mansion costing $350,000.

The Ring had been in power five years and felt it could continue indefinitely. Tweed had mocked the reformers, *"What are you going to do about it?"* But Tweed's power had peaked without his knowing it. In a few weeks after the statue was proposed, he would be fighting for survival. A great cartoonist, a newspaper, and a weekly magazine had at last aroused the city to move toward reform. Evidence was being dug up; turncoats on the fringe of Tammany were offering to turn state's evidence.

The New York Times and *Harper's Weekly* almost alone had raised the cry that Tweed be brought to justice. Thomas Nast had continued to carry the biggest club—his pen—and he still set it to paper and had his images transferred to woodcut blocks.

Again and again Nast drew Tweed and his gang—sly, dishonest, gross, revolting, gamy. Tweed felt ashamed that his family should see him drawn as so evil a figure, with his huge nose, his paunch, portrayed now as a dark and sinister brother to the devil, now as a convicted thief in prison stripes, now as Lord of Darkness.

Thomas Nast was offered half a million dollars to leave the United States and go away to study and to improve his art in the delightful capitals of Europe. Nast is said to have answered to the bribe offer: "I don't think I'll do it. I made up my mind not long ago to put some of those fellows behind bars, and I'm going to put them there!"

The New York Times was offered half a million to lay off Tweed. George Jones, the publisher, also refused it. "I don't think that even the devil himself will bid higher for me than that." Jones and his imported English editor, Louis Jennings, most likely read Niccolo Machiavelli:

> No well-ordered republic should ever cancel the crimes of its citizens by their merits; but, having established rewards for good actions and penalties for evil ones, and having rewarded a citizen for good conduct who afterward commits a wrong, it should chastise him for that wrong without regard to his previous merits. And a state that properly observes this principle will long enjoy its liberty; but if it does otherwise, it will speedily come to ruin.
>
> For if a citizen who has rendered some eminent service to the state should add to the reputation and influence which he has thereby acquired the confident audacity of being able to commit any wrong without fear of punishment, he will in a little while become so insolent and overbearing as to put an end to all power of the law.

By September 1870 public outcry was growing. The *Times* insisted the citizens could turn the rascals out with their votes. Civic responsibility was the theme, and well-off New Yorkers were pointed to as being indifferent and not taking enough interest in fighting the evils in City Hall that they all resented.

The Tammany dam began to crack through an accident. In January 1871 James Watson, Tweed's man as county auditor, died in a fatal sleigh mishap. To replace him, Matthew O'Rourke was appointed as the Tweed Ring's man in the office. But he turned out to be a weak vessel. He carried a deep grudge against Tammany—having at one time made a claim against the city that was denied payment.

Tweed was careless in placing a disgruntled follower over the city's books and accounts. For Matt O'Rourke began to copy out the more odorous of the doctored figures and facts from books kept according to the Tweed Ring's idea of bookkeeping. These he turned over to the *Times*.

Tammany had also nurtured, unknown to itself, a rebel group calling themselves the Young Democrats. Seeking power, they, too, wanted to bring Tweed and his old boys down. One of the Young Democrats, Jimmy O'Brien—the former sheriff—pretended that he had broken with the rebels and begged to be taken back under the blanket of Chief Tammany. Jimmy, too, carried a grudge against the organization—he had claimed a huge sum due him while sheriff, but again Tweed made the mistake of refusing to pay off. These two men—O'Rourke and O'Brien—were *not* reformers, but merely boodle hunters, thieves themselves, who had not been able to collect their "honest graft." O'Brien got one of his men into the comptroller's office and there copied the city's voucher records, including county liabilities, clearly a nest of frauds for anyone who could read.

Tweed knew blackmail when he heard of it, and he gave O'Brien more than $20,000 and also promised that he'd see O'Brien was put in the way of "making $130,000 on property deals." Jimmy O'Brien, not trusting Tweed, like O'Rourke, turned his material over to the *Times*.

And the *Times* began to drop its bombs: THE SECRET ACCOUNTS: PROOFS OF UNDOUBTED FRAUDS BROUGHT TO LIGHT. Everything was there in print—padded payrolls, contracting swindles, the Ring's way with judges and courts. A "Committee of Seventy" was formed by the city's important people. And it moved while Tweed and his boys seemed to slumber and feel safe. The Tweed downfall was in the works. Criminal charges against the Ring came in October 1871. The opening gun was 190 vouchers that revealed the stealing of nearly $6.5 million.

On November 2, 1871, the "Committee of Seventy," at a meeting at Cooper Institute, presented a hot report:

> There is not in the history of villainy a parallel for the gigantic crime against property conspired by the Tammany Ring. It was engineered on the complete subversion of free government in the very heart of Republicanism. An American city, having a population of over a million, was disfranchised by an open vote of a legislature born and nurtured in Democracy and Republicanism, and was handed over to a self-appointed oligarchy, to be robbed and plundered by them and their confederates, heirs and assigns for six years certainly, and prospectively forever . . . the political paradox of the New Charter of the City of New York the people of this State gave to a gang of thieves, politicians by profession, a charter to govern the commercial metropolis of this continent—the great city which is to America what Paris is to France—to govern it with a government . . . which substantially deprived the citizens of self-control, nullified their right to suffrage, nullified the principle of representation—which authorized a handful of cunning and resolute robbers to levy taxes, create public debt, and incur municipal liabilities without limit and without check, and which placed at their disposal the revenues of the great municipality and the property of all its citizens. . . .

The reform groups put up a ticket of candidates to battle the Tammany men. The citizens reacted violently. Aroused by the exposures and the charges, the reformers got the votes to beat Tammany in an election as it had never been beaten since its rise to power. They carried New York State, but Tweed's ward, the 7th, held fast and reelected him alderman by a 10,000-vote margin.

For the next two years indictments were issued as investigations turned up many other frauds. Everyone from Tweed down to bribe collectors and many small-time chiselers was ordered to stand trial. Legal actions to get back the boodle were set in motion.

The first to run for it was Pete Sweeney, who made it across the border to Canada, there to join his brother.

Slippery Dick Connolly, who had tried to make a deal offering to give some small aid to the reformers, was arrested in January 1873, and had bail set at $1 million. Prosecutor Samuel Tilden denied he had double-crossed Slippery Dick. But Slippery Dick managed to get hold of $6 million and took off for Europe.

Oakey Hall, the dapper New Yorker, decided to stay and fight. He was brought to court four times, and stood three trials. He was a marvelous actor on the stand, well-tailored, witty, sure of his innocence.

He treated the jury like a theater audience, and his three trials were better attended than any of the plays running on Broadway. He candidly admitted that he had an aversion for details and could not recall ever having done anything wrong as claimed by the evidence presented.

The first trial ended with his going free, but being told he was "careless and negligent." But there was enough new evidence to bring him back before another jury. Hung juries and showmanship ended his days in court. He remained in office, then retired.

William Marcy Tweed was the big stud animal the courts really wanted. Yet, on January 30, 1873, the jury agreed it could not reach a verdict. Tweed decided to visit California before facing the ordeal of a second trial.

The first jury was most likely bribed. One member was an ex-convict, another a Bowery bum who suddenly flowered in new clothes. Tammany men were observed feeding jurors at Delmonico's, and another juror admitted he was a professional jury sitter who found "it paid off."

In November the second trial began. Tweed's signature was produced on warrants that documented $6 million in frauds against the city.

The jury found Tweed guilty as charged on 204 counts. No "plea bargaining" here. Tweed stood for sentencing, calm, with just a little quiver of his lips. He received a prison sentence of twelve years and a fine of $12,750.

However, there was no need to pity Boss Tweed, for his lawyers were skilled at legal mumbo jumbo. Tweed still had friends, or people in high places, who feared what he could expose about their dealings with him. The Court of Appeals turned him loose after a year in prison and a fine of $250.

He was not free for long. The reformers tossed him into Ludlow Street Jail in a new civil suit for robbing the city. Bail was set at $3 million. He didn't dare use his own money because he couldn't have accounted for it. But his second year in jail wasn't too bad. A carriage took him home every day. Mrs. Tweed always had a tasty, nourishing dinner waiting for him, with the best china and silverware on the table. This privilege became a habit, and the escort grew careless. On December 4, 1875, he escaped "while escorting his wife upstairs."

Tweed hid out in New Jersey and his trial went on without him. He was convicted and $6 million was demanded of his estate, all of it money stolen from the city.

He ran for Florida, a disintegrating bulk, moving in panic. He managed to reach Cuba, then shipped as an ordinary seaman for Spain.

He was deported to New York in November 1876. Ludlow Street Jail, with no outside visiting privileges, was again his home. He was no longer the sure and able leader but a trapped man and a sick one. He suffered from bronchitis, diabetes, and heart trouble, and the great bundles of loot were gone. Lawyers and others had managed to strip him of most of his boodle. He offered to turn state's evidence, confess all, and turn over all his remaining assets to avoid the $6 million in claims of the thirteen indictments against him. Tweed wrote out a confession and expected the promised deal to be kept.

Meanwhile, "Sly" Sweeney had come back on a deal of his own to stand trial. It was a strange arrangement, never fully explained. "Sly" settled for $400,000, not of his, but his brother's money. He himself kept all his graft and was turned free. "Sly" was better at bargaining than Tweed, and reformers in power often have tainted moral values themselves. Tweed was double-crossed by the courts. His confession was refused. The deal to free him in return for his assets was called off. The Attorney General, people said, was a man of little faith. The *Times* spoke up, "Could Mr. Tilden not afford to have Tweed's story told?"

It seemed not. It was dangerous stuff. The Tweed confession contained too much information about highly placed respectable people who were involved with the Tammany gang. Twenty-one senators had taken his bribes, and there was "a list of gross amounts paid to the following persons. . . ." Other private papers of Tweed's that were repressed could have, as someone with knowledge put it, "exploded the lid off the city."

Tweed was a shattered wreck, barely alive, double-crossed by Sweeney and others of his Ring and by the courts of justice trying him.

A few days before his fifty-fifth birthday, April 12, 1878, William Marcy Tweed died of what was listed as "pneumonia" in Ludlow Street jail, a structure Tweed had voted on to be built when he was on the Board of Supervisors.

While many criminal action suits were on the docket against the Tweed mob, none ever came into a court to face a jury. It was estimated that the Ring had stolen $200 million. The only money recovered was from the estates of two dead men. Watson's and Pete Sweeney's estates amounted to $94,525.44—and this at a cost to the taxpayers of nearly $260,000.

In time the Tammany Tiger recovered to produce its Crockers, Murphys, Walkers, and De Sapios, and keep its claw hold on the city.

12
The Fox and the Sullivan

In 1876 a feisty little Irishman, Richard K. Fox, took over a faltering weekly newspaper, *The National Police Gazette*. The paper owed him money and was a wreck. Mr. Fox was to make it the champion reporter of the sporting life in text and daring woodcut pictures and to enliven journalism by covering national events of a sensational and sensual content. He shunned the aesthetic, cultivated the physical. He was also the father, the promoter of the modern prizefight ring and the giver of grand-sounding awards to champions, near champions, and the mere freaks.

Richard K. Fox was born in Belfast, Ireland, in 1846 of Scotch-Irish parentage—and, as his own paper, the *Banner of Ulster*, wrote of him (with his approval), "The solid grit of one and the mental acuteness of the other are both equally represented in him."

He began early as a newspaperman with the *Banner*, the official organ of the Presbyterian Church in Ireland. In 1874, after ten years with the *Belfast News Letter*, Fox, like so many Irish before and after him, landed in New York City.

Overcoming clamoring trivialities and hard times, he soon was working on the *Commercial Bulletin.* Here he became entangled with the

Police Gazette, and one morning found himself owner and editor of the oldest (founded 1845) weekly in America.

Richard K. Fox was not impressive in a day of large men with paunches, turkey jowls, and wild growths of hair cultivated with bear grease. He was slim, boyish-looking, and just forty years of age when the weekly became his.

There were debts, and Fox borrowed $500 from William (The Great) Muldoon, who was the pride of Harry Hill's Sporting Resort, a splendid muscle fanatic, an example of a clean-living athlete, a member of the New York Police Department, and about to become "Wrestling Champion of the World."

Fox purchased new type and printed the weekly on the pink paper soon to become notorious as background for indiscreet woodcut pictures of sports figures, actresses in exuberant attitudes, big-time criminals, and a grab bag of crimes of passion. The *Police Gazette* was to become an international favorite and a sports authority.

Prizefighting was in disgrace, and outlawed in most states. Serious newspapers paid it little attention beyond a casual sneer at its brutality. Fox at once saw his opportunity to attract the followers and lovers of the sporting life to news of the square ring.

In 1880 he began to promote interest in a fight between Paddy Ryan and Joe Goss for the "Heavyweight Championship of America"—whatever that meant, for the prize ring's ethics and honesty were then, as now, a bit of a joke. It was furtive, smelly, dishonest, raucous—a mean business. Goss was the "champion" recognized by the sporting set. Ryan, called the "Collar City Giant" (Troy, New York), sported calcified ears and brain, a game heart, and seemed a good butcher's block for a champ.

Actually, Fox had little interest in boxing but, since he had just added a sports section to his paper, he saw a chance to increase circulation by ordering his sports editor, William H. Harding, a writer, and some artists to cover the fight in quivering prose and dramatic pictures. The first thing was to find a place for the fight. Outlawed in most of the United States, it was set for Canada, but British soldiers in red coats rushed the fighters and their unsavory entourage back across the border.

At last, on the bare turf at Collier's Station, West Virginia, the two fighters squared off one June morning. The old London boxing rules were still in force; a round consisted of a knockdown, and when the fighter got up—if he could—that began another round. Bare fists were the weapons. While Fox's artists sketched and his writer wrote, the bloody conflict went on for eighty-seven rounds (an hour and twenty-four minutes) to the cries of the sporting bloods, with Ryan emerging as the winner.

The other papers, busy featuring the Garfield–Hancock campaign for President of the United States, hardly covered the fight. The *Police*

HARRY HILL'S DANCE HALL AND SALOON
The music was good, the drinks fair, and the ladies all bad. The sporting set hung out here, and John L. Sullivan was featured. Note girl on the right smoking. (Author's collection)

Gazette rushed out special extra editions that sold out again and again in the next four weeks. Four hundred thousand copies were sold.

Fox was not one to miss a chance when it came along, and so he became the backer of Paddy Ryan, the "new champion"—a backing that included a $5,000 offer for a fight with "The Boston Strong Boy"—John L. Sullivan—whose drinking was matched by his ability to hammer opponents down to defeat with the grunt of an articulated oboe.

It was the Great Muldoon, the wrestling champion and one of the original backers of Fox, who brought the Great "Jawn L." to New York City to fight Steve Taylor in the cleared dining room of Harry Hill's ever-popular resort. Sullivan won handsomely with an annihilating punch. He was a fine figure of a man and the clamor was on for him to fight Mr. Fox's own Paddy Ryan, "the champ." Fox had developed a dislike of Sullivan so strong it goaded him for years to find a man who could batter Sullivan to the canvas.

It all began the day Mr. Fox and his sports editor went to Harry Hill's place to enjoy some of the resort's famous roast beef. The place was crowded and Mr. Fox noticed a well-made young man who was the center of loud attention. Mr. Hill said, "It's that young fighter, J. L. Sullivan. He fought a fine brannigan here, in this very room, with young Steve Taylor, just two nights ago."

Mr. Fox, always looking for sports figures to add to his growing empire, said, "Tell Sullivan to come over and see me."

Flushed from his recent success in Harry Hill's place and full of the charge from several hearty gulps of whisky, Sullivan responded to Harry Hill, Fox's messenger, "You go tell that Mr. Fox if he wants to see John L. Sullivan to come over to *my* table."

Not surprisingly, Sullivan's rejection of Fox's invitation was regarded by the latter as an affront to his position and dignity and started the great Fox–Sullivan feud.

ఆర్ర

John Lawrence Sullivan's story is not one of moralizing sobriety. He was born in Roxbury, Massachusetts, in 1858; his five-foot-three father came from Tralee in County Kerry, his five-foot-two, 200-pound mother came from Atholone in County Roscommon. John himself in his prime was never the giant that legend made him, being just five-feet-ten, and at his best fighting strength weighed 185 pounds of beef and bourbon.

Perhaps because of some deep psychic scar he was handy with his temper and his fists, and when he lost jobs from bosses who "didn't like to take a punch," John L. turned to semipro baseball, earning the unthinkable sum of $100 a week in an age when that was a traumatic experience besides being a fortune. From baseball he went into the prize ring.

John became known as the Boston Strong Boy, with a right-hand smasher of a punch like the new Krupp cannon. Soon he was rallying his followers in any bar with his famous saloon boast, "I can lick any man in the house!" His followers—rummies, sports, and barflies—cheered and bought him whisky, knowing his great fondness for its temporary glow of total, incomprehensible joy. He had a chest like a prize pigeon, shoulders and arms that resembled ropes of solid muscle.

In the ring his menacing stance and scorn—suggesting disciplined outrage would soon take place—would beat a rival before the bell rang. He was a simple fighter and tremendously aggressive. It was the Sullivan style to rush across the ring and pump his fists into the other fighter's face and body until the victim fell.

Sullivan fought a man named John Flood on a barge anchored opposite the city of Yonkers, for a purse of $800. "Sullivan," wrote one reporter, "hit Flood so hard in the neck that it swelled his ankles."

Fox had offered a stake of $5,000 to back Paddy Ryan against Sullivan. He ballyhooed the match, and sold thousands of extras of his paper. The fight was scheduled for February 7, 1882, *if* a place could be found to stage it. The match was finally held on the lawn in front of the Barnes Hotel in Mississippi City, Mississippi.

The *Police Gazette* devoted eight pages to the fight and to information about the fighting colors of the two men. Sullivan, it claimed, was un-American, and had had his colors made abroad. The *Gazette* insisted they were not as attractive as the colors of the *Gazette*'s champion, Paddy Ryan, whose robes and trunks were so colorful that the *Gazette* was selling copies to readers at prices ranging from $10 to $50 each.

Not too much was made of Sullivan's colors, or the fact he was just as Irish as Paddy. As for the battle—it was Sullivan all the way. In nine rounds—in eleven minutes of barefisted battering—Paddy went down for good on the Southern lawn.

Soon Fox had new challengers—an Englishman, Tug Wilson; Slade, a New Zealand Maori; then another Englishman, Charlie Mitchell. All in good time went down before Sullivan's furious, two-fisted onslaughts. Fox eventually blew $20,000 promoting anti-Sullivan fights, but it was money well spent, for it helped the sale of the *Gazette*. A return match with Mitchell was promoted, and Madison Square Garden in New York was packed with nearly 14,000 people. Then came dismal, shocking news for the fans. In staggered Sullivan from the street, dead drunk. He held onto the ropes, and said in alcohol-blurred words, "Gents—*hic*—I am sure sick—*hic*—just not able to box t'night—*hic*—the doctor himself is here and this—*hic*—is the very first time I'm disappointing—*hic*—you."

The crowd did not take kindly to these words, and Sullivan was assisted from the building amidst boos, outraged cries, and hisses.

A thorough and extravagant search for Sullivan killers continued. In November 1884 Fox tried again with Alf Greenfield, who was so destroyed in the ring by Sullivan's blows that Police Captain Williams arrested *both* fighters as "not boxing but engaging in physical combat."

The Paddy Ryan–John L. Sullivan fight had been attended "by newspapers from all over the world." A London sheet hired Oscar Wilde to report on the fisticuffs. Sullivan was only twenty-three years old when he was declared the World's Champion Heavyweight Boxer. As time passed he proved he was also a champion long-distance drinker of whisky.

On tour as champion he no longer appeared on stages of theaters offering $50 to anyone who could last one round with him. Now he was the star attraction, appearing once as a blacksmith hammering on red-hot steel, always exhibiting his muscles, his diamond-studded champion's belt, and doing a little shadowboxing. But after the show—or before—he'd appear in some elegant saloon and order "Drinks for everybody. Bellies to the bar, boys." Then he'd ask, "What's the record now in this here establishment?"

If the barman didn't know this was the Great John L., or didn't understand, Sullivan would add, "I'm meaning now, what's the most drinks a man's been able to drink in this saloon and *still* stand up?"

Whatever the record, Sullivan would proceed to beat it, never losing his equilibrium. There is a report that in a Western mining town the record was seventy shot glasses of prime bourbon—each glass holding two ounces of 90-proof whisky.

Sullivan slapped the bar hard. "Call *that* a record! I'll show you now what a real man can do. I'll start meself off with six drinks."

Sullivan in a cataleptic calm drank down eighty glasses. Inevitably, he soon became the ex-champion, a has-been, a mockery of the great fighter he once had been. All his income was spent on whisky; the period also marked the end of his diamond-studded champion's belt. He grew fatter, sloppy, anatomically grotesque, a wheedling drunk mooching for drinks. In 1905, not yet forty-seven years of age, he was a pathetic wreck, seated in a saloon, very close to a state of delirium tremens. He managed to get to his feet, stagger to the bar and put down a few coins. "Whisky, man, a drink of the best whisky you have in the house."

The barman shrugged and poured. Sullivan, a thwarted, baffled look on his face, glanced around the barroom and its dozen or so citizens. He lifted the glass. "Here's a toast, gents, a toast to me, John L. Sullivan."

No one cared; there was not even coarse indulgence for the sodden wreck. Slowly Sullivan tilted the glass and poured its contents in the cuspidor by the bar rail. "So! If I ever take another drink of whisky, I hope I choke, so help me God!"

The citizens laughed. Old John L., drunk and bragging again, reeling from intoxication to intoxication. They were wrong. John L. Sullivan never took another drink as long as he lived. For thirteen more years, until he died, he drank nothing with alcohol in it. He joined the Anti-Saloon League and toured the nation, lecturing in his bourbon-burned voice on the evil of Demon Rum and John Barleycorn.

He died in 1918, and his obituaries were larger than the headlines of Mr. Wilson's war to "Make the World Safe for Democracy." Roxbury, Massachusetts, never had a bigger funeral, not even for a Lodge or a Cabot.

As for Richard K. Fox, who unwillingly made Sullivan great to build interest in the *Gazette*'s sports reporting, his backing of other fighters went on. Fox began to award belts to other champions—to Jack Dempsey the Nonpareil (not to be confused with the later fighter whose name originally was not *Jack* but William Harrison) the middleweight belt; to Jack McAuliffe the lightweight; to Ike Weir, the "Belfast Spider," the featherweight.

There was also the Richard K. Fox Six-Day Go-As-You-Please Trophy for the winner of a race of blistering days of walking. Annie Oakley, the lady sharpshooter, got a Fox medal, and Fox awards were also given for wrestling and fencing.

The Fox awards began to run downhill when they were dedicated to a champion rat-catcher, a one-legged dancer, a steeple-climber, an oyster-opener. All these, while perhaps still in the field of minor athletic prowess, seemed to lack the ravenous vigor of proper sports. Once the best bartender and drink-mixer got the judges fully inebriated tasting the mixtures. The hair-cutting contest for champion barbers caused some freak hair jobs, the winner coming in just under thirty seconds, the victim dazed and wondering if he still had ears.

A reputation the *Gazette* made through one of its stories concerned Steve Brodie, a newsboy, who, it claimed in woodcut pictures and text, made "a flying leap from the big Brooklyn Bridge." Facts seem to indicate he never made the famous leap, but the publicity made him a celebrity and he opened a popular New York saloon.

BOOK FOUR

The Twentieth Century Begins

13
The New Century on Stage

The end of the nineteenth century found New York one of the major cities of the world, certainly the greatest city of America, locked on its island between two rivers. In social position, in money, in hustle and bustle it was vigorous.

There were as yet no great leaps forward in the city's façade. The rich lined the avenues with French châteaux and German castles, built Italian villas at Newport and Tudor country homes on Long Island. Just ahead in the new century were the first skyscrapers, the Flatiron Building and Woolworth's Gothic tower, incorporating structural methods that would change the appearance of the city. It was still a horse-drawn city in the late 1890s, with the few autocars owned by the sporting rich. The more daring ladies drove an electric automobile, which they steered by means of a lever. Overhead the streets were hideous with strung wires, and in some places the iron legs of the "El" supported iron-wheeled cars that rattled overhead. Edison had invented the incandescent lamp, but gaslight still gave its glow to most night life—which featured such names as John Drew, Chauncey Depew, and Stanford White.

THE STEAM CARS TO NEW YORK
A late nineteenth-century railroad poster showing the day coaches, the parlor cars (note curtains), and the freight carriers. (Library of Congress)

Society preened itself as part of the élite and exclusive "Four Hundred," and the Astors and the Vanderbilts and the Belmonts were the Best People—or so they insisted to each other, even if they had begun as scow builders, fur buyers, and worse. On gala nights they collected at the Metropolitan Opera for Italian opera or the voices of Schumann-Heink, Nordica, and Melba.

In art one collected Meissonier; the better clubs and saloons featured the pearl-waxed, Percheron-rumped nudes of Bouguereau, and someone repeated the stale joke that of the 3,000 pictures Corot had painted, 5,000 were in America. Sargent painted portraits that gave one social status in oils; Chase did still lifes and shiny fish; Richard Canfield was bold enough to collect Whistlers—a mistake, people said.

The true genius of the time was neglected. No one bought a Ryder, and both Homer and Eakins were not selling well at all. Mary Cassatt, living in Paris (her brother was president of the Pennsy Railroad), insisted her rich American friends buy a Dégas now and then. But the other impressionists had not yet found collectors in New York.

The Hudson River School of Inness showed taste on a wall; a Church or a Cole might grace a fashionable living room (it was hard to believe Cézanne and Picasso were busy covering canvas). The Ashcan School of New York, Henri, Sloan, and contemporaries, was just preparing for the new century, using New York streets as prime subject matter.

The theater, too, was dormant, locked into repeated patterns. Joseph Jefferson was to play *Rip Van Winkle* 2,500 times; James O'Neill, father of Eugene O'Neill, was to perform *Monte Cristo* almost as many times. Among popular, solid plays were *Sherlock Holmes*, starring William Gillette, and *Arizona* by Augustus Thomas—"a Remington come to life." For real theater one expected imports of glamorous women who had sinned freely and so thrilled the public: Eleonora Duse, in 1893, in *Camille*, Sarah Bernhardt in *Phaedra, La Tosca*, and such passionate items.

Ibsen? Shaw? Strindberg? No, thank you. Burlesque (not the later Minsky variety) music hall items did well with fat girls in tights—Billy Watson's Beef Trust, each girl weighing 180 pounds. Finally, there was Lillian Russell in a pirated version of Gilbert and Sullivan.

American literature, too, was at a low ebb. Edgar Allan Poe's cottage and Walt Whitman's house had not yet become New York shrines. Herman Melville was a sour harbor customs officer in New York City. William Dean Howells wrote books rooted in dry and sterile realism.

Stephen Crane, unwashed, with nicotine-stained fingers, found his New York realism unacceptable. He published *Maggie, a Girl of the Streets* himself, and his *Red Badge of Courage* was considered a kind of freak. His poems, such as "Black Riders," which foreshadowed the symbolists, were known only to a few. John Dos Passos, F. Scott Fitzgerald, Ernest Hemingway, and William Faulkner were very young.

Sports were mainly brutal—dog fights, cock mains, bloody prizefights. And in the slums pit terriers fought giant rats. College football was played without helmets, and baseball players wore whiplash moustaches.

Music consisted mainly of ragtime and echoes of Stephen Foster. The weepy ballads of Paul Dreiser were big hits. Paul, the brother of the author of *Sister Carrie*, produced "My Gal Sal" and "On the Banks of the Wabash." Weber and Fields with their fractured ethnic dialects, Negro cakewalks, Tony Pastor's vaudeville—all made for lively entertainment. But the American musical, an original art form, was not yet in production. Jazz—often to be spelled *jass*—was just beginning to take form in the New Orleans' Storyville sporting houses.

The finest cuisine, if one could afford it, was a gourmet's delight. New York was never to eat as well as it did in those years. The quality would hold up in some places until 1914, before it declined into the twentieth century's mere imitation of a great gourmet past. Rectors, Delmonico's, Shanley's, Claremont Inn, and a dozen others saw Jim Brady's eating contests with Lillian Russell. Oscar of the Waldorf was pleased to have a chef producing the crêpes in orange brandy for them.

The press flourished. Twenty-five New York dailies existed, as well as a Yiddish press and Italian and German dailies. Hearst and Pulitzer had brought to journalism a combination of excitement and entertaining vulgarity, and soon the funny papers, now called comic strips, were added.

My Uncle Roc swore the twentieth century in New York City could not begin until midnight December 31, 1900. But my aunts, his sisters, on Murray Hill and on Riverside Drive, celebrated at the stroke of midnight December 31, 1899, and never felt any ill effects from it. Certainly New York cheered in the new century with crystal-ball visions of its future. I could fill this book with the rosy dreams the wise heads, the politicians, authors, and ministers of God predicted, promising the most peaceful, civilized century, with no wars and the evil in men boiled out of them.

Wrote my pessimistic Uncle Roc to a girl he didn't marry:

> Western Civilization is a humbug—based on the ruins of Greek temples, St. Peter's, the British Museum, Tolstoy's peasants, French food, and the good manners of English servants. Here, civilization is a pride in owning Standard Oil shares, supporting the New York baseball teams, having a house designed by Stanford White containing several Favrile glass screens by Louis Comfort Tiffany.

There were more hopeful men in New York in 1900 than Uncle Roc. J. P. Morgan welcomed the New Year, aware he had helped forge a powerful nation by investing in steel and copper and finished products, most of which were controlled at an outrageous profit by his Wall Street bank. A religious man—he contributed large sums to his church—with mistresses stashed away in Europe, Morgan had given a lying-in hospital to New York City (and town wits said, "He's going to try and fill it all by himself").

That year, as the bells and harbor whistles rang in the century, there were young men waiting to make their mark in history—Franklin Delano Roosevelt, Fiorello La Guardia, and Jimmy Walker were all in their teens. In their thirties and forties were Teddy Roosevelt, John Singer Sargent, Alfred E. Smith, and William Randolph Hearst.

THE SIDEWALKS OF NEW YORK
By 1906 the East Side was overcrowded, and people were dreadfully housed, many in buildings owned by the Astors and Vanderbilts or by churches. (Library of Congress)

Land values in New York were still rising. Uptown shopping was passing 34th Street, and who knew *where* it would end? There wasn't much education for the New York masses in their slums and ghettos. Nearly 200,000 New Yorkers spoke their original tongues and not English.

The Irish had seized the city government, policed it mostly with their own, and held on. "Shanty Irish" was turning to "Lace Curtain Irish." The 700,000 Jews—the Litväk, Glitz, Russian *shul*-goers—were still trapped in poverty on the East Side. The Italians, menaced by Black Hand terrorists, didn't get around to starting the first Columbus Day parade (in 1900) until there were more than 140,000 of them.

The Negroes didn't organize any parade. Sixty thousand of them existed by shining shoes, portering, toting and carrying, cleaning and dusting.

Visitors did feel the invasion of the automobile. Autos were banned from Central Park, and a speeder was arrested for driving recklessly at 12 mph. In 1900 mass production of autos began (up till then they were custom-built jobs on order), but only for the rich. That year the original Madison Square Garden held an auto show with over fifty makers of cars presenting their horseless carriages. Tall, often tiller-steered, hand-cranked, with gas headlights, they featured lots of brass to polish.

Uptown was now going up Fifth Avenue where the great mansions of the robber barons of former generations were settings for the twentieth-century spending of inherited fortunes by fast-living heirs.

My Uncle Roc was an auto car buff. I remember pictures of him driving a Simplex, a chain-driven monster with a red undercarriage. He was one of the clockers in 1901 when a car ran a mile a minute at the Long Island Automobile Club meet.

At a time when license plates cost $1 per year, Uncle Roc protested that Henry Ford's Model T would ruin the middle class. He didn't like the double-decker buses, introduced from France, on Fifth Avenue.

He cursed taximeters in the new motor cabs, but he was there to see the first traffic-control standards go up on Fifth Avenue in 1922. They were topped by a naked metal figure of the god Mercury wearing a World War I helmet.

Uncle Roc did very well when the Belmonts and the English Rothschilds set up the Rapid Transit Construction Company, and subway trenches were first dug in March 1900. Four years later the mayor and a lot of starched white shirt fronts went down into the bowels of the earth that was City Hall Station and entered the first train.

Whistles and a cannon made noises about the event, and the train

The Brooklyn Bridge when It Was Young
The bridge connecting New York and Brooklyn, in the days when sailing ships were putting up a losing fight against steam.

CENTRAL PARK IN WINTER, 1872
A cold clear day in the park and great for skating. The little bridge beyond
the pond is still standing. (*Harper's Weekly*—author's collection)

started off. It went to Grand Central, crossed to Times Square, and at last reached the wilds of 145th Street—end of the line. New Yorkers went mad over this new way to travel—many of them spent the rest of the day riding the train. And the price was only a nickel a ride.

⊷§§⊷

As New York had grown from a village into a town, and from a town into a city, the more respectable citizens wanted more reputable names for the streets that began usually as colonial alleys and muddied lanes, and were often disreputable in their history. So Smell Street Lane (hardly needing explanation) became Broad Street. Tinpot Alley was renamed Edgar Street, The Street-that-leads-to-the-Pie-Woman became Nassau Street, Windmill Lane was turned into Cortlandt Street.

There remain streets that do not belong to the city but are owned by associations. Washington Mews was pointed out to me—it lies between Fifth Avenue and University Place and is owned by the Sailors Snug Harbor Association. Thomas Street, between Broadway and Church Street, is owned by the Society of the Hospital of the City of New York. Other privately owned streets and sidewalks in the city I discovered while working on this book are such out-of-the-way places as Shinbone Alley, MacDougal Alley, Henderson Place, part of Vanderbilt Avenue, Sniffen Court, Extra Place, Bishop Lane, and Shubert's Alley.

There were more pleasant uses of the streets. The Easter Parade up and down Fifth Avenue toward St. Patrick's grew slowly from some strollers in the 1850s. From 1869 on the newspapers began to feature the Easter Parade. By the 1900s it was one of the annual events in New York City, like the appearance of the hot chestnut man in the fall, the organ grinder with his monkey in the spring, and the Diamond Horseshoe gala night at the Met after society had returned from Newport or Europe.

In the beginning, the strollers went around from Madison Square and up Fifth Avenue into the fifties. The press reported "elegant equipages at church doors, manned by pompous doormen. . . . The throng was almost exclusively composed of churchgoers . . . prancing horses, glittering harnesses, shining carriages."

Already, by the turn of the century, modes of fashion and a kind of social status-seeking had crept in. The paraders and strollers were hardly churchgoers, rather fine-feathered exhibitionists in many cases. But the Holy Day promenade did not reach the commercial use of professional models and eye-bugging stunts until after World War I.

My uncles grew up in the age of the last horsecars. They remember as small boys riding with their father in a horsecar across town on Canal Street. Later I, too, was endangering my limbs leaping off New York City trolleys in my art school days. Times Square was a steel griddle of trolley

CENTRAL PARK IN EARLIER DAYS
Concerts under the trees on Saturday afternoons were a regular event. (Author's collection)

tracks crossing north, south, east, and west. The Fifth Avenue buses in those days, for me, weren't for transportation, but for riding with a girl on top of the open double-decker. Or for just sketching the city, sitting warmly dressed, hunting the first green buds of spring on the Central Park trees. But like the steam locomotive and the El trains, the very last trolley of New York City went offstage with its final clanging run on April 7, 1957.

One letter writer wrote to me as follows, recording the event:

> No wonder a poet wrote, "April is the saddest month." Old 601 was the trolley that made the last proud route of the Queensboro Bridge; from the Manhattan side to Queens Plaza in Long Island City. The sickening fumes of today's buses, the frayed nerves of harassed bus drivers seems to we Nostalgia Hounds to lack something. The Dickens-style character of the 1907–1914 old conductors, their big feet in bulldog-toed shoes, the way they punched a transfer. And the sound of a trolley pole sparking as it hunted its overhead live wire, the thump, too, of its not always truly rounded wheels, the clang of the motorman's foot bell: *all* gone. Trolley 601 rests in a trolley museum on Staten Island.

14
The General Slocum's *Fate*

"Few people understand that great disasters often create a historic social standing based on the importance of their victims." So my Uncle Roc told me after the Wall Street bombing of the early 1920s. "To have lost an uncle, better yet a parent, on the *Titanic*, I've observed, is something that enhanced one's social position. To have had most of your family killed in the picnic steamer accident, well, it only placed you among the socially unimportant."

Death by accident retained its own kind of snobbery, no matter how tragic.

The people who boarded the *General Slocum* on June 1, 1904, were not slum dwellers or Tammany Hall picnickers rewarded by a ward boss with a day on Long Island Sound in return for their votes. They were decent middle-class families, yet not one of their names has entered folklore like Casey Jones or the Unsinkable Molly Brown. I have, myself, been informed over the years of the names of famous New York theater people, department store owners, publishers, society movers and climbers who went down with the *Titanic*—and always with a kind of pride.

On that fine June morning the white three-decker paddle-wheeler *General Slocum,* loading at the 3rd Street pier, had good thick plumes of smoke coming from its twin funnels. Two thousand holiday-makers were headed for a day's picnic at Locust Sound Grove on Long Island Sound. Most of the gay and cheerful passengers were women and children. The Rev. George Haas from St. Mark's German Lutheran Church on East 6th Street was taking his parishioners for a day's outing.

At nine o'clock, just after the boat siren sounded, bells clanged in the engine room and the white paddle-wheels began to churn. A band was playing good music, including Luther's hymn "A Mighty Fortress Is Our God." As the boat moved up river picnic baskets were opened and toasts given, *"Zum Wohlsein!"* Children played, laughing, exploring among decks covered with picnic baskets, sunshades, musical instruments, folding chairs.

Then, opposite 145th Street, someone smelled smoke, saw flames coming up from below. At once the panic cries of "Fire! Fire!" horrified the passengers, and slowly a milling, unreasoning movement began. The forward part of the ship was transformed almost at once into a raging,

A BURNED-OUT HULK
The charred remnants of the *General Slocum* after the disastrous fire that claimed 1,021 lives. (Wide World Photos)

orange-colored mass of fire. There was no great outcry at first. In fact, many of the passengers, their features frozen, stared in silent horror at what could not be.

Suddenly the ship began to buck and vibrate. Captain William Van Schaik ordered the wheel spun about to head the burning craft toward North Brothers Island. This proved to be a tragic mistake, for the increase in speed fanned the leaping flames to greater intensity.

Blackwell Island's shoreline was filled with people watching the steamer burn briskly as it moved toward North Brothers Island. Boards, planks, towboats, barrels were launched from Blackwell toward the burning vessel. But the *Slocum* ignored them and went on, a flaming torch, with utter panic on board as mothers and children helplessly floundered along the pitching decks.

Tugboats began to move out to assist the *General Slocum*, but Captain Van Schaik—like some demented Flying Dutchman—drove his vessel inexorably onward toward that point of land he had decided to reach. He had obviously lost his ability to reason, for the only sensible solution under the circumstances was to bring his ship to a halt and wait for assistance to come to him.

Crying and screaming in panic, people began to drop over the sides. Men first, then women—some with children in their arms.

The river suddenly seemed full of floating, struggling shapes. Many of the bodies the tugboat men fished out of the water were badly burned, limbs charred. All the members of the band, with the exception of Julius Woll, the clarinet player, perished. It was just less than an hour since the cheerful holiday start from the 3rd Street pier. Of the 2,000 people on board, 1,021 were dead or dying in the fearful agony of burns, or drowning, while watchers on shore stood helplessly by.

Afterward, there were the usual investigations. It was quickly apparent that rules had been broken. There had been serious overloading; engine room carelessness existed and oily wastes had been permitted to lie around in the boiler area.

In the end, Captain William Van Schaik went to Sing Sing for several years. In a certain sense he was made the scapegoat. He had not sold the tickets, planned the overloading, or neglected the fire-fighting precautions—these things were up to the owners to supervise. He had been aware that the paddle-wheeler was overloaded, but most of the New York excursion boats usually were overloaded.

15
The Hedonists

The most famous name in American gambling and the most impressive and respected figure in all of New York's gambling history is Richard Canfield, a man neither eccentric, capricious, nor self-infatuated. In 1893, at the peak of his career, he bought control of the Saratoga Club House, in Saratoga Springs, New York, which had fallen on shabby times since the rich socialites who made the best pigeons to pluck at roulette and faro had gone elsewhere for their gambling. Canfield soon changed all that. He knew wines and put nearly $50,000 worth of the best vintages into the cellar. He brought in two dozen expert waiters who made $50 a day in tips but got only $1 a day from Canfield. He also knew that a fine cuisine was needed to attract the rich; even those who couldn't eat the gourmet specialties served by chef Jean Columbin could take joy in seeing and smelling his culinary delights.

Actually, the splendid food was only a come-on for the gamblers to feel satisfied in the stomach before their wallets became thinner. Canfield lost at least $70,000 a summer in the dining room by serving fine food, but he made it up neatly at the gambling tables.

Canfield was an imposing figure of a man, five feet eight or nine inches tall, weighing 200 pounds in his prime, and going to 240 in his decline. His brown hair and gray eyes gave his head the look of a Roman emperor, a man who seemed never to stress the qualities in which he excelled. He was clean-shaven for most of his life in an era when the moustache and the beard were still a sign of male virility.

He was a neat, even fussy dresser, owning forty suits and fifteen pairs of shoes. He ran honest clubs, used no ropers or cappers, never welshed on a payment.

A Canfield club ran seven days a week. The arrangements were impressive. The first floor was home for ten roulette wheels and four faro layouts. In the private rooms upstairs there were two double-end wheels and a faro layout. There was no dice playing in his clubs or card games other than faro.

Thirty highly skilled croupiers, case-keepers, and guards were under Canfield's eye and order to keep it calm. Play was with chips valued at from $1 to $1,000. Winners were paid by check, unless they preferred cash from the big safe, which was supposed to hold a million dollars.

In his clubs Canfield claimed he did not pay bribes to police or city officials, but in fact he made "friendly loans" to them that were *never* repaid, so it came to the same thing. In New York City the graft was collected by police and city officials from all gambling places: 25 percent of the house take *plus* $1,000. Canfield himself paid off the boodle to the police collector monthly, usually over a table at Delmonico's.

Canfield's actual losses when he closed his last gambling house were $250,000 in uncollected IOUs, some from the best families and the richest men. Reggie Vanderbilt welshed on a $300,000 IOU and settled for a payment of $130,000. Canfield himself was a great spender—he was a magnificent collector of paintings, statues, and etchings. Chinese porcelain was a favorite, and he had two peachbloom vases valued at from $8,000 to $12,000 each. Chippendale furniture also delighted him, and his twelve chairs cost him $60,000.

Canfield was an impeccable gentleman, unlike Bet-a-Million Gates who didn't mind matching pennies for $1,000 a turn, and who would even bet on two raindrops racing down a windowpane. He once won $22,000 playing the raindrop game on a train from Chicago to Pittsburgh.

❦

What was Richard Canfield's background? He was born in New Bedford, Massachusetts, in 1855, and the claim of his mother, as a Howland, was that she was descended from those Howlands who came over on the *Mayflower*. Also that she was related to the notorious Hetty Green, the Witch of Wall Street (whose son became a fabulous sport and gambler).

Canfield's father was crippled on a whaling ship when he was a young man. Later he tried publishing a newspaper and failed, and ended up running a saloon—what we today in neater language call a bar.

There were six children, and Richard was the smart one of the litter and a most persuasive child. He had hopes of becoming a famous runner. After his father died of dropsy, he attended public school, became a fine talker, and was a commencement speaker. Canfield worked for a while in a Boston store's shipping department and saw this was no way to wealth. At the age of eighteen he and a partner set up a small poker game in Providence, with a dime limit. When the police shook their heads at this way of life, he traveled around New England as a professional gambler, and claimed that in 1876 he took in $20,000 in a run of luck. He spent it wisely, he thought, by going to Europe and getting a traveler's polish at Monte Carlo and other casinos—seeing how they gambled over there.

He returned with no assets left and became a night clerk in the Union Square Hotel, which was managed by his mother's cousin.

He moved on to work at a better hotel, read a lot of good books, became manager of Monmouth House, and a Knight Templar of the Masons. Finally, he decided it was time to spread out, so he and a partner opened a poker game in Pawtucket, Rhode Island. In 1885 he felt well enough established to marry Genevieve Martin, of whom we know very little. One of his faro setups was raided, and Richard, on his thirtieth birthday, went to jail for a six-month sentence.

With another partner (he had charm and could always get a partnership) he set up in New York, on Broadway, a gambling house that ran from high noon to midnight and paid off to its owners with smooth efficiency $4,300 a week in the first year.

Canfield and other partners went into business as the Madison Square Club on West 26th Street. Here he was in the big time, his magnetism and charm at its best. From twenty-five and fifty-dollar limits the stakes went to a hundred limit, and gradually to higher and higher stakes. The boast was that there was always $50,000 in the safe to pay off winners. Canfield soon bought out the partnership and became sole owner. The value placed on his club at the time was $1 million. How this figure was obtained was not explained, but Canfield became a very rich man. It was at this point in his career that he moved in on Saratoga and became the owner of the Saratoga Club House.

The club ran smoothly under Canfield's cool gray eyes. And it was safe for the women in boas and puffed sleeves to wear hundreds of thousands of dollars' worth of jewels to the place. And no man's wallet was in danger from pickpockets or holdup men.

If the ladies were most welcome in the public rooms to fill the deep ottomans, they were not admitted to the gambling sections; neither were citizens of the town. One of the frequent female guests in the club's dining room was Lillian Russell. The great plump American beauty was an actress, gourmet, and friend of rich men. She came nearly every night to test Chef Columbin's artistry, and he never let her down, nor she him in her flowing-sleeved chiffon.

Lillian's official escort for many years was Diamond Jim Brady, but it would seem they were never actually lovers; Jim, being a great feeder rather than woman lover, had no delusions about his sexual abilities. He neither drank nor smoked but could consume six dozen Lynnhaven oysters, a saddle of mutton, a breast of chicken with caper sauce, a few lobsters, a dozen venison chops, a twelve-egg soufflé and all the trimmings of a twelve-course dinner, washed down by a gallon of orange juice. Then followed the crêpes suzettes, which had been invented for him by the great chef Henri Charpentier.

↔

There was a library for the guests in a Canfield club, but no record has come down to us of the contents of the books shelved there. (He himself preferred well-bound, rare classics.) Perhaps it was law books he collected in the public room, for he was beginning to have trouble with the bluenoses and the reforming bleeding hearts. The Saratoga Club was shut down for one entire racing season. The following year, however, the club remained open. But the Canfield clubs in the city were raided.*

It was all very complicated. Canfield spent two years in court defending himself; for with his New Bedford jail days on record he could have gotten a long prison term. He was fined $1,000 and his lawyers cost him about $1,000 more.

For Richard Canfield, someone said, the clock was striking midnight. More laws and outcries and pressures were put on him, and by 1904 he had had enough of New York City.

He closed the dining room, which was a blow to many gourmets. In 1908 he sold the upstate club to the city of Saratoga for $150,000. (Today it is the Saratoga Historical Society—a shabby display.)

Canfield had made a fortune on Wall Street by speculating and was said to be worth $12 million. His take at the Saratoga Club House in fourteen years was figured at $2.5 million. Most of this fortune he lost in the financial panic of 1907. In 1914, at fifty-nine, he fell down a flight of

---

* The success of his first club led Canfield to expand his operation so that, prior to the raids, his New York City gambling clubs were located on Broadway between 18th and 19th streets, on West 26th street, and the most famous on East 44th Street between Delmonico's and Sherry's.

THE HOFFMAN HOUSE BAR
The most famous clubman's hangout, and on the wall the most notorious nude painting in town, Bouguereau's *Nymphs and the Satyr*. No females permitted, of course. (Ross Collection)

stairs, and died of a fractured skull. His estate was appraised as being worth $841,485.

◈◈◈

Two New Yorkers served as a kind of transmission belt between the hedonism of the city in the last part of the nineteenth century and the beginning of the twentieth. Louis Comfort Tiffany and James Gordon Bennett were not mere playboys, idle rich men's sons. Tiffany gave his name and skill to an era of graceful décor. James Gordon Bennett made the New York *Herald* an even better newspaper than his father had, and he established the first good English-language newspaper on the continent, the Paris *Herald*. Both died after the end of World War I. Both brought forward into the twentieth century some of the ideas of pleasure from a more leisurely age.

Louis Comfort Tiffany's stained-glass lampshades, tree trunk art patterns, and flower forms in metal and other substances were just a few years ago revived, first as "camp" and then as genuine American genre. His fame and décor were not merely American but international. Modern design of the turn of the century found him its most celebrated and most salable artist. His logical fantasy, his fine, bizarre use of metal and glass once decorated the best New York homes.

He was born in New York City in 1848, the son of Charles Lewis and Harriet Young Tiffany. Charles Tiffany, with nothing but a fine and honorable background, got together, on loan, $1,000 in 1837 and, with a partner, opened a tiny dry-goods and stationery shop at 259 Broadway.

From such beginnings grew the present-day world-renowned Tiffany & Company. But young Louis wanted no part of that small, safe life of struggling, earnest shopkeepers. He was a redheaded child, wild, headstrong, and not easy to control. He was packed off to the Flushing Academy on Long Island, and there, somehow, he became interested in the arts. His parents, like good, middle-class climbers into society, decided Louis should go to college. The salient characteristics of a degree would improve the family's image. But Louis had no desire for a formal education, no wish to enter the family business; he wanted to study art. The parents finally consented, and he went to the studio of George Inness, whose mild, genteel landscapes were a romantic feature of the Hudson River school of painting.

The youth was eighteen at the time, but not a typical New Yorker, for he loved the cozy, paint-stained life of the studio, the painters and writers who came there to smoke cheroots, drink the rye whisky, and talk of Paris, of the artist's pleasant, unquiet life, the great collections of art.

Paris was Louis' goal, and somehow when he was twenty-one he got his parents to let him go there to study at the studio of Louis Bailly. Study is too strong a word; Louis loved and lived in Paris the way that

Whistler and the heroes of *Trilby* ordered their lives—a sort of aesthetic delinquency with a denigration and condescension to ordinary existence.

Louis' teacher painted imaginary landscapes of North Africa and the Near East in his Paris studios. Louis was delighted with the subject matter. With another American artist in Paris, Samuel Coleman, he went to seek out the color and glow of North Africa, sample the women, the couscous, the rafa brandy, perhaps inhale the opium pipe.

Certainly he took delight in the color and confusion of an Arabian Nights' world. Islamic fabrics and design pleased him with their rhythmic structures that kept a decorative distance from nature. Popular in America were pseudo-Oriental and the brass, beady, inlaid Near Eastern art. Mansions had "Turkish corners," Moorish rooms, divans from Arab harems, camel saddles. Americans brought back Turkish rugs, harem divans to Bohemian studios.

Louis Tiffany, his head whirling with color and patterns, returned to New York in 1870 with a cargo of his North African paintings. Sales were good at $500 each. But the young man was more interested in crafts, in industrial arts, in home décor.

By the turn of the century he had perfected his working in glass for fashionable New York buyers. "I took to chemistry and built furnaces." Soon the city's best salons, houses of the rich, were displaying his "Favrile Glass," as he called it.

His screens had been the sensation of the Columbia Exposition; even Paris featured his work in a dealer's Salon de l'Art Nouveau. His lamps, boxes, glassware, screens became the Tiffany touch in a social setting, and the Tiffany lamp a must in the best houses in New York. He worked his molded glass into delicate shapes of marvelous colors. Louis used mosaics, opalescent, iridescent precious stones and pearls, and copied the tails of peacocks, the petals of flowers in glass, metal, and enamels.

As his fame spread between Paris and his atelier in New York—he hardly would call it a factory—Tiffany became a very busy man. By 1909 he had a stock of 5,000 art objects on hand for buyers.

He was in business in a very big way, establishing the Tiffany Studios in New York, where hundreds of girls applied his décor. They were called *craftsmen*, these girls, rather than factory hands, although their pay was hardly more. Glass, bronze, ceramic, enamel—Tiffany used them all on lamps, vases, penwipers, pin trays, stemware, lighting fixtures, art jewelry, tiaras, necklaces.

A born hedonist of the Stanford White set, a cheerful Silenus, his parties in New York drew international attention. He was a striking-looking man with his flaming red Edwardian beard, his frantic gestures— a man fully aware of his worth and his own intense desires.

The years approaching the Great War didn't much diminish Tiffany's ideas. With talk of the conflict drawing close, he gave, in memory of his wild times, a Peacock Dinner for his male friends—the rounders, sportsmen, sensualists of his set. Roast peacock was served—in its retrieved feathers—by young girls wearing transparent Greek garments and carrying the trays of birds on their shoulders in a colorful procession around the table. It was a farewell to the realm of dreams before the guns of August sounded.

In 1914 he published his own memorial, *The Art Work of Louis C. Tiffany*. As a British statesman said, "The lights are going out all over Europe, we shall not see them relit in our time."

His own light was going out as a pioneer maker of expensive art objects. Tastes and times were changing in a world of incoherent horror. He retired to his estate, Laurelton Hall, on Long Island. "A retreat for artists," he called it in 1918, "the Louis Comfort Tiffany Foundation." There was to be, he announced, "no formal instruction," instead he called for "art by absorption."

Lillian Russell liked Tiffany products. A few close friends admired most a gift she got from her friend Diamond Jim Brady. As a clerk of Louis Tiffany's once confessed about Mr. Brady's taste, "He asked Tiffany to make for Miss Russell [and we made it] a solid-gold chamber pot; in the center of the bottom, peering up, was a large eye."

❧

If in the first half of the twentieth century the antics of Joseph Pulitzer and William Randolph Hearst were to make one wonder at the methods of New York City journalism at its peak, they had an early model in James Gordon Bennett, the Younger. He was a true original, a cocksure hedonist. The limitless opulence of his $1 million-a-year income (after taxes) afforded him his excesses, his vulgarity, his drunken escapades, his strenuous unorthodoxies and permitted him to sneer at all social and moral conventions.

His father, the stern maker of a great newspaper, the New York *Herald* (after Horace Greeley was gone), raised young Bennett to anticipate a rich gold mine as publisher. Later, when Bennett established the Paris edition of the New York *Herald* (wrongly called the Paris *Herald* by most), he was to have two sources of power in two important newspapers. His life was that of a man constantly endangered by his wild dashing about as a sportsman, by overeating, by predatory games, by sexual liaisons with all manner of willing women.

After his father died young Bennett soon gained the reputation of being a mean boss in his role as the *Herald*'s new owner. On the other hand, he did possess a fine newspaper sense. He hired Mark Twain to write a series of travel letters—the "Quaker City Letters"—based on a trip to the Holy Land, which later were used to produce Twain's first best-

GOLD DIGGERS OF 1900
A poster showing three beauties—when hips were larger, corsets tighter, and garters a sex lure. Ziegfeld was soon to start his *Follies* and produce a different kind of beauty. (Library of Congress)

seller, *The Innocents Abroad*. Bennett also hired Henry M. Stanley to find (not to rescue as claimed) the missionary David Livingston in unknown "Darkest Africa."

Just what sent James Gordon Bennett, that New York citizen, to Paris? What made him an exile from his native land? The answer: one of those society scandals that today seem merely foolish, a boozy caprice. In 1877 it caused a social shock that sent Bennett eastward to Europe for good. It began with the idea that since he was a very rich young man with valuable New York properties, he should marry, even if just for the sake of producing heirs.

He found Caroline May, who came from one of those stiff and proper families who were very much aware of their ancestors' world, in Maryland. Caroline was beautiful, and her family was solidly entrenched in a grand house in New York City, upholding the highest social position in "a society made up of descendants of former fur traders, slavers, whisky sellers to Indians, land thieves, and robber barons."

On New Year's Day 1877 the Mays were holding open house in their Manhattan mansion, the festive seasonal atmosphere properly gay with eggnog, old wine, tidbits, game birds, and sliced beef ready to welcome the New Year.

Bennett arrived at the Mays' in a two-horse cutter on thin steel blades since the streets were blanketed from a recent snowfall. He was enveloped in buffalo robes, and it was apparent that he was already filled with a great deal of New Year's cheer, the result of imbibing generous potions of his favorite brandy. He managed to get into the house and greet the guests, his bride-to-be, her parents, and Caroline's brother.

A good fire burned in the ornate fireplace. Bennett seemed only vaguely aware of what was going on around him, as he continued drinking, or perhaps he mistook it all for that male retreat the Union Club, and the fireplace for a urinal. Whatever he thought—if he thought at all—he opened his fly and proceeded to urinate into the leaping flames.

The reaction of the guests was horror, panic, and revulsion. Suddenly the New Year's celebration at the Mays' came to a silent end. Four men quickly helped Bennett through the front doors to his cutter.

News of Bennett's vulgar action circulated quickly, and the incident was greeted with much raffish and bawdy comment. Lunching the next day at the Union Club ("on a broiled Southdown mutton chop and part of a bottle of Pommery Brut"), Bennett believed the worst was over.

Then, in front of the club, as he prepared to leave, his way was barred by Frederick May, the twenty-five-year-old brother of Caroline, his once intended bride. Frederick began to flog James with a horse whip, and they progressed from there to a rolling fight in the snow.

The fight was stopped before any serious damage was done. Bennett sailed for Europe, to live mostly in Paris, returning to New York only on visits—business trips to see to the New York *Herald*.

Bennett was dedicated to the images of owls—an owl, he claimed, saved him once from shipwreck off Long Island. Bennett held there was some mystic, shaman-like quality to owls. He covered his material possessions with images of owls, when there was space. When the new New York Herald building was erected on Broadway and 35th Street, the roof line showed two huge bronze owls with electric eyes that blinked off and on, and two giant figures beat hammers on a bell to announce the hours to the citizens of New York.

JAMES GORDON BENNETT'S NEW YORK HERALD BUILDING
One of Bennett's famous owls is on the roof. To the left is one of Herald Square's horsecars going down Broadway. (Author's collection)

Bennett wanted to enter eternity with an owl as the bearer of his remains. He decided that he wanted to be buried inside a 200-foot-tall, hollowed-out stone bird. A staircase would lead up to the eyes of the owl, the eyes serving as windows and observation balconies. On chains hanging inside the bird's head, James Gordon Bennett's casket—with his body reposing inside—would be suspended, free of the rot of earth burial. It was a plan for a mausoleum that dwarfed anything any other rich New Yorker or American had yet conceived.

Early in the century Bennett commissioned Stanford White to draw up plans for the burial owl and hired sculptor Andrew O'Connor to create the entombing bird in glazed Vermont granite.

But Bennett had time for other thoughts besides death. The impression most people had was that Bennett died a bachelor. Actually, in September 1914 he left the Catholic Church of his mother, became an Episcopalian, and married the widow of the Baron de Reuter, née Maud Parker of Philadelphia. The baron had been related to the founder of the famous news-gathering organization Reuters. Bennett always kept his life in touch with some form of journalism.

But his major project remained the plans for his New York owl tomb. Bennett wanted to supervise its progress himself, domesticate himself, as it were, to the owl's interior, its roominess, view, and comfort. The price? Stanford White said it would cost $1 million if all of Bennett's ideas were to be worked out. Bennett said $1 million would satisfy him.

But the project never got past the planning stages. Stanford White was shot down in Madison Square Garden's roof restaurant by Harry K. Thaw, the playboy husband of a woman with whom White was once entangled.

James Gordon Bennett predicted in a clairvoyant moment that he would die on his seventy-seventh birthday. In 1918 he fulfilled his prediction. No New York owl tomb existed. Bennett was buried at Passy, across the river from Paris. There are a pair of owls—like emblematic devices—carved on his gravestone. But they lack the wise look of the New York City owls from the Herald building.

As for the gaudy, wonderful journalism of New York, it did not last. The *Herald* in time combined with the *Tribune*, becoming the *Herald Tribune*—a hybrid—and in the end it entered an alliance with three other dying newspapers and they expired in each other's arms.

16
Ordeal by Fire

By the time the first decade of the twentieth century had passed, nearly one-seventh of the city's population was foreign-born. In addition, the ethnic composition of the people flowing into the country from Europe was altering drastically. The middle-class Germans and Austrians, as well as the Scandinavians and Irish, were being replaced by people from Eastern Europe—Hungarians, Poles, Czechs—and Italians and Greeks. And most of them were merely shifting their living quarters from their home country ghettos to similar areas of urban blight in New York City.

What changed the city at first were the markings of the newcomers on their streets and shops—signs in strange languages as well as the odors of odd spices in the air, the appearance of stores with foods untasted by the native New Yorkers. Blintzes, dolmades, bagels, cervelatwurst, goulash, cacciatora dishes. Women with shawls, some even wearing ritual wigs. Hordes of youngsters new to public schools and with accents that caused laughter. Pushcarts full of tainted bargains, seconds, and hand-me-downs, serviced by Talmudic students with beards and earlocks, or Italian peasants, stood at the curbs of Houston, Delancey, and Essex streets.

The foreign-born worked hard and cheaply. Their own kind exploited them; the German Jews, of long standing in the city, went to the immigrant enclaves to secure workers for their ready-made clothing factories, usually located in dismal lofts and dusty spaces turned into desperate little businesses called "sweatshops."

The pictures in the newspapers of society people showing off their glittering jewels at the Met's Diamond Horseshoe, or of a Vanderbilt driving his tallyho coach and four matched bays down Fifth Avenue, didn't lower the poverty level of New York. The city still remained a great mass of have-nots on which floated, like a pie crust, the haves.

Under that crust of plenty, misery and despair sat heavy. Children staggered through mean streets under great bundles of half-finished garments from clothing contractors, to be finished at home—basted and sewed in dismal cold-water flats, called railroad flats because they had no hallways, with one room leading into the next and the next. Women, often three generations of a family toiling in one room, sewed these bundles for pennies a section, or twisted paper and wire flowers.

Those women of the East Side who worked in sweatshops "were the slaves of the needle"—as one radical poet wrote—and the sewing machines. The shop owners usually bribed city inspectors to permit all kinds of health and safety violations in these lofts—lofts that herded young immigrant girls and women together over the whirring Singer machines to produce garments for a few dollars a week for the rapidly growing, but cutthroat ready-made clothing industry.

By 1911 there was a kind of horror hovering over these shops; some impending tragedy seemed moored above the rooftops. On March 8 this feeling of disaster decided the destiny of the young girls at the Triangle Shirtwaist Factory located on Greene Street, east of Washington Square.

The factory consisted of the top three stories of an old building. It was a Saturday, but the two-day weekend holiday was not yet acceptable. The girls were working this Saturday afternoon but were scheduled to leave early at 4:30. The machines were just coming to a halt and the operators were stretching their limbs from their demanding tasks over the flashing needles. Then there was smoke, followed by the cry of "Fire!"

The place was a bomb of lint and dust, scraps of the flimsy stuff from which the shirtwaists were made. How or where the conflagration started was never fully discovered, but it was *there*, and terror surged through the trapped women as they fought their way outward—toward a fire escape or into a hallway with a staircase, or to an elevator.

But for most there was no escape. The fire escape was a mass of twisted, misshapen iron. Much of the mortar in the brick wall to which it was originally anchored had long since eroded, and now it failed. Over-

A Home Sweatshop
Photographed by Jacob A. Riis, an early twentieth-century reporter, who did much to expose the dreadful working and living conditions of the poor. (Ross Collection)

loaded with desperate, struggling humans—like a lifeboat of a sinking ship—the metal structure tore loose and fell to the pavement below.

As for the exit doors, they opened *in* and not *out*. The press of bodies prevented most of them from opening. One door had been locked permanently to prevent pilfering. The two elevators functioned at first as the operators tried to remove as many of the girls and women as possible to ground level. But as the fire grew in volume, it filled the elevator shafts with smoke, and then flames attacked the greasy cables and walls, forcing disruption of service.

Below in the street a crowd was gathering around the twisted mass of iron that had been the fire escape and the shattered bodies of girl workers who had been carried to their deaths.

AFTERMATH OF DISASTER
Workshop of the Triangle Shirtwaist Factory in the Asch Building after the
fire that raged so furiously that many of the trapped young female workers
leaped to their deaths from the flame-wreathed windows. (Wide World Photos)

Meanwhile, fire alarms were being turned in, and in fifteen minutes
10,000 people were milling around the smoking, burning building watching the top stories turn into an incinerating torch. They were not just idle
watchers or thrill seekers. Many were Italian and Jewish relatives of the
trapped and dying girls. It was a slum district below Washington Square,
and many people lived near their jobs.

Police lines were formed to keep the screaming, weeping people
back. The pressure to reach the burning building went on as the thick
smoke and the orange-red plumes of fire continued to roar overhead.
Now those below could discern the figures of girls clinging to window
ledges, handgrips slipping, flames setting their hair and clothing on fire.
Desperate cries in English, Yiddish, and Italian urged them to hang on.
But one by one their strength gave way and they plummeted to the street.

It was one of those swift and dreadful city tragedies that strike
without warning and leave great shock; the fire itself was brought under
control by the firemen in eighteen minutes. All that remained was a smell

New Americans
on the East Side.
During the 1890s the flood
of immigrants from Europe
grew constantly. These pictures from *Illustrated American* are among the very few
taken in the city during that
period. (Author's collection)

of burning cloth, charred timbers, a soggy, water-soaked staircase, *and* the bodies—some burned through so that only bones remained.

Firemen and police began to lower bodies to the street by block and tackle. As night fell, trucks brought up searchlights to illuminate the macabre packages that swung about as they were lowered to the sidewalks. The crowd had grown; moaning and weeping were heard—also mixed curses and shouts against the bosses, against City Hall, with added calls on God asking why he had permitted this horror to happen.

There was a shortage of coffins. Only sixty-five were sent by the city morgue. Some of the bodies, naked and burned, lay on the cold walk, though a few were covered by canvas. Actually, the morgue had no room for the 146 workers who lost their lives in the fire. An annex was set up on the Hudson River pier at West 23rd and 24th streets.

Sunday was a true Doomsday. Two hundred thousand people walked through the rows of mostly open coffins on the pier, trying to identify a daughter, wife, relative, or just a friend.

The Jews held services for their dead, the Italians gathered in church for masses to be said. Lamenting in the Jewish ghetto was as heart-rending as was the keening for the dead amongst the Italians.

The Jews were clustered together in decaying buildings, many of them owned by some of the best families of the city. Along Rivington, Division, Orchard, Hester, and Baxter streets, millionaires owned whole blocks. Most of the dwellings were cheap, jerry-built tenements, built on lots that measured 20 feet by 100 feet and often housing 300 people. From 1905 up until World War I, a million and a quarter Jews were to enter the United States (one-seventh of all the Jews in Europe), mostly through Castle Garden and Ellis Island in New York Harbor.

It was from the squalor of these dwellings—heatless and usually without plumbing—that the girls who died in the Triangle Shirtwaist Factory fire came. There were, of course, official investigations, exposing misconduct of safety inspections and bribes paid to overlook violations of building regulations. Laws were eventually passed concerning maintenance of fire doors and establishing fire prevention and safety standards.

BOOK FIVE

The Dancers and the Intellectuals

17
The Art of
Giving a Party

On Tuesday, January 31, 1905, James Hazen Hyde, a turn-of-the-century man-about-town, dangerously shook the foundations of New York society and the social structure of the entire nation. He gave a ball that shocked simple Americans at the way money was lavishly tossed away.

Slim, with a nicely pointed blond beard, James Hazen Hyde, at twenty-eight, was a Francophile, obsessed with the notion that France possessed the only noble culture, food, wines, way of life, and was the true, suavely gracious setting for such people as himself.

In addition to his convictions about France, Hyde had inherited from his despotic father control of a giant insurance company. Hyde was first vice-president, held a director's seat in forty-six subsidiary companies that did well-rewarded business with the all-engulfing insurance firm. He also owned the big family estate in Bay Shore, Long Island, and a private Pullman palace car on wheels, the exquisite, comfortable *Bay Shore*. His stables held the best horses, his coach house the finest carriages, and as a member of the Coaching Club, with its braided whip *esprit de corps*, he drove a four-in-hand up Fifth Avenue.

To encourage the wheeled sport, he set up twelve coaching stations, one at New Brunswick, New Jersey, where the coaching parties, out to roll along the roads south to Lakewood, could dust off and refresh themselves on the eighty-mile ride with Alssop's lager on draft, Stilton cheeses, Melton Mowbray pies, and some good sparkling wine.

The costs for all this were borne by the insurance company, or rather the stockholders, who were as exploited as the peasants in the *ancien régime*. Hyde's own salary with the company was $100,000 a year, free of taxes. The company was a half-billion-dollar organization, and Hyde's personal outlays slipped past the bookkeeping department.

Hyde had visited France and came back a convert—an Orpheus—awakener of the "dead" Americans to life overseas. Everything French dazzled him, from the actresses to the great writers, the splendid cuisine, the museums and châteaux, the gossipy literary salons of French society.

So it was that in 1905 Hyde planned a grand gala to surpass anything the Astors and Vanderbilts could mount. It would be no mere Quat'z Arts Ball, no copy of life on the Côte d'Azur. His ball would glorify his love of *old* France, with all arrangements being carried out with the proper costumes and food, drink, music, and setting. New York would be amazed. Guest of honor would be Mme. Gabrielle Rejane, usually referred to just as Rejane. While few thought her much of a success as an actress, her languorous posturing and melancholy grace were being admired at the Liberty Theatre in *Ma Cousine*.

The staff of Sherry's was called in by James Hazen Hyde, and the restaurateur, the most fashionable provider to society parties, nodded and didn't appear to be shocked. Nor was Hyde when it was estimated that his royal shindig could be staged at the amazing high cost of $200,000. Hyde knew he could charge it all to the insurance company.

The final plans called for the re-creating in Sherry's ballroom of the golden court of Louis XV. The society architect Whitney Warren was hired and went to work to make a replica of one of the wings of Versailles inside the grand ballroom.

As Hyde stood to greet his guests at the entrance to the new Versailles, they found him attired in knee breeches, silver-buckled pumps, olive-green tailcoat (the color of the Coaching Club), his beard trimmed to a Henry IV point, and wearing all the decorations the cynical French government doles out so easily to well-heeled strangers. He was hardly aware that in this happy moment he was calling down upon himself a force that Henry James had warned against:

> Living as we do under the permanent visitation of the deadly epidemic of publicity, any rash work, any light thought that chances to

escape us, may instantly, by that accident, find itself propagated, and perverted, multiplied and diffused, after a fashion poisonous, practically and speedily fatal, to its subject . . . to our foolishly blabbed secret. . . .

And Hyde (no reader of this whiplash sentence) had arranged for his trial by deadly publicity and its rash aftereffects by hiring Joseph Byron and his cameras and his photographic staff of five to take pictures of *everybody* and *everything* bizarre that night.

Among the early arrivals was Mamie Fish, trailing an entourage of sixty or so diners who formed her court. Meals were to be served in series; three full twelve-course dinners would be available one after another, and Mrs. Fish's own group of guests would feed off her personal solid-gold table service.

Mrs. George Gould and many of her diamonds came. She was costumed as the Queen of France, wife of Louis XV, in green velvet with a lining of white silk, and in between could be seen the gleam of emeralds.

The hard, tough past of the mining camps of the West was represented by Mrs. Clarence Mackay (related to a woman who had been washerwoman and pants-patcher for miners before the bonanzas were found). Now Mrs. Mackay was the wife of the message king, owning the nation's telegraph and cable lines. She had dressed as Phédre, from the play of that name as performed on stage by the actress Adrienne Lecouvreur, all in velvet and watered silk.

As more people moved in from the cold and adjusted wigs they hoped had been picked clean from their last use in a masquerade, the entertainment had begun—eight unhappy college boys and a matching number of the season's debutantes doing what passed for a gavotte to music played by the forty-piece orchestra of the Metropolitan Opera House. Then on came the full Metropolitan corps de ballet.

But all this was prologue. The star of the evening, the one to be honored this night, was late. It was midnight when a sedan chair was carried in by four footmen in powdered wigs. Mme. Rejane rose from it as from a chaise longue in naughty French sex dramas. Hyde uttered a little speech in his still awkward French.

Mme. Rejane walked past rose-covered walls onto the stage. A special little play had been written for the event—one of those excruciating, unreal French bedroom dramas, *Entre Deux Portes*. Everyone who knew told his neighbor it meant "Between Two Doors." With its disquieting chatter it hardly seemed to be a thing to have amused Louis XV.

A gaggle of trumpeters blew air into their gold-colored horns as they led the guests, now numbering more than 350, to the floor below, where supper was laid out in what was still another segment of Versailles. Mme. Rejane recited a poem about how France loved America and America loved France, which pleased all present, and the turtle soup and the white champagne ('98) were served at once.

⋑⋐

For all the talk by William K. Vanderbilt of "the public be damned," and the scandals of Congressional grafting and lobbies, or old John D.'s Standard Oil trusts wrecking rivals, shooting strikers, the average American enjoyed his version of the rich at play. Teddy Roosevelt would rouse them a bit by his grandstand attacks on the trusts, the poisonous meat packers, and the scandalous looting of oil and railroads. But when average Americans picked up their newspapers, they liked the drawings of drunken girls in the arms of leering men in evening clothes, of champagne being poured—that wine of sinners.

The ball given by James Hazen Hyde wasn't useful, but it filled the need of the people who didn't go to fancy parties and who were a little fed up with the puritan ideal—the notion that all functions of the republic had to be useful. People who had little took vicarious gratification in the glow from above. However, they could be spurred to resent it all by the vulgar press media, the coarse journals and papers they read. It was a time when the newspaper, in yellow jingo journalism, was discovering its power, not to educate or speak with gravity of the true situation, but to excite, to exploit murder, crimes of passion, high living with its sexual detail, and the special sins of the rich.

So while the second meal at the great French ball was being served to the sound of opera horns and oboes, the cameramen were recording the scene and the actors. And while the local city prison, the Tombs, was modeled not on the Bastille but on some Egyptian fake, the real outraged attack would come not against a jail but against the insurance company, not with society heads on pikes, but with grand juries and investigations, all sired by the party in progress.

Back at the ball, after the second dinner, those who could went upstairs again where they would dance until three o'clock in the morning. A third dinner was being served, and some guests ate all three.

Dawn came to Manhattan, and the still sleeping Four Million waited for their dollar alarm clocks to ring. At six o'clock the sun began to tint the East River and the pealing of church bells called some to mass.

Finally, after the last guest had left, the waiters and charwomen began to clean up. The cameramen, still in evening dress, packed their last exposed glass plates in boxes to be developed. They produced an amazing assortment of pictures, and some of them escaped, or were stolen or sold to the New York *World*, to do their deadly work of showing how fortunes were spent by rich idlers—not even their own money but the assets of an insurance empire, whose cash belonged to stockholders.

The photos were lulus. Mrs. Potter Palmer, her tiara perched like a nervous bird on her head. The host himself standing in abject pride at the side of the Countess de Rougemont (born plain Edith Glass). Mme. Rejane posing in fastidious zeal as she leaned on a long white cane entwined with ribbons.

Somehow they turned out as preposterous cartoons of all the best names reproduced by a too righteous press: "robber baron," "bloodsucker," "makers of trusts and cartels." All lovely game for the yellow journalism in Pulitzer's *World* and Hearst's *Journal*.

There was William Harriman, railroad gobbler and a director of the insurance company, in hunting coat and knee pants. Stanford White in bored audacity (soon to be shot to death by millionaire Harry K. Thaw). There were Burdens (Vanderbilt heirs), James Henry Smith and friends, the easily rich (inherited) and the hard way (making it).

Hyde had meant the photographs to be placed in an album as a souvenir of a grand party. But when they were stolen or sold to Joseph Pulitzer of the New York *World* (who was not invited to the ball), the old man, blind though he was, knew a good story when he heard what the pictures showed. Henry James's warning about publicity and its evil was about to come down like a monsoon storm on Hyde.

The *World*, publishing the pictures with simple captions written for lip-moving readers, exploded in outrage to wonder at the doings of these rich "bloodsuckers" while the worker's dinner pail was hardly full. $200,000? Yes, the cost was $200,000! (Had there been a leak from Sherry's accounting department, too?) It brought up the subject just *who* had paid for this party? Who paid for these perverse French (!) scenes? How innocent, people asked, was this French ball? Could the rich really just eat and dance and drink up imported booze? Or had there been an orgy?

Soon there was talk of the wild cancan dance performed by the Metropolitan corps de ballet, of champagne drunk from slippers (always for early twentieth-century Americans this slipper-sipping was the final hedonistic perversion). The insurance company suddenly found itself in trouble. The public was interested in learning how a corporate giant with its vast power and influence could be mulcted by a young whippersnapper in a long pointed beard and fancy knee pants. Astute politicians scented a situation in which they could establish a reputation. Insurance companies were to be investigated and found guilty, and Charles Evans Hughes, as head investigator, rose to the limelight to expose all the managements of insurance companies.*

* His popularity as a result of this crusade was almost enough to take Hughes to the White House in 1916; in fact he went to bed as president of the United States, but woke to discover that California returns had turned him out. But he had nearly gotten his profile on a future postage stamp, and it all started by exploiting Hyde's Palace of Versailles party.

And James Hazen Hyde? The inner paneled offices at the company were full of hard words, of arm waving, of desperate men. There was talk of the dismal publicity, the notoriety. The insurance business had no wish to expose its bloated profits and odd methods of doing business or to reveal how shabbily the policyholders were treated and how vast sums of money went *here* and *there* among directors, as well as salaries hardly earned. For Hyde was not alone in stripping the money tree when it was always so beautifully in bloom.

William Harriman, as a director of the company and forgetting his image of himself in royal knee pants, felt that silly ball was just a boyish escapade. Scandals pass, new headlines take over. But William Cohen, a Tammany judge, wondered about some of the compromises that were discussed to whitewash Hyde. No, Hyde's removal from the company was the *only* answer. The whole economy of the firm had to be examined in order to keep the policyholders and the public in line.

The state legislature, heavily greased though it was by special interests in the insurance business, was compelled to back Charles Evans Hughes and his committee exposing the games of the directors, their dovetailing interests, kickbacks, all the high financial hanky-panky among them that lined their pockets.

Hughes came out with a scalding report of the company's nepotism, political corruption of many kinds, a business morality like that of the Jesse James gang that ran through the entire organization from top to bottom. Hughes also made it clear in his report that all the big insurance organizations and corporations were no better.

James Hazen Hyde did not wait for the full storm of the scandal of the looting by the insurance companies to burst over his head, or to be called to testify. He slipped out of the country on the French Line's *La Lorraine*, giving out the information that he did not, of course, have any plans for living permanently in France. He merely stayed away for forty years, enjoying life as a well-heeled expatriate in Paris. He died in 1959 at the age of eighty-three.

18
Early Greenwich Village: 1900-1914

Although New York had long had a Bohemia, as we know from the lives of painters like Winslow Homer and from Edgar Allan Poe's circle of poetasters uptown, the word "Bohemian" was not native to Americans. It had been given new meaning by a French writer, Henri Murger, whose stories, gathered into a book in 1851, *Scènes de la Vie de Bohème*, told of a rather sloppy romantic way of poverty, pathos, love, and creative activity among a group of artistically bent people living on Paris' Left Bank. It became a play, *La Vie de Bohème*. Later Puccini gave it more of a romantic gloss as the opera *La Bohème*.

The New York middle class at the start of the twentieth century could only agree that like Murger's art tramps, certain creative people in New York led immoral lives, wallowed jobless in poverty, and that most of them were loafers, drunkards, and worse.

Greenwich Village, from about 1900 until our present era, was where the uptown folk and the visitor to New York hunted out the Bohemian life. Actually there have been several Villages, not a continually evolving one, beginning with a district of poverty and cheap rents, followed by the early radicals of all kinds, mixed with painters who turned from the Ashcan School to the modes of Paris after 1913.

Then came the Depression, which spawned the Marxist years of the thirties and forties, shading into the smart pads and hippie joints of the fifties and sixties where one could get high on a lid of grass, recite Allen Ginsberg to jazz, or—one of the In things of the seventies—read the *Village Voice*. And always there were well-heeled intellectuals from advertising, publishing, and the Broadway theater who moved into new flats and caused the rents to rise.

◈

Laura B., a young art student in 1908, set down for me the city as it was in its O. Henry days. She was then two years out of Dublin, Ireland, with a desire to paint and taste the city's pleasures:

I had come down from Boston to New York after living with a sister of my mother. Grand Central Station, they were just building it, was a mess, like a wedding party in Cork. It stayed that way for years while they raised up the place. The tracks were all in open ground running along Park Avenue. I was a real scared Mick—"a reuben" as George M. Cohan put it. I got a room on 12th Street, near Broadway, with "a good Catholic family," and went out to see my Aunt Bessie—mother's other sister—in Brooklyn.

The subway was just a few years old. It began at Van Cortlandt on the West Side and ran to Brooklyn, to Atlantic Avenue. I had a long walk to my aunt's house where I got a good meal and a wet kiss—a proper colleen he said—from my uncle Luke, and a warning against the vices of the city and sins waiting to trap country girls from Ireland. I could hardly wait. My uncle Luke was a baseball knut (as it was spelled then) and a week later he took me on the subway to the 168th Street Station to watch the Highlanders play baseball in the park up there. The Highlanders were the New York baseball team before the Yankees came along.

I didn't care for it, but George Bellows, whose studio I used to visit, thought the game "Bully!" The only home-cooked food I had was when visiting Aunt Bessie and Uncle Luke. Corn flakes, Coney Island franks, pretzels were all new to me. I was studying with artists connected then, or later, with the Art Students' League.

The Public Library at 42nd Street was new in 1908. Not yet finished, and I figured if I could sell some illustrations—in a style combining Remington and Howard Pyle—to *Colliers* and *The Saturday Evening Post*, I'd make it. (But I—like so many other would-be illustrators, didn't make it.) But then I got a job, with somebody in the Village who read the *Masses*—painting scenes in rich uptown hallways of forest glades and fauns playing pipes.

It got me enough cash to walk in the Easter Parade with Walt, the boy my ears were giving off steam for. He was working in the department store as a change watcher of the girls, and sent little trolleys with money and change along rails to sales people and customers. We heard High Mass in St. Patrick's.

I suspected Walt had some arrangement with a rich Catholic girl who was supporting some radical magazine in the Village. Her name was Kate, she had gold on one front tooth. I was to meet her a lot at Mabel Dodge's, and she was a friend of John Reed's. . . .

The Easter Parade was fun. I had a Merry Widow Hat with impossible flowers on it and hat pins holding it to my pompadour and curls.

The newest hotel in town was the Plaza; we walked past it like we were bored with it. But it was not in our price range.

Uncle Luke did take me and Walt to the Knickerbocker several times, and to the King Cole Bar "to look at the fancy whores." As Walt claimed the girls we saw in the Peacock Alley of the Astor were.

Uncle Luke had something to do with city inspection of boats in New York Harbor, so he seemed to have certain rights in certain places. I mean he grafted a lot—the truth—without paying. Maillard's restaurant on 23rd Street I remember when he, me and Aunt Bessie went to eat there, he never got a tab. Just a wave from the maître d'.

Somebody in City Hall sent Luke tickets for the Metropolitan Opera from time to time. "They can't use 'em tonight, Laura girl." So me and Aunt Bessie, we'd go, bug-eyed, eyes on stems, looking around at all the scarlet plush and the balconies and all the well-dressed folk. . . .

I suppose it encouraged me to city boldness, seeing all those doings in Venusberg, because I got Walt up to my room and we got into bed together, and he was no virgin and soon I wasn't.

I said afterwards, "What took you so long, kiddo?"

I wondered myself. Some people might say I was what was called *fast* in those days. I don't mean they felt I was a tramp. Just that I came down to live in the Village with two other girls and talked of Omar Khayyam, and the silk strikers and IWW. . . .

I kept feeling I should ask Walt about the rich radical Kate. But didn't. We three went to see Mabel Taliaferro in *Polly of the Circus*, which Kate said was "boors-wash-cee," but she enjoyed it I thought. Walt and me, Sundays, we'd stay in bed—I had moved with my three hat boxes, no bags—and we read the *World*, a marvelous newspaper such as they don't have anymore, and make love and drink terrible coffee brewed on a gas ring. Near noon, we'd dress and go to a place off 14th Street where for 35 cents you'd get all the pasta with meat sauce you could eat. . . .

Walt became a small part actor on Broadway for a while—and we two—we felt we owned New York . . .

The name of such a place in the decade from 1900 to 1910 was Bohemia, and its location was Greenwich Village, that section of New York where those with money and tradition clustered around Washington

READY TO WELCOME THE TWENTIETH CENTURY
The Talisman "Spring" scene from the ballet of *Versailles* at the Manhattan Opera House—once a rival of society's Metropolitan—showing that leg art was also present in the operas staged at that time. (Author's collection)

Square. A Bohemian streak went back to the age of Edith Wharton and Henry James, but the Village did not actually become Bohemia until around 1900, and saw its first period of fame or notoriety expire in 1915 when the Great War changed attitudes, life, and drinking habits. What followed in the 1920s was another kind of Village.

The young and middle-aged who gathered there before the war were mostly artists, writers, truth seekers, and sex seekers who had come from west of the Hudson, from farms in Nebraska, from Chicago—yearners for culture and who felt the closer to Europe the better. Some were classified: the tramp, Harry Kemp; the dreamer, Floyd Dell; the realist and magazine editor, Theodore Dreiser; even a Yale man, Sinclair Lewis. Most of them, however, were people in beads and sandals who had little talent and no serious ambition to paint, write, or compose music. They just liked the life, wanted experiences not found on Main Street or in places like Pasadena, Detroit, or that mythical Zenith, home of Babbitt and Elmer Gantry.

There were so many of the seekers that the Village expanded from Washington Square and MacDougal Alley into the Tweed old 9th Ward (once solidly Tammany Irish) to Charles and Grove, Perry and Bank streets. Also invaded were the Italian blocks of pasta and bambinos, the home of the Black Hand and girls going to Holy Communion in white as little Brides of Christ. Soon the Bohemian, or an imitation of him or her, was on Bleecker, Bedford, Carmine streets, and in Minetta Lane.

Laura wrote in her unpublished memoirs:

Of course when Walt and myself decided to merge our daffy lives together, we couldn't afford any of the pink brick park houses—Georgian, Walt called them—on Washington Square.

We did look at a place John Singer Sargent had lived in on 10th Street; the rent was too damn high. We got a place on Grove Street, three flights up, smelling of cat pee and fresh paint. A bit of a skylight, south *not* north, but I didn't paint all the time. The skylight leaked when it rained and the wind blew up from the rivers. But we stayed warm in bed.

There was a toilet in the hall, and there existed off the room we called the studio, in what was a doll's house-sized kitchen, a sink. I brought over my ice box and bedding and my wardrobe on hangers. We washed in the sink, stripped, towelling ourselves, once or twice a week.

Kate lived on the Square and the houses all around had name plates like Van Rensselaer, Buckalew, Lydig. She had a big oak-bound bathtub and a rubber hose attachment with a shower head. Walt and I bathed there at least once a week.

Kate smoked Turkish tobacco, had a Bagdad corner of a dozen colored cushions and a camel saddle. She was studying Russian, "So I can read the greatest novels in the world in their original."

We drank Chianti which we didn't call red ink as some claimed. Later I painted hotel lobby pictures. This was 1912 or around then. The women were marching, me among them, in suffrage parades. Girls down from Vassar and Smith; Henrietta Rodkan, Inez Mulholland, Crystal Eastman and a woman whose name I forget, she was a magazine artist, and the mother of the actor Humphrey Bogart.

Some of the couples we knew around us were married, but said they weren't. It was called free love in New York in those prewar days.

After hotel pictures, I was painting theatre backdrops for the Met, the Opera. I don't mean I designed them, but I was part of a crew and I even painted part of *Moxie*—a soft drink sign to be displayed high over Times Square—dressed in a man's overalls. We used to meet, our group, at Polly's basement eating joint on MacDougal Street—two painters, a few actors, three writers, and a model with a beautiful body.

When we had extra cash, rarely, we went to the Italian table d'hôte, Ginfarone's on 8th Street. Kate, who was asking Walt to marry her, usually once a month, took us to the Lafayette where the food was marvelous and the swells greeted each other very politely.

It was becoming fashionable to come slumming among the Bohemians. To see women smoking, men wearing sandals and no socks. Being waited on—that thrilled their gizzards—by a real anarchist at Polly's; that was Hippolyte Havel. You'd find Boardman Robinson, one of the radical cartoonists there, and Marsden Hartley who talked of Cézanne.

Kate knew Upton Sinclair, who had written a book *The Jungle* that made him famous, and he watched us eat meat and spoke of vegetables as the only food, and argued with Alfred Kreymborg about Ibsen and Shaw. All these names maybe mean nothing now. Who remembers Orrick Johns, and people like George Cram Cook? A forerunner of the fascists, some said later of Cook, always talking, with a fine head of bone-white hair, and in a cape. He was full of yammerings of Greek culture and later he found Eugene O'Neill and started the Provincetown Playhouse.

There was a bookstore over Polly's basement, and a stove there. When we were out of coal, we'd go up there and look over the books. A couple named Boni ran it, and they didn't expect you to buy a book, and were pleased when you did. I met Max Eastman there, I think he was editor of the *Masses* then, and teaching up at Washington Heights.

New York's Bohemia had a rich variety of people with strange ideas, causes, or creeds out of which the rest of the country got an impression of New York as an up-to-date Sodom and Gomorrah.

Mabel Dodge, who had a lot of money and didn't like existing in Buffalo, and had tried Italy, had a big white apartment up at Fifth Avenue and 9th Street. The food was good, and there was lots of tobacco smoke and talk and waving of long cigarette holders. The guests often included people who seem to have slipped out of New York history but were very well known then. Ernest Poole, Hutchins Hapgood, Carlo Tresca, Lincoln Steffens, and Carl Van Vechten.

Carl was always talking of Harlem, and ten years later he really put the place on the thrill-seekers' map as a smart territory to dance and get beginner brown and yellow girls, *or* boys. Later, too, Carl sponsored Covarrubias, a Mexican painter, and got his work into *Vanity Fair*. Before the Great War the Village wasn't as artsy-craftsy or tearoomy and fake as it later became.

19
Murder among
the Best People

How sporting is the crime of passion? Or is it the demented act of the male, or female, driven by loss of dignity, a wound to the ego, or injured vanity, to take in frenzy a weapon, or some other method of doing harm to another person, or group of people, destroying a life or lives? Certainly the best people also have that sudden impulse to murder.

From a social-historical viewpoint the most famous of these inconsistent outbreaks has been the crime of passion involving the world-famous architect for the rich Stanford White, a dedicated fifty-two-year-old hedonist by reputation.

The other man was Harry Kendall Thaw, thirty-five years of age, heir to one of Pittsburgh's greatest fortunes made in railroads and coke, items much in demand by a nation still expanding in 1906. And the woman, the lovely houri? She was known as Evelyn Nesbit, once an artists' model, sometime show girl, mistress to both men, and finally the wife of Harry Thaw, eccentric, playboy, sadist with hardly any true adjustment to real-it. All three were full of arbitrary caprices and intrinsically selfish.

Evelyn, one of the most beautiful women of her time, or any time, was born in Tarentum, Pennsylvania, and entered with pliant zeal the gay life called at that period "the primrose path." At fourteen she became an artists' model, and posed in what the novel *Trilby* called, with eloquent evasiveness, "the alltogether"—nude. Soon she was in the great musical hit of the Edwardian period on Broadway, *Floradora*, as a minor show girl.

Stanford White, an impressive and handsome figure of a man, gave the first parties in which nude girls emerged from large cakes at a festive dinner. He was well known as an escort of chorus girls. A married man with children, he was nevertheless still a stage-door Johnny, indulging, as age advanced, in sexual desires with willing and nubile female partners.

His clients were mostly the rich of New York, Long Island, and Newport. It was among people of high social standing whose tastes ran to elaborate ornately styled homes that White erected handsome mansions in a style that was slightly French château and somewhat "white marble wedding cake" in décor. His pride, his grand achievement (in addition to the Washington Arch and the Century Club) was the second Madison Square Garden, located on Madison Avenue between 26th and 27th streets (there have been four in all, the current one being atop Penn Station at Seventh Avenue and 33rd Street).

Still in her teens, Evelyn attracted the attention of White, that portly, charming man, described once by a Village poet as, "A man to whom woman is a slave and accomplice—an available rapture."

She claimed that one night while they were alone in his apartment he deflowered her, as the expression of the time had it. She also claimed his pleasures included seating her naked on a red velvet swing and pushing her very hard until she nearly touched the ceiling, while she held on.

White lost her to Thaw, who took her to Europe with him for two trips, showing her the continent. On their last trip she had a falling out with Thaw, and went back to White and the red velvet swing. She explained that Thaw had gotten from her the details of her life with the architect and then with great delight had taken a whip to her pale flanks.

In 1905 Evelyn married Thaw. Then on June 25 of the following year, a musical, *Mademoiselle Champagne*, opened on the roof theater of the Stanford White-designed Madison Square Garden. Among those in attendance were the architect and Mr. and Mrs. Harry Kendall Thaw. As the singer on stage began a forgettable tune, "I Could Love a Million Girls," Harry Thaw left his table, walked with care among the ice buckets cooling wine, and approached White. Thaw calmly drew a pistol and shot White three times.

Thaw walked back to his table, and Evelyn asked, "Good God, Harry, *what* have you done?"

"It's all right, dear. I have probably saved your life." He bent over and kissed her. A fireman on duty took away the pistol and a policeman led Thaw from the disrupted performance. White, the philandering hedonist, his face powder-burned, lay dead in a pool of his own blood.

The trial for White's murder saw Harry Thaw hire the most expensive lawyers Pittsburgh steel fortune money could buy. Evelyn, then twenty-two, was in court, dressed in a schoolgirl's Buster Brown collar and black bow, to testify about her seduction by White.

The trial lasted three and a half months, and the jury in self-indulgent lassitude could not agree. A new trial brought in a verdict of "Not guilty, on grounds of insanity."

There was much speculation about whether that jury had not been reached by Pittsburgh money to sidetrack the members' integrity.

For fifteen years Thaw lived in various asylums. After his release and return to society he continued to stay in the news as he had run-ins with police and reporters. He died in 1947, after a life of hallucinations and ineffectual but deadly gestures. Evelyn went downhill, going through several lovers, divorces, eventually becoming a show business performer in sleazy Mafia-ridden clubs. She died in poverty at eighty-two.

20
Shifting Images,
Changing Colors

When I was a young New Yorker, Harrison Smith, publisher of *The Saturday Review of Literature*, introduced me to Sinclair Lewis at one of his parties. I had met him several times before. I was to assist him with facts in writing a novel about an American painter, but we never got very far in the project. Rather, Lewis spent most of our time talking about his Bohemian days in New York. He was always a good talker and somehow he seemed to look at his early days in New York with a kind of glow he rarely produced during the bad last years of his decline. I still have my notes of some of his talks on the city in its first decades of the century.

"I was twenty-five, and a bit callow, you know, but bushy tailed. Yep, I was getting $12.50 a week working for Frederick Stokes, the publisher. 1910 it was, and the literary life was like corn popping on a cold night. Exciting. Always something, always somebody to drink with and talk, God how we yammered and beat up ideas.

"Mostly all gone now, Harry Kemp, Howard Brubaker, Susan Glaspell, Albert J. Nock, Mary Heaton Vorse. That horse's ass Ben de Casseres, a fake intellectual. And the little magazines. I never did get anything printed in the *Masses*. I did try a story with *Seven Arts*, but I think Waldo Frank turned it down. I had been knocking out story plot ideas for Jack London, getting peanuts for them. But he was hot stuff there before the big war, and he kind of infected me with his socialism."

In fact, Lewis in 1911 became a member of the Socialist Party, Branch One, New York local. He also attended the Anarchists' Ball, and these two facts made him a New York intellectual; it was radical chic to be very much for change. Theodore Dreiser was at the ball.

"Dreiser had this wonderful novel out, *Sister Carrie*, and I was impressed. He was a kind of slob to look at, but his way with women was wonderful. He was more than just a garter snapper.

"You know, H. G. Wells had the same magic for women. They were both girl-crazed galoots, and very successful. I was, well, I was engaged to Grace, and she liked things like Toscanini waving his baton at *Tristan and Isolde*. I preferred the Heretics' Club and the short-haired women. But they talked *so* much. We all did, I guess. I didn't much take to the fancy Bohemians, they hung around Jack, John Reed that is, and his mistress, Mabel Dodge. What a salon of tea tasters and art lovers.

"I remember going with Grace to the Armory show in 1913 when Picasso and his crowd really set everybody on their heels. But it didn't give me the sock it did most of the younger New York artists. It was pretty much a stunt, you know, and all the boys like Sloan and Henri and Bellows and Kuhn who backed it, they got kind of washed out as painters from then on. Everybody was Picassoing."

⋞§⋟

Lewis was not popular; some people felt he wanted to take over, carry on, amuse people, and he tried too hard.

But he did move on at Stokes from reader to publicity, and then to editor. He was still trying to be a girl chaser, and prewar girls, now forgotten, avoided his amorous attempts. Sonya Levien, Frances Perkins, Edna Kenton, and Rose Strunsky are mentioned in some memoirs as his failed targets. Once he and B. W. Huebsch had a date with two girls they took to dinner at the Lafayette—very expensive and impressive to literary girls. After the meal they drove to Port Washington, a beach that was supposed to be a good place for love-making. But Lewis' girl lost a brooch in the sand, and wept until the brooch was found.

Soon after that he had met Grace Hegger, he told me, in the freight elevator in the Fifth Avenue building where he worked. He spent $20 taking dancing lessons, and wrote home to say that he was thinking of getting married. She became his first wife, a charming person, but not Bohemian. Rather, her desires were to move in the best society.

"I don't suppose I belong with the Jack Reed, Lincoln Steffens group, and all the bleeding-heart brigade," Lewis said. "Not that I didn't feel injustice being done. But they were such humorless Serious Thinkers —capital letters, please. They marching in the funeral of Valentino Modestino, a picket the police murdered, and some of them getting jailed in Paterson, New Jersey, and sitting in the calaboose. Or staging pageants in Madison Square Garden.

"I always felt Jacob Riis did more to expose the misery of the city's poor in New York than all the do-gooders who marched and howled. Riis's text and his pictures in *How the Old Half Lives* reached the right people. I wonder why I never wrote a big novel about all of that?"

The New York of O. Henry was fading fast in those years, 1910–1915; the chess players and diners in the Café Monopole on Second Avenue and the Café Boulevard were growing older. Little Hungary, with its goulash, chicken paprikash, and *palatachinken*, was getting the artistic crowd and the uptown slummers. And those who hadn't sold a play or a story or a painting could, if they were broke or hungry, go to Riggs where a big basket of rolls was served at every table.

The gamblers and sports ate at Reisenweber's on Eighth Avenue near 57th Street, and in 1912 the talk was of Herman Rosenthal, the gambler whose career ended abruptly at the Metropole restaurant on West 43rd Street. A crooked cop, Lieutenant Charles Becker, was charged with setting up a gambler named Jack Rose, who owned a car, to drive the killers with remarkably expressive names—Lefty Louie, Dago Frank, Whitey Lewis, and Gyp the Blood—to the restaurant to punish Rosenthal, who had been talking publicly about the police payoffs and tie-ups with New York City criminals.

The whole shocking story of police payoffs had first come to a head in 1912 when the New York *World* began to print a series of stories about the clear-cut tie-up between high-echelon people in the New York Police Department and the top layer of the underworld open to police protection—racketeers, gamblers, whorehouse madames and brothel owners.

Lieutenant Becker, head of one of the city's strong-arm squads, was ordered to crack down on gambling houses. He raided the supposedly protected gambling establishments where big games went on, one of which was Herman Rosenthal's place on Broadway.

Rosenthal felt doublecrossed, betrayed by those to whom he paid protection money. He made a statement about the police protection racket, first to District Attorney Charles A. Whitman, then to the *World*. The raid, he claimed, was rigged—he had been warned about it—and his real partner in the gambling setup was none other than Police Lieutenant Charles Becker, who wanted a bigger cut. Rosenthal stated he would testify to all facts—which he put in writing—to a grand jury.

Warned to get out of town and keep his mouth shut, Rosenthal, nevertheless, was at the Metropole on July 16 at two o'clock in the morning. He was well known there to the night birds—the gamblers, actors, and political figures. Since it was a hot, humid New York summer night, Rosenthal was seated at an open window, reading a paper, when a gangster named Bridgy Webber greeted him loudly with a "Hello, Herman," a voice signal of identification.

Rosenthal strolled out to the steps of the Metropole finding the night was no cooler. The four killers had driven up in the car of the gambler Bald Jack Rose. A pistol was fired and Rosenthal dropped dead. The evening papers had carried an account of the gambler's affidavit to the district attorney.

Becker denied everything tying him to the murder, declaring it was all a frame-up and that he was being convicted by the newspapers and by the desire of the D.A., Charles Whitman, to become governor of New York, even president. (He did become governor.)

However, Becker and the four hoodlums were found guilty of murder. The electric chair at Sing Sing in which the five men died was still a new enough instrument of execution to horrify the weak-stomached and yet fascinate the nation. Pulitzer's *World* and Hearst's *Journal*, given to sensational details, delighted in describing the wisp of smoke that appeared when the current to the chair was turned on, and the faint odor of roasted flesh that hung in the air.

❦

The other shocking sensation of the year 1912 was the disaster of the unsinkable new British luxury liner, *Titanic*. An iceberg sliced her open on her maiden voyage one night in the North Atlantic. She sank quickly with hundreds of passengers. There were not enough lifeboats, and the icy waters swallowed up a couple of hundred of the best-known citizens of New York and many luckless steerage passengers.

❦

A truer celebrity than any of the *Titanic* victims was known as the "uncrowned King of Bohemia" and the "Village's Mikado." So said Stanton MacDonald-Wright, over eighty when I helped him write his autobiography. He told me a great deal about Sadakichi (meaning "Fortunate" or "Constant" in Japanese) Hartmann, 1869–1944. His father was German, his mother a native of Japan. Raised in the United States and in Germany, as a young man he wrote of the theater and art, even visited Walt Whitman in Camden, New Jersey.

Soon he was listing himself as: "DR. SADAKICHI HARTMANN, Art Critic, *First Prophet of Symbolism in America*." He also wrote religious plays, the first being about Christ, for which he was arrested and convicted on charges of obscenity. "His Jesus is a lover of several women, not excluding his own sister" (MacDonald-Wright). Hartmann was a heavy drinker, a poor husband, a writer of good poetry. By the time he was King of Bohemia, the intellectuals of the city knew they had a true eccentric talent among them and a character playing a character.

He had the appearance for it: tall, thin as a crane, with the eyes of his Japanese mother and a face rather like that of an actor playing a demented ghost in a Hokusai print. He spoke best in cafés, wrote a great deal, and was a woman chaser and hunter.

Hartmann not only delighted the city's artistic culture seekers, but his work from the turn of the century until 1910 appeared in such magazines as *Harper's, Forum,* and *Cosmopolitan.*

In his Hollywood studio John Decker, the painter, used to collect Hartmann, Fields, John Barrymore, often Errol Flynn and Gene Fowler, to drink and cut up hair-raising gossip. Decker remembered Hartmann "as a walking wreck and if you got him really oiled, I mean taking on a load of free hootch, he'd start on his New York days, and he was King Piss there and getting all the girls, and all about Bessie McCoy who sang the 'Yama Yama Man' in some show, and how she married some writer, Richard Harding Davis. But Sadakichi, if his teeth weren't too loose, could talk about Buddha and Forbes-Robertson in *The Light That Failed,* and Whistler—he wrote one hell of a good book about Whistler."

❦

> All New York was demanding a new man, and all the new forces, condensed into corporations, were demanding a new type of man—a man with ten times the endurance, energy, will and mind of the old type. . . . As one jolted over the pavements . . . the new man seemed close at hand, for the old one had plainly reached the end of his strength. . . .
> —Henry Adams (1905)

One wonders if Henry Adams—crotchety, spoiled, bigoted, brilliant —ever met James Gibbons Huneker (1860–1921), who was as popular in the downtown artistic political circles of New York as among the uptown intellectuals. He was, like Hartmann, a man of diverse talents, a modern voice certainly, calling out approval of Cézanne, Ibsen, writing of the rediscovery of El Greco.

Huneker had begun as a pianist and then a teacher. He went on to become an art critic and music historian. From 1906 to 1907 he wrote over 400 columns on music for the New York *Sun.*

James Gibbons Huneker's critical works are not read today. Just as the city was always seeking new images, so there was always a turnover of styles, modes, and methods in accepting comment about them. But his exotic novel of scented vice in New York's Edwardian period, *Painted Veils,* is still in paperback reprint. It is a special portrait of the city's richly endowed, talented playboys and voyeurs of the Stanford White type (who appears to have been a model for the major character).

In our time, when someone was to suggest that casual fornication "is like putting a letter in a mailbox," *Painted Veils* remains a period piece. It's pumped-up champagne bubbles, in settings a bit too overripe; it suggests a more leisurely time of high-button-shoes sinning. A New York of intimate parties in red velvet dining rooms.

Huneker produced one disciple, H. L. Mencken, "a rather crass and intolerant word slinger who came to New York like a tourist" (Mac-Donald-Wright). Mencken's bad taste in baiting New York's Jews is shown in the line, "History will accord the Nazis at least one white mark for having thrown Freud out of Vienna."

Hartmann and Huneker were the forerunners of an age of splendid theater, music, and art critics to follow in a generation or so and change the taste of New York: Men like Brooks Atkinson, Walter Pach, and Deems Taylor. For "Bertha the Sewing Machine Girl," Sousa's band, and "September Morn" would not please all New Yorkers.

❧⚬☙

When he first saw New York's Flatiron building, Edgar Salter was quoted as saying: "Its front is lifted to the future. On the past its back is turned." Salter also wrote an often-asked question:

"What do you know of New York?"

And his answer was:

"Only what I have read in Dante . . . Dante told of the inferno, he told, too, of paradise. Manhattan may typify both."

It was certainly a new city arising, lifted to the future, but as for its being Dante's circles of punishment or reward, that depended on the setting of the individual in society—his position, fortune, or habits. Certainly New York was becoming aware of enough change to please the progressive viewers and readers of the new art forms and imported philosophies (Freud's texts were seeping in). The hints of a new culture in the city were causing frowns on the faces of those individuals who were solidly entrenched and expected only their real-estate holdings to show any movement away from old values. How wrong was the French writer Paul Bourget when he visited New York, "Money cannot have much value here, there is so much of it."

But it was not money that was remodeling the shape of the city, adding to its colors, its way of looking at itself. It was the strange importation of the most advanced and despised new art from Paris, shown in New York a year before the Great War, that changed everything for the worse in the new century.

THE FLATIRON BUILDING
The most amazing structure in the city. Built in 1901, it produced such a windy corner that eye-popping males would gather there to watch the women trying to keep their skirts in order while boarding the streetcars. (Library of Congress)

Americans are still rather too inclined to suspect this new art, hailing for the most part from Paris, as the outcropping of a decadent and worn-out society. Characteristically, foolishly, pardonably, perhaps, we cling to a nationalistic idea of art, priding ourselves on our immunity from such alien and disrupting influences. . . .

—Ralph Flint (1913)

While New York, as a whole, had not accepted the Armory Show of avant-garde art in 1913, it did change the viewpoint of many painters, collectors, and students of art. Actually, there were forces at work in New York City long before that, manifestations of what was going on among the fauves and cubists of the School of Paris.

From 1900 on, most of the new American artists were traveling to Europe, their usual goal being Paris. They were aware, if their eyes and temperaments were alert, of what was going on. Men like Hartley, Sheeler, Marin, who had seen the postimpressionists—Van Gogh and Gauguin—and even some of the brash young men such as Picasso, Braque, and Matisse. While there was little of the work of these French painters among private New York collectors (Frick and J. P. Morgan cherished the past) and nothing in the museums, the visiting Americans, and a few New York galleries, recognized something new in them.

Alfred Stieglitz's Photo Secession Gallery, at 291 Fifth Avenue, announced it was going "to advance photography as applied to pictorial expression . . . to draw together those Americans practicing or otherwise interested in art . . ." and also to show works of art, including the first New York exhibition of Rodin drawings, and later Picasso and Matisse.

Stieglitz was a sly eccentric who knew how to attract attention in the city. Certainly he wasn't interested in the work of painters labeled The Eight, or the Ashcan School (because of their realism), and artists who came late to the styles of Manet, Goya, Daumier—men like Henri, Sloan, Davies, Prendergast, Luks, Shinn, Bellows, and Glackens. They had a love of the city and a great slapdash skill in painting New York street scenes, the dramas of the El tracks ("The rapid transit is poetry and art; the moon but a tedious, dry body moving by rote" [O. Henry]). They reproduced the ferryboats, McSorley's Saloon, vaudeville acts, and dusty theater interiors. They captured on canvas the women of the city in their feathered hats, the men in derbies or shirt-sleeves.

The city's realistic painters owed little or nothing to the new values being found in Paris through African fetish figures and South Sea tattooing—all to invade the city at the Armory Show. As Amy Goldin, a social critic, was to write of the Ashcan School:

The creative force of the American social realists was vitiated by their historical tardiness. By their time the artistic action was focused elsewhere, on the problems of abstraction. Neither in style nor iconography would social realists draw on a broad frontier of artistic concern.

Yet what was lost to modern art nevertheless impressed Henry James during a visit to New York. He had to admit, "the city . . . in certain lights almost charming . . . an element of mystery . . . and wonder entered into the impression." But the "assault of the streets" was in bad taste. Kipling also snarled at the city—where he was to lie near death and to lose a daughter, so he can be forgiven.

Meanwhile, the city had remained just as reactionary in its art tastes. Uptown did not take to the street scenes of Hassam and Bellows, but preferred its paintings to be done, at great cost, by Sargent, Chase, and Duveneck. It was only a later generation that was to view with delight the images of that transition period of the New York scene in O'Keeffe's flat streets, Joseph Stella's Brooklyn Bridge, the club night boxers of Bellows. No one bought Sloan's *Dust Storm* swirling around the Flatiron Building, a structure of which an early guide book stated that the wind-storms around the Flatiron Building were wild events, often resulting in the smashing of many windows in the vicinity.

Most likely no camera captured the flavor and atmosphere of the city better than those early black and white images by the Stieglitz group connected with his Photo Secessionists—Gertrude Kasebier, Frank Eugene, Eva Lawrence Watson, Edward Steichen, and Alfred Stieglitz himself. His picture *The Steerage*, as Sinclair Lewis told me, "is a greater symbol than that dumpy Statue of Liberty."

There was, of course, a vast community of New Yorkers who were not interested in the new art (or much of the old)—either in Isadora Duncan, in town to dance barefooted "The Blue Danube," or Pavlova, to die as The Swan for the thousandth time. "The Irish Players"—Sara Allgood and Cathleen Nesbitt—gave New York the fey dramas of Lady Gregory or William Butler Yeats. But Diaghilev's Russian Ballet didn't outdraw Houdini at the Hippodrome.

Vaudeville was at its height in New York just before 1914. No one suspected the coming of the great film palaces that were destined to move headline acts to second place. (Today the wrecker's ball has bowled down most of the great movie palaces—the Paramount, Roxy's, the Capitol—and vaudeville, at its worst, is back—on television.)

The luminaries of vaudeville seemed so permanent to New Yorkers. Joe Jackson and his bicycle act, the Seven Little Foys, the Dolly Sisters, Rozika and Yansci (the first Hungarian sexpots to grab the spotlight), Nora Bayes and her husband, Jack Norworth—he wrote the songs they sang, "Shine on Harvest Moon," "Take Me Out to the Ball Game," and "Smarty." Elsie Janis, who was soon to bill herself as "The Sweetheart of the AEF," Eva Tanguay throwing herself about the stage with "I Don't Care."

Broadway regarded itself as the place of the hoofer, the "him and her" gags, the slapstick, the soft-shoe dance, the feckless duos with straw skimmers and canes, thinking they were George M. Cohans.

New York was becoming sophisticated, for it was also a time of tea dancing at the Ritz, going mad over dance acts, infatuation for Vernon and Irene Castle, setting the steps to which New Yorkers, first, then the nation's more daring couples, would dance and cavort, while the hand-wound Victrolas played "Everybody's Doin' It" (for the Turkey Trot) and "You Made Me Love You . . . I Didn't Want to Do It." Specialties of this famous married team were the Castle Walk, the Maxixe, and the Grizzly Bear. Then one night they boldly improvised the Fox Trot.

At the Winter Garden there was a blackface singer named Al Jolson who cried out in his own way songs of a never-was South, produced by the city's Tin Pan Alley—an imaginary street in New York where song-writers and song pluggers tried to guess the nation's needs in popular ballads, love songs, comic capers, and snappy tunes.

In 1947 when I was writing the screenplay of *The Jolson Story*, he was a forgotten figure—aging and bitter at being passed by . . . "They wouldn't even listen to my jokes at the Hillcrest Club" (Los Angeles' most important and exclusive Jewish country club, to which nearly all rich Jewish entertainers from New York belonged and where they amused one another). I still have the notes of some of my conversations with Jolson while writing the screenplay. They give an excellent picture of Broadway before World War I.

"You don't know nothin' if you didn't promenade 'round in New York in 1910, 1911. My brother Harry and me, we died there on stage—sure—a few times before with our act. But in 1911, the Shubert brothers—two momsers—they had this new gorgeous place, see, The Winta [Winter] Garden, and they needed something ho-ho big, so they had Jerome Kern, he did this score for *La Belle Paree*. Paris, you see? I was part of a deal when they took over Dockstaders' Minstrels for the Garden. Now I didn't come on openin' night all corked up until the show, it's been runnin' three and a half hours. I sang 'Paris Is a Paradise for Coons.'

"You understand me, we didn't have no hard feelin's then about minorities feeling bad about their part in show business. 'Coon,' 'Yid,' 'Dago'—we all used them. Well, I felt I was a flop. The critics, they had mostly gone, and the audience, too. I just walked the streets after the show. New York is a cold burg, believe me, when you're not making it.

"But, yeah, I did get one good review. So I got a better spot and I started to play my tricks. Oh, I got to whistling during where the lyrics should be. I got 'em right in the palm of my hand. Uptown, downtown, at parties with my singing of 'He Had to Get Out and Get Under' and 'That Devilin' Rag.' Then there was Gaby Deslys, a dish from Paris; we did *Vera Viletta*, and I felt I was a star and in New York, and only New York counts in show biz. Know what that meant? For me a fur coat and a secondhand car, all shiny, you know. There was a girl in the show, in the chorus, you guess who? Mae West, yeah Mae. I made my first Victor record, 'The Haunting Melody,' then I did 'Brass Band,' 'Ephraim Jones,' and 'Snap Your Fingers.' I got the original records someplace.

"There was this nineteen-year-old song plugger named George Gershwin. He pushed his way into a party I was at, and got to the piano, began to play his tune, and the lyric writer, Irving Caesar, sang 'Swanee, how I love you, how I love you, my dear Old Swanee.' And, of course, I hadda have it for *Sinbad*."

BOOK SIX

Tong Wars
and the
Great War

21
Chinatown Violence

The wars of New York's Chinatown from 1900 to 1925 created a great deal more interest among the populace than other manifestations of violence and mayhem. The cloying musical notes of slowly played "Chinatown, My Chinatown" brought to the minds of New Yorkers a miniature city within their own larger boundaries—a city of incense-smelling little shops and crimson-painted surfaces scarred with dragons, inhabited by mysterious slant-eyed people spouting deadpan philosophy without an "r" in their sentences, smoking opium, sexually enslaving white girls, or serving up pungent dishes highlighted by such legendary items as bird's-nest soup, *ching yu* ("shark's fins"), *pei tan* ("100-year-old eggs"), and heaped-up dishes unknown in China such as chow mein and chop suey.

Actually, the district around Mott Street was merely an enclave, one more set of minorities settled in New York. All of these areas boasted their own cultural patterns, cooking odors, and rituals to some special godhead. However, in the space of two or three generations most of the other racially knit neighborhoods lost much of their distinct atmosphere and local color, the people gradually intermarrying with citizens from other sections of the city.

New Yorkers saw Chinatown—all the district from Pell and Mott streets as well as the color and smells of Doyer Street—as mysterious, spine-tingling country. Actually, twentieth-century New York's China-town was, for a long time, the battleground of the *tongs* for the control of the area's gambling, drugs, traffic in women, and the profitable honest trades of merchandising, importing, and feeding white visitors.

The tong, like chow mein, never saw China. It grew out of the thousands of Chinese coolies imported to help build the Western rail-roads. The tong was a protective group organized against the mobs of Western racial bigots, and in time the tongs became power clans control-ling the rackets and business of the Chinese communities across the nation. *Hongs*, on the other hand, were business associations.

The first Chinese man to settle in New York had been Ah Ken in 1858. By 1900 the Chinese in New York were a prosperous community. The most powerful enemy and problem of the Chinese was the Hearst press, which kept up a cry of "the Yellow Peril" coming out of Asia by the murderous millions to seize America and the world.

There were, too, certain stage melodramas of evil, saffron, slant-eyed masters of crime who lurked, with their four-inch-long fingernails, in dens behind the antique shops, lusting—in early films, also—for the pale flesh of white virgins, while puffing on their opium pipes.

Actually, behind the eating places, laundries, and sellers of dried duck, *my tuy* ("water chestnuts") and *mo yee cha* ("a tea"), there was an active world of gambling in *fan tan, pi gow*, and even American poker. *Gow* ("opium") was considered a relaxing addiction after facing the white devils all day in trade. White and Oriental slave girls were also available in rooms along Doyer, Pell, and Mott streets, bowing, reciting "*Chang dzai lai*" ("Please come again"). The entire district was quite crowded and, by the turn of the century, at least 250 Chinese gambling houses were busy.

They all operated with New York police protection. The Chinese owner paid $18 to $20 a week to the cops, and also gave a share of the take to the Gamblers' Union and something to the tongs for protection.

The twentieth century saw its first East Coast tong war between the On Leong tong, which controlled most of the gambling and vice in New York, and the Hip Sung, a weaker organization working only the fringe of Chinatown. Power reposed in the On Leongs because their boss, Tom Lee, had votes for Tammany when election days arrived.

The city expected no Judeo-Christian moral values from its Chinese. All New York knew Bret Harte's* poem:

* Bret Harte's father was the Hart (Bret added an "e" to his last name) who helped start the New York ready-made clothing firm of Hart, Schaffner, and Marx. Wearing one of its suits was a status symbol to a young man on the rise in the New York social order.

Which I wish to remark,
And my language is plain,
That for ways that are dark
and for tricks that are vain,
The heathen Chinee is peculiar.

That a great many of New York's Chinese were hard working, and even exploited, and were plagued by domestic and economic problems, hardly penetrated the consciousness of the average citizen.

There was little interest in the fact that the Chinese paid their taxes, ran their own newspapers, created healthy diets and better cooking methods, and produced tastier food. No, the city needed its shiver and its wonder of "What are the Chinese *really* like?" Only a few studied New York's Chinese seriously and realized they were not of the Peking or Mandarin class. Or that the food was not the Peking cuisine but rather mostly Cantonese—items from Kwangtung Province.

So if Tom Lee was pointed out as the "mayor of Chinatown," it didn't matter. It was only an honorary title and Lee kept things quiet most of the time.

As the mayor of Chinatown Tom Lee held a nonelective office, and Tammany saw to it that he became a deputy sheriff of New York County. Lee was a huge man with two *boo how doy* ("gangster") bodyguards and a coat-of-mail shirt. His rival, Wong Get, was a nobody.

As is the case with all absolute rulers, there were always new rivals, and in 1900, in time to greet the new century. a fat fellow named Mock Duck—ironic, mean, fond of *she juploong har* ("lobster") and *yew toe* ("fish gut")—had appeared in Chinatown. He, too, wore the coat-of-mail shirt (an XXL size) and carried two Colt .45s and a razor-sharp short-handled hatchet. He was as ready for a shootout as Bat Masterson.

Mock Duck also had a shrew of a wife, and she was known to slap and kick him down Pell Street if she caught him nested away with some younger singsong girl. Mock Duck's gambling fixation went beyond any of the wild surge of recklessness in most Chinese. He'd bet on the number of pips in an apple or an orange.

A Hip Sung man, he joined forces with Wong Get and began to recruit and train boo how doy. He then went to Tom Lee and demanded to be cut in on half of all the gambling rights in New York's Chinatown. If Lee refused, he threatened there would be trouble.

Lee had no fear of the rival Hip Sungs. But he changed his view when two of his tong members died in a mysterious fire in the tong's sleeping dorm on Pell Street. In return, On Leong killers went out with their hatchets and chopped up a Hip Sung member. The big tong war, the first in New York, was on. The Four Brothers group joined the Mock Duck gang and Lee became the main target. He was followed and shot at.

PIGTAILS IN NEW YORK
As the new century began, the Chinese in the city were divided into powerful tongs and were preparing to control the legal and illegal economy of their community. (*Illustrated American*—author's collection)

Mock Duck, with the mind of an economist, decided to hurt Tom Lee where he would suffer most. He went to the white anti-Tammany reformers and revealed where all the gambling houses, opium dens, and whorehouses of the On Leongs were located (of course the police already knew—as their protectors).

After the On Leong's places were raided and closed, Mock Duck and Wong Get took over the premises and ran them for the Hip Sungs, and naturally for themselves. It wasn't all profit; the police continued to be paid off, and new boo how doys had to be imported to replace the dead—for the prolonged first tong wars went on until 1906.

The City of New York finally decided the situation had gone far enough. Visitors didn't like to be stepping over hatchet-chopped bodies. A judge of the Court of General Sessions called for a peace conference of the leaders of the two tongs. Terms were worked out. The On Leongs would hold on to Mott Street as their fief, and the Hip Sungs would boss their own section. As for Pell Street, it would be open country, a sort of buffer zone free of pistols, hatchets, snickersnees, and krisses.

A week later the war was on again, both sides claiming the other had fired the first shot. The judge called for help from the Chinese government, which worked—by the simple device of arresting fifty close relatives of the tong leaders still living in China and ordering that their heads would fall to the great sword *if* the tongs didn't make up at once. This forced peace lasted until 1909.

Mock Duck had an adopted daughter, Ha Oi, who was born of a white mother. When Mock Duck was found with a relative deep in an opium daze, Ha Oi was taken from him. He sorrowed, went to court, lost his case, and left town on a national gambling spree.

When Mock Duck returned, the tong wars warmed up, and while he was known to have killed, or caused people to be killed, he himself escaped knives, bullets, and hatchets—until one bad day when three On Leongs caught him walking down Pell Street, and they went into the group-firing squat position, hugging the ground, eyes shut, firing. It's amazing they got Mock Duck in the hip.

After a few weeks in the hospital, Mock Duck was ready for a Chinese Gettysburg. It was a time of great knifings. The New York press loved to write up the tong wars. Business in Chinatown, between periods of bloodshed, was good, with most of the sightseers showing keen interest in viewing the signs of the latest battles.

Mock Duck was brought to court, but the evidence against him as a gang leader was weak (or else, as some suspected, the police were seeing that key witnesses remained mute). Mock Duck was sent to Sing Sing for a few years for operating a gambling game. Once free of prison, he decided, at least so he told the press, that he was finished with gambling, with tongs, and with city wars. Later he proclaimed he was a citizen of Brooklyn, happy in his comforts there, and Chinatown would see him no more. But before that the destiny of the great Chinese comic actor Ah Hoon had been worked out at the old Chinese Theater. Ah Hoon was an On Leong tong member. So his ad libs and comic material about the Hip Sungs really rocked Chinatown with laughter. Ridicule hurt like bullets.

The Hip Sungs decided to silence the mocking comic Ah Hoon. Many times he had to leap off stage as some fight broke out in his audience. Once an On Leong had his throat cut, ear to ear, during a show, and no one noticed until the last of the acts was over. As a result, Ah Hoon was given New York police protection.

One night in November 1909 an Irish police sergeant sat on stage while the comic, now in grave fear of his life, performed rather nervously while deleting his more acid lines. A good crowd was present. Word was out that Ah Hoon was scheduled to get the deep six. Killers were actually present, but so thick was the crowd inside and outside, the assassins felt it just wasn't a situation roomy enough to do a proper boo how doy job.

The police took Ah Hoon back home, and his tong brothers in the hallway, armed and armored, guarded his locked door.

However, a Hip Sung killer had let himself down from the roof on a seat attached to a pulley, and through a window shot the comic dead.

The tong war broke out again in all its fury after the loss of Ah Hoon. On Chinese New Year's night, listed as a "truce night," Mock Duck and his killers were preparing for slaughter at the packed theater. A marvelous show was put on with jugglers, shrill female impersonators, and even a scene from an old play, done without props, wherein the hero lifts one leg, like a dog at his favorite tree (in Chinese drama this signi-fied the man was mounting a horse). At that moment someone set off a packet of firecrackers and flung them over the heads of the customers. The series of explosions had many thinking of more deadly sounds: It was the signal for firearms to appear—at least by one side, for the police found five dead On Leong members still in their seats.

Mock Duck and some of his gangsters were arrested. But again, no one talked and no witnesses came forward. There was a victory feast of stewed shark's fins, with pork and duck among the dishes.

It was during the Ah Hoon trouble that the worst tong war in New York started, and it centered around a girl. Bow Kum (Sweet Blossom) had been sold by her father in Canton for a few miserable coins as a slave girl and sex object. She was smuggled into San Francisco, passed through by a bribed customs officer, and auctioned off to Low Hee Tong for $3,000. He kept her as his concubine for four years, but lost her when he could not produce a wedding certificate and pious white busybodies put Sweet Blossom in a mission to graft a Christian soul onto her.

However, one Tchin Len saw her, fell in love with her, and married her. He came with her to New York's Chinatown. Low Hee Tong followed—wanting the return of his property. As the original owner, he wanted Tchin Len to pay him back the $3,000 he had paid for the slave girl. Tchin Len refused.

Tchin Len was an On Leong and he was backed by his tong in refusing to pay. This brought out the Scarlet Flag of the Highbinder (a banner that was unfurled on buildings when a tong war was declared). One does not know if all this turmoil over the girl was for love of her or the money involved. What we do know is that a tong killer got into the Tchin Len house on Mott Street and butchered Sweet Blossom.

A murderous series of tong battles followed the death of Sweet Blossom. The lowest estimate is that more than fifty Chinese were killed in the Bow Kum war.

Merchants of Chinatown saw the ruin of the principal legitimate trade the district offered—food and "art" objects. They spoke out, making it clear that if the wars continued, the white man would force the closing of Chinatown and drive them all out of the state.

The On Leongs demanded, as the price of peace, that the Hip Sungs in abject humiliation present them with a Chinese flag, ten thousand packets of good-sized firecrackers, *and* a large roasted pig.

So the war continued and no pig was roasted, no firecrackers presented. By 1910 the Chinese Ambassador to Washington was called into the situation. A Committee of Forty of the highest Chinatown citizens was established and peace seemed again in order.

But in 1912 someone saw the need for a new tong of active young hot-bloods, and the Kim Lan Wui Saw tong, the newest gun in town, was ready. It offered to take on both the older On Leongs and Hip Sungs in a bloody power struggle. Again it was only the threat of the Chinese government to use the official ax on the necks of relatives back in the old country that brought a new peace treaty.

The next tong war in New York broke out in 1924, caused not by women or tong loyalty, but by some good old American-style embezzling of funds. This war lasted only a few months, and it seems to have been fought by a Chinese Expeditionary Force, for the dead were mostly restaurant workers and laundrymen in Brooklyn and the Bronx.

Through the years since then, the hatchet men were phased out and modern Capone-type weapons brought in. The young gangs were modeled on the New York's Mafia rather than on the now fairly respectable tongs and their aging boo how doys. The Chinese Merchants' Association members became pin wearers of the Rotary, the Lions, the Elks.

22
Love with a Blue Flame

Before World War I began a woman of thirty-five, described as "buxom, comely, muscular, nerves and laughter and hearty heat," stood at the rail of an ocean liner with her young son as the ship moved toward the skyline of New York. She had lived abroad in luxury and excitement for many years. She now said to her son:

"Remember, it is ugly in America. We have left everything worthwhile behind us. America is all machinery and money-making and factories—it is *ugly, ugly, ugly.*"

The woman, Mabel Dodge, was to found one of the most impressive New York literary and political salons of the twentieth century in a white-painted apartment on the second floor of a brownstone house (owned by a one-legged Civil War general, Daniel E. Sickles) at 9th Street and Fifth Avenue, near the Hotel Brevoort.

Mabel had been the one spawning of a very well-off couple in Buffalo, New York. She was raised to expect a life of luxury, attention, and Prince Charmings offering themselves to her. Mabel had been married twice, if not to princes—first to the father of her son, John, and then to Edwin Dodge, who set up the ménage with her at 23 Fifth Avenue.

But Edwin's days as a husband to her were numbered. He was failing in some mystic test her mates had to pass. For three years before settling in New York, Mabel had lived in a magnificent setting—her Villa Curonia in Florence, Italy. She had mixed in circles of writers and painters, mostly Americans like herself.

In New York Mabel painted and papered the apartment white. White helped her moods, for she felt herself the product of an unhappy home life in Buffalo (she made this claim in her many-volumed autobiography, *Intimate Memories*) that influenced her development into a stoic, able to face the problems of life without showing her true emotions.

One of her attending New York friends, Carl Van Vechten, used Mabel as the character Edith Dale in his novel *Peter Whiffle*, where he described her as "a dynamo . . . a face that could express anything, or nothing, more easily than any I have ever seen. It is a perfect mask."

After she married Edwin Dodge, a very rich architect, Mabel described herself as one who wanted "to be alive like fire." She experimented sexually as if with styles of hairdressing.

Settled in New York, part of a country she found *ugly, ugly, ugly*, snug in a fine apartment, with guest rooms, a few servants including a very proper butler, Mabel carried her fetish for personal décor to installing a white marble fireplace, a polar bear rug, gilded mirrors, chaises.

She candidly admitted it was all "so beautiful . . . I have always known how to make rooms that had power in them . . . it diminished New York, made New York stay outside."

But not for long. She was absorbing the uptown intellectuals, homosexuals and straights, the Village radicals. Always there was Carl Van Vechten, very chic as a critic on a New York paper, who was keenly interested in modern music and in what he saw as the Negroes' sensual charms, their watermelon colors, jazz, and their intimate ways of surviving among upper-class whites who sponsored them.

Mabel remained bored but admitted that Carl "animated my lifeless rooms." Her marriage was soon to end. She was a pioneer, being among the first to lie down before a Freudian practitioner of psychoanalysis. It didn't help, and another doctor said her tonsils should come out.

The tonsillectomy was performed in her own bed in the apartment. To entertain her, Edwin Dodge brought in a friend, Jo Davidson, a burly sculptor. Davidson, like most artists finding a hostess appetizing to look at in her big white bed, sensed that here was an ideal patron and more.

Davidson came again and again, and, a sharer by nature, he brought in Walter Lippmann (just starting a career as a journalist philosopher), Lincoln Steffens, and Hutchins Hapgood from the New York *Globe*.

Her salon grew, the butler and the maids served more food, whisky, laid out cigarettes, counted the ash trays later. It became the place to meet bed partners, intellectuals, rebels, strike leaders. It all had a new, exalting flavor, like the 1913 Armory Show of modern paintings at the 69th Street Regiment Armory. The postimpressionists, fauvists to the cubists and futurists talked of it at Mabel's Evenings.

Marcel Duchamp's notorious *Nude Descending a Staircase*, called "a rather minor second-rate cubist work" (Stanton MacDonald-Wright), captured the attention of the public by its title. Where the nude? Where the stairs? asked the Philistines, and laughed. But at Mabel's Evenings the show—all agreed—was just what the nation needed, and it was admitted that Mabel had done good work in arranging the exhibition.

Mabel—Edwin having departed for good—was now a crowned hostess in her long white dresses, green chiffon scarves, among vases of dying lilies, blue larkspur, and snapdragons.

It was not, Sinclair Lewis told me, a salon for mere dilettantes or party snackers. A hundred people usually gathered for one of Mabel's Evenings, and the talk was daring for that period. Discussed, dissected, torn to bits were many subjects (all in capital letters)—Psychoanalysis, Sex Antagonism, Sacred Names and Scarlet Mores, Birth Control (Margaret Sanger attended). Also Union Organization, Revolution, Revolt of the Masses, Women's Rights, and Anarchism.

> And life is very fair,
> In Washington Square.

So wrote John Reed, one of her guests, who was known as The Golden Boy to the Villagers, and as a romantic revolutionary to the radicals. He was to be drawn into the Mabel Dodge circle, into her ample arms, to fall in love with her. He was only twenty-six, a poet of sorts (the quote above is from his "The Day in Bohemia"). He wrote short stories, articles, even for the Establishment's *Saturday Evening Post.*

Reed was tall, handsome, his brown hair usually in Byronic disorder over a thinker's brow, while his nose was too small over a child's mouth.

He first met Mabel, not at an Evening, but in a shabby studio where Mabel and her friends were discussing the Paterson Mill strikes.

The Paterson, New Jersey, mills, many of them silk mills, had been the testing ground of union organizing and the scene of labor strife since the turn of the century. Owners wanted no unions, and insisted on long working hours. They fought laborers with lockouts and hired guards, so that the strikes that broke out from time to time for a living wage and union rights took on the semblance of true warfare.

After World War I, intellectuals, radicals, and the Marxists discovered the Paterson strikers' cause and began to get newspaper coverage. Support for the Paterson workers, Art Young (the *New Masses* artist) told me, "became a kind of testing ground to see if you were a true radical, a true liberal against the system, and a friend of the working man and woman."

Later, after the invention of nylon, the mills either went south for cheaper, unorganized labor or closed as the chemical threads replaced the work of the silk worm.

During the studio gathering someone suggested that a mass meeting ought to be held for the strikers' cause. When Mabel was asked for an opinion about where the rally should be held, she replied, "Why not Madison Square Garden?"

John Reed whispered to her, "My name is John Reed." And to the room he shouted, "I'll do it."

He had been sentenced to twenty days in a Paterson jail for being involved with the strikers. Freed after five days, his ardor for the strikers increased.

The rally was a success and 15,000 people packed the Garden to view the Paterson Pageant. Even the press, which usually played down anything favoring strikers, gave the event space. It was a triumph for Mabel and for Jack. The love between them in the days that followed rose to a steaming pitch. But they had not yet gone to bed together. To rest up from the excitement of the strikers' pageant, Mabel suggested that they go to her Villa Curonia in Florence.

Jack Reed was raging—as only one with a bottled-up romantic desire can—for physical possession of the older woman. But after their ship sailed, when he tapped on Mabel's stateroom door, she addressed him through a crack and shook her head. "Darling, we are just on the Threshold [her capital letters in her memoirs] and nothing is ever so wonderful as the Threshold of things, don't you *know* that?" (There was also the obstacle that her young son was with her on the ship.)

All throughout the sea trip, Jack kept pressing for copulation, but Mabel insisted the Threshold was not to be crossed just yet. It was in Paris, with the son on his way to the villa, that the Threshold was passed by the lover. Once firmly rooted between her thighs, the realist in Jack fell away and the poet returned to whisper to her, "I thought your fire was crimson, but you burn blue in the dark."

The love affair endured for a long time, though on less purple language, even with Jack going to Mexico in 1916 to follow Pershing's pursuit of Pancho Villa, visiting home in the West, writing in bouts, plugging for the glorious, nebulous revolution. Life at 23 Fifth Avenue became a lament by a woman ten years older than her lover, she feeling when he did not cross the Threshold regularly that she had lost him.

Eventually he fled her clinging arms, leaving a note that gives us vital information on his state of mind:

Goodbye my darling. I cannot live with you. You smother me. You rush me. . . . I love you better than life but I do not want to die in my spirit. . . . I love you—I love you.

Was the blue flame no longer burning? But it was not the end of the affair. They made up, they parted. They went to Italy, then to Paris. The war was busy in the ghastly slaughter at Verdun. For Jack, as a radical, it was Woodrow Wilson's dirty little J. P. Morgan Loans war, the Capitalists' war, the British Empire's colony-bloated war. Mabel, however, was all for the war against the Germans.

23
War Times—
River to River

The Great War (as World War I was once known) was destined to
modify the well-lived New York existence. But signal alerts of the twilight of the Edwardian sporting life-style were already there by 1910–
1913; signs of a loss of vitality and decline in the hedonistic ethic. For, to
exist in its glossy prime the good life needed money, fortunes, a free
economy, where much can be piled up and used without restriction and
with no feeling of frugal pressures that funds might run out. In 1913 the
forests of great fortunes were being thinned out.

A Congressional committee headed by one Arsene Pujo called a
hearing on the "Money Trusts" that it claimed owned the nation, ma-
nipulated its credits and stocks, were its corporations. It pointed out that
a small group of men—J. P. Morgan, George F. Baker, James Stillman,
the Rockefeller family among them—ran the American money market
and controlled its wealth. The committee stated that these men and their
underlings held jobs as directors in thirty-four banks and trust companies,
which companies had resources of over $2.5 billion.

As for transportation systems—railroads and other things on wheels
—among these same persons half a dozen were major directors in 105 of

them, and in 32 transport systems with assets of $12 billion. Also captive were thirty directorships in ten insurance companies, with resources of nearly $2.5 billion. In public utilities the trusts held twenty-five director-ships with over $2 billion in capitalization. Adding it all up, the dozen or so men named held nearly 150 directorships in 111 corporations, and the money they controlled amounted to $22 billion.

That all this was true was no secret to those who knew the big money, the juggling and fixing, the rigging of stocks and trusts. But that the federal government should step in and call an investigation on this tight little group was a blow to clubmen, old families, and sportsmen.

When Congress's Sergeant at Arms attempted to serve J. D. Rocke-feller with a subpoena to appear before the Pujo Committee, he declared a personal war against the United States. Rockefeller refused to accept the subpoena, withdrew within his walls, and turned his New York Fifth Avenue house into a fortress. He hired tough Pinkerton men to protect him, while the USA, in answer, hired Burns Agency men to break through if they could and get the monopolist to listen to Congress.

A state of siege took over Fifth Avenue around the Rockefeller home. Police kept traffic moving, Pinkerton and Burns men set up battle positions, while cameramen and reporters elbowed each other for the best coverage of this war against the government.

The Rockefeller war against the United States lasted four days. Then his lawyers made a small concession—their client would appear "when his health was better," for at the moment he had a sore throat. This was all window dressing, for Mr. Rockefeller had disappeared.

He turned up in Nassau in the West Indies, taking the sun on his wrinkled features. Two versions of his escape were given—one declaring that he had crossed a hastily built bridge between his house and the next one in the dark of night and taken it on the run like a ferret; the other version, as one of the directors of the Consolidated Gas Company stated, was that, dressed in the guise of a plumber, J.D. had been spirited away in the repair truck of Consolidated, dispatched to sniff out a gas leak.

To make amends Mr. Rockefeller said he would meet with Congress representative, Mr. Samuel Untermyer, at an island stronghold—the Jekyll Island Club, off the coast of Georgia, free from the prying eyes of the public and its reporters. The hearing there was canceled almost at once because of "Mr. Rockefeller's physical breakdown." He had long supported with bribes some senators and congressmen, who spared him.

The other men of power who did testify defended free enterprise and denied that they acted against public interest or were in accord as trusts, fixing prices and services. Nothing much, of course, came from the Pujo Committee hearings, but the public was left with their suspicions about a few rich men who ran the nation.

The end of one giant of the era of what the muckrakers called "the Robber Barons," and others called "Empire Builders," came with the death in March 1913 of J. P. Morgan, noted for his consuming allegiance to gold, banking, yachts, and to the power of the vast corporations he formed, the trusts to dominate copper, steel, railroads, and banking. He died regally in Rome, far from the Pujo hearings.

His son, J. P. Morgan, Jr., was no replacement for the blunt, sensual, powerful figure of his father, nor did he ever achieve the public dominance of the older Morgan.

The change was slow, hardly noticeable at first; the façade of the good New York life went on. The visible clash was between the wives of the rich. It resulted in the creation of a new opera house as a showplace, one group fighting off the more mature social dodos who had taken over the old Academy of Music. The Academy, run by the old Dutch and English families, had refused boxes to Whitneys, Rockefellers, Vanderbilts, Goulds, Harrisons, Morgans, and Bakers to show off their jewels under the incandescent gaslights. So the rejected group had opened the Metropolitan Opera House, with enough boxes in tiers on the Golden and Diamond Horseshoes for them all to be seen as incontrovertible evidence they were *the* society.

❧

When the city became unbearable in the summer heat, the best people left it for Saratoga, for Newport, for Maine or the northern lakes and woods. But as society competed for exclusiveness, the signs of decline that Herr Spengler was to write of in his history of the decay of Western culture were already worrying some social leaders. Mrs. Cornelius Vanderbilt, Jr., realized the last-stand character of her position: "Dear poor Marie Antoinette, I feel so sorry for her. If revolution ever came to this country, I would be the first to go."

It was a society well past taking secret home-lessons from *The Quadrille Dancing Book*. There had been many changes, and the early days of being ashamed of spending, of gaudy collecting of what one liked were over. There were dancing attendants to advise one on what was art, what was taste, what was costly and rare. A supreme confidence—a last mad ball—was taking over.

The best people, as they saw themselves, set up and solidified the aspirations that made Newport the summer society capital, so that palaces, mansions, villas were built and decked in trellises and arbors. Mrs. Pembroke Jones spent $300,000 a year entertaining, and Newport's best-attended balls cost $100,000 to $200,000.

But the enemies of the good life and lace were moving up. A great waiters' strike began in New York City; *canard à l'orange* and *filet de boeuf* were endangered. The lobster palaces, the splendid dining places were suddenly without the polite, skilled help needed to serve their guests. One hundred fifty waiters dropped napkins at the Folies Bergère, 2,000 refused to debone trout; instead, they massed near the Hotel Knickerbocker, grimacing and howling at expectant diners. Chefs, pantrymen, waiters, valets, kitchen help, salad men, pastry cooks, all moved out to the streets, dropping aprons, peeling knives, meat cleavers.

Waiters demanded a three-and-a-half-hour dinnertime period, day waiters wanted a seven-hour serving period, with pay for overtime. And they demanded one day off a week.

The strikers broke windows at the Knickerbocker, at the Hotel Belmont, the Waldorf Astoria, Ritz-Carlton, the Astor, and Delmonico's. The *Tribune* wrote an obituary to the Age of Reason and Plenty, saw the guillotine already erected in Times Square and the mobs carrying the heads of Astors and Vanderbilts on spikes. "Scenes comparable to the Commune took part in the hotel and café zone all day." This was nonsense, for after a day and a night of the strike the police in their beehive Keystone hats began breaking heads—hickory staves on bone ringing like gongs—and bundled off the bleeding and the injured in patrol wagons.

The strike failed. But it frightened society; behind it was seen all the radical International Workers of the World (sneered at as meaning "I Won't Work"), a native-American direct-action organization. What horrified the best people was that the waiters' strike and the one against the Paterson silk mills were masterminded by two of their own kind—a Harvard man, John Reed, and his rich mistress, Mrs. Mabel Dodge.

Another blow to respectable high life, with its investments in pale-silvery Corots (usually fakes), Meissoniers, Rosa Bonheurs, and Millets, was the opening in 1913 of the imported avant-garde art show at the 69th Street Armory.

The levels of complexity of raw color and abstracted forms baffled people who loved the covers of the *Saturday Evening Post*, the blues of Maxfield Parrish. The show not only rocked an America that could read the *Atlantic Monthly* and the *Literary Digest* and had some notions of art beyond that of *Washington Crossing the Delaware*, but it made the rich collections of so-called Old Masters and the mild, nineteenth-century storytelling paintings seem dark and stuffy, and living in a backwater.

Theodore Roosevelt rose to defend the old art of the *Belle Epoque*, and said, "All modernists are lunatics." But while his opinion on teddy bears, big-game hunting, and digging the Panama Canal have value, the forces of the new art, the modern style, compared with the often "false Renaissance *merde*," were to sweep the young collecting world, and a new set of the rich would take over art buying and press deeper into the background the wealthy old collectors of social status.

As Elliot Paul was to remark (in the 1920s, at Harry's Bar, in Paris),

"No matter what is the fashion, what senseless crescendo of nonsense, no matter how crazy a path the mode takes, society will grab it up someplace along the line. Just let it be touted by shifty art dealers and paid-off critics. It's social status the good livers want."

The young were welding indolence and action; they wanted felt experience rather than lives of social mannequins. If there were still those who bred horses and dogs, and rode and leapt fences, the younger set— their sons and daughters, their grandsons and granddaughters—began to take to ragtime and the early jazz by the time the Great War was just hinted at on the far horizon.

From four to six every afternoon the devil's tea dances moaned at the Ritz, at the best ballrooms and tearooms. Dances of expuisite excitability called the Grizzly Bear, Turkey Trot, Bunny Hug, Dip, Chicken Scratch, Crab Step, Knut Dance, the Kangaroo, and to the music of "Everybody's Doin' It!"

❦

Later there were New Yorkers who felt that the twentieth century did not really begin until August 1914: Before the Great War they had basked in the last lingering moments of nineteenth-century New York, with both the aeroplane and the motorcars remaining toys for the rich.

There was tap code wireless for distress calls at sea, but no radio as we know it. Not all New York homes had bathrooms *with* tubs, or electric light. The first tall, steel-spined buildings in the city were called skyscrapers; the latest exciting monster opened in 1913—presenting the Gothic form of the Woolworth Building, modeled on the style of the British Houses of Parliament by Cass Gilbert. Nothing could be more daring and modern than that edifice on Broadway, standing between Park Place and Barclay Street. Sixty stories high, just under 800 feet of stone lace. Raised up that tall at a cost of $13½ million, and no mortgage or building loans either. Frank W. Woolworth had paid in cash, just as his customers did in his 684 "five and dime" stores.

Its viewers were admiring its dangerous height when *The New York Times*, in June 1914, got out its heaviest black type:

HEIR TO AUSTRIA'S THRONE IS SLAIN WITH HIS WIFE
BY A BOSNIAN YOUTH TO AVENGE SEIZURE OF HIS COUNTRY

Events followed quickly to end a New York era, a changeover that those who had grown up a generation back were always to recall with heavy doses of the Old Nostalgia.

By the end of July the New York Stock Exchange closed, and the city began to look at maps of Europe. The Germans, soon to be referred to as the Huns, were tearing apart the peaceful world; France, England, and Russia were sinking into full war.

In November of that year, New York had a new mayor, John Purroy Mitchell, the youngest mayor, aged thirty-four (he took office in April 1915). He was that rare thing in City Hall politics—an honest man. Mitchell was efficient, and he cared about the welfare of the city.

Mayor Mitchell got his reward that November—an attempt at assassination—a mild ear wound inflicted by a Michael P. Mahoney, who had some vague paranoiac grudge against the city.

New York had a large German population and their newspaper the *New Yorker Herold* cheered the declaration of war, *Macht est Recht*, by der Kaiser, soon to be dubbed "Kaiser Bill": ALL GERMAN HEARTS BEAT LIGHT TODAY. Hearst's *Deutsches Journal* also came out against the Allies. Hearst had a deep dislike of the English, never fully explained.

Rooting for the Allies was the banking firm of J. P. Morgan and Company, housed in its new fortress building at 23 Wall Street.

During the war J. P. Morgan and Company floated $3 billion in loans to the Allies, of which it kept a commission of $30 million for itself. It was to become the opinion of many Americans, among both the radicals and the general public, that the Morgan loans forced the United States into the Great War. The shipments of war material out of New York harbor to the Allies increased as 1914 became 1915, then 1916.

Then the *Lusitania* was sunk by a German U-boat.* Meanwhile, New York harbor, on both the New York and New Jersey sides, continued to be active in shipping millions of tons of high explosives and weapons across the sea.

New York, unaware of it, was sitting beside a huge bomb. In the dark of a July night in 1916, at Black Tom, just outside Jersey City, two million tons of explosives went up with a tremendous roar.

The city of New York took shock after shock. Buildings vibrated like tuning forks, windows and skylights shattered in Brooklyn and Manhattan. All windows in the House of Morgan on Wall Street, among others, were blasted out.

Proof was to come later that German agents had set off the great $45-million disaster. The press pointed out nervously that "only seven people had been killed."

Chase National Bank held the $150,000 the German Ambassador had on deposit there. His agents worked out of a brownstone house on West 15th Street. Here, TNT, bombs, and fire-setting devices were kept handy to be used against shipping, factories, and supply storage areas. The

* The *Lusitania* was carrying munitions, a secret that was finally admitted by documents presented in 1973.

R M S TITANIC

APRIL 14, 1912.

LUNCHEON.

CONSOMME FERMIER   COCKIE LEEKIE

FILLETS OF BRILL   •

EGG A L'ARGENTEUIL

CHICKEN A LA MARYLAND

CORNED BEEF, VEGETABLES, DUMPLINGS

FROM THE GRILL.

GRILLED MUTTON CHOPS

MASHED, FRIED & BAKED JACKET POTATOES

CUSTARD PUDDING

APPLE MERINGUE   PASTRY

BUFFET.

SALMON MAYONNAISE   POTTED SHRIMPS

NORWEGIAN ANCHOVIES   SOUSED HERRINGS

PLAIN & SMOKED SARDINES

ROAST BEEF

ROUND OF SPICED BEEF

VEAL & HAM PIE

VIRGINIA & CUMBERLAND HAM

BOLOGNA SAUSAGE   BRAWN

GALANTINE OF CHICKEN

CORNED OX TONGUE

LETTUCE   BEETROOT   TOMATOES

CHEESE.

CHESHIRE, STILTON, GORGONZOLA, EDAM,

CAMEMBERT, ROQUEFORT, ST. IVEL,

CHEDDAR

ed draught Munich Lager Beer 3d. & 6d. a Tankard.

TWO TRAGIC RELICS OF THE TITANIC AND THE LUSITANIA

Left: Menu from the "unsinkable" *Titanic*. Right: Warning published by the German Embassy the day the *Lusitania* sailed. (She was carrying a cargo of contraband and rifle cartridges.) Two hundred and twenty-four Americans lost their lives when she was sunk by a German U-boat, and the tragedy precipitated America's entry into World War I. (Author's collection)

Mata Hari in charge of New York affairs was a plump version of the Goddess Germania named Martha Held. There was a plot to kill President Wilson, which was silly, as he was being re-elected in 1916 under the slogans: HE KEPT US OUT OF THE WAR and HE GAVE YOU PARCEL POST.

It was a close election. Tammany "hated his guts," for Woodrow Wilson made no secret of the fact that "New York is rotten to the core."

On election night Charles Evans Hughes went to bed in the Astor House Hotel on Broadway, convinced he had won and was the president-elect. Morning brought the cold news that California in its late returns had turned the tide toward Wilson. "The Peace Keeper is still President."

⋗§⋖

In Europe the Germans, proud in their iron purpose to win, yet pinned down in the ghastly Western front trench stalemate after a slaughter of half a million men at Verdun, ordered unrestricted warfare at sea against all shipping suspected of supplying the Allies.

The New York press was about to enter the war with cries of greater horror against Germany. The nation was mostly pro-Allies, romantic in its concept of warfare, as if it were just a bigger cavalry fight on the Western plains.

In April 1917 President Wilson asked Congress to vote a war with Germany. British propaganda had played him like a fish on a line with a delayed coded German cable. Four days later the United States was at war with the Central Powers, including Austria-Hungary and Turkey. Federal agents moved in to seize eighteen German ships, five of them anchored in the Hudson River. A steel net was sunk across the Narrows to keep out nosy U-boats. And New York would become the port of embarkation for the AEF (American Expeditionary Forces) to sail for France, singing "Over There," by George M. Cohan.

THE FIGHTING 69TH GOING "OVER THERE," 1917
New York was the great embarkation point. These ladies don't seem very happy about their posed farewell. (Library of Congress)

Waterfront fires and arson on ships did some damage, but in the main the port of New York was busy and prosperous in supplying the war effort, and spending money in riotous living. For the middle class, the poor, New York had meatless Tuesdays, and people began to cultivate their garden plots, not on the advice of Voltaire, but at the request of Herbert Hoover, National Food Administrator. People hoarded sugar and flour, and a black market existed and soon expanded.

❧

For most, New York was a safe city in which to work and play. The war extended the activities of night club cafés, whorehouses, gambling dens. Music, drink, food, body pleasuring saw no dangers.

However, one man planned to bomb New York with a weapon that few in the end believed in. Führer der Luftschiffe Peter Strasser never lost his faith in zeppelin power. Toward the end of the war Strasser went to see Admiral Reinhard Scheer at his headquarters in Berlin. He had a new zeppelin, the L-70, and his plans were grandiose. While the admiral listened, Strasser pulled some papers from a briefcase and laid them on the desk. Here, he told the old sailor, were the plans to "attack the United States by zeppelins!" He pinpointed the first target: New York City as the main objective.

The admiral showed his surprise and some wonder at this strange scheme. Kapitan Strasser went on talking. The L-59, he explained, had flown nonstop from Bulgaria to the Sudan and back. A newer ship, the L-70, could go even farther. Two more L-70s were under construction. With three ships, Strasser said, he could drop bombs on New York City, ruin it as a port, strike the terror of German might in American hearts.

The admiral told Strasser to leave the papers. He sent them back, marked in pencil, "R.S. *Nein.*"

Experts agree the zeppelins could have crossed the Atlantic from French soil the Germans still held. New York City had no antiaircraft guns and no planes armed to attack the big bags. It is doubtful the zeppelins could have made it back home—but they could have landed in Mexico or Brazil.

❧

In 1918 the war finally came to an end and in 1919 an epidemic of influenza hit the nation. 13,000 New Yorkers succumbed to the disease, with half a million in America and 22 million throughout the world.

An actress relative of mine, Aunt Fran, in a letter to another relative, made some comments about the end of the war and the epidemic, which are revealing of the mood of the times:

> On the 7th Nov. [1918] there was such a caterwauling in the streets and on Fifth Avenue, fit to bust eardrums. Armistice! Vans were being

WORLD WAR I IN NEW YORK
The officer and his lady could have been Jay Gatsby courting Daisy, as is shown by the bare-shouldered ladies in this polite hotel setting in the summer of 1917. (Ross Collection)

overturned, pots, pans being banged. The End of the War! Everyone in the flats and lobby yelling and the cross streets down to Times Square, 34th, were like the Johnstown dam had burst again, and everyone was running in all directions with flags.

Roc says Wall Street and Union Square were the same bedlam. You could get all the free kisses you wanted on 57th Street, and at 34th and 5th Avenue, the snake dancing was holding up everything, everybody—to ear bursting noise. Certainly every office in New York was getting rid of its wastepaper and other things being thrown into the streets.

We were drinking champagne at Emma's. Riverside Drive going like into a St. Vitus seizure, when it was clear there was no peace move at all. Some waterhead had started a rumor and fools passed it on. Was the last of papa's good champagne, so we finished it. As you know, four days later it began again with bells, horns and tug whistles—noise from the Jersey factories across the way, and this time it was Armistice. This time I made us all hot toddies and stayed indoors.

So now maybe, it's peace and a million or so young men coming back, but will it mean taking up their old life again? I wonder. Remember Uncle Ned coming back from Cuba, a drinking man and a gambler and running the Madison Avenue business into the ground? Until he died, he never did anything but shuffle a deck of cards.

Then there was grandfather's brother, the Customs inspector at the Battery, who never stopped yammering about the fun in the barns of Virginia with yellow girls in the Civil War. I think I'll get out of New York for good. It's not going back as [what] it was when we were girls.

My Aunt Fran didn't leave New York or her West End Avenue apartment (she always called it a flat). She survived the flu epidemic:

It's been here big now for two weeks. Dr. Zimmermann calls it Spanish influenza. But why blame it on the Spaniards? Emma says it came off the docks from those rundown people coming over from Europe. I'll murder the next person telling the joke, *"I had a little bird and its name was Enza. I opened the window and in-flu-Enza."* Sickening.

Nell [another aunt] was down with it, chilled and feeling her spine was made of slush, beetles dancing in her eyes and ears. No sense of balance and coughing so you'd think she'd end up in Denver. Some jackass, Dr. Royal [S. Copeland], the city's health commissioner, has issued a statement, "The City is in no danger from an epidemic." That's a time to worry when officials get cheerful as your ship sinks under your feet. Hospitals are filling up, and there is talk nearly a thousand people a day are dying. You can't get central on the phone, and the cops and the fire boys are also hard hit by this plague in a modern city.

Aunt Fran was a small-part actress who hoped to do Chekhov and Strindberg. She never became a star but had, she always insisted, a few "good walking on parts" in Kaufman and Al Woods. In August 1919 she was walking as a picket for the Actors Equity Association against the really dreadful conditions actors and actresses worked under—exploited by the old-time producers. She used to come home to soak her feet in hot water and mustard powder, and curse George M. Cohan for an hour.

Cohan, a partner of the producing firm of Cohan and Harris, was violently anti-union. He set up a company front, Actors Fidelity Union, to smash the actors' group. Aunt Fran went down to Wall Street to take part in a rally with a couple hundred show girls. She kicked a policeman's horse and was arrested. The family had to bail her out.

After the strike was won, she cherished some signed pictures of some of the strike supporters. I remember on her walls photographs of Marie Dressler, Ethel Barrymore, and one of Al Jolson. As an old lady, she came to see the film I had written about him.

⁓⧸⧹⁓

Ever since the tumultuous days of the Civil War it had been obvious that the city would have to find new means of transportation for its growing population. During the next hundred years millions poured in from Europe, and the streets became more crowded, the buildings to house the people taller. But the city could not expand its Manhattan land area because it was an island, running from the East River westward to the Hudson River, and from the Battery north to the Harlem River. Horsecars had replaced the lumbering white stagecoaches, and the horse would be replaced by the streetcar, which drew its power from overhead wires or underground cables.

There were two ways for metropolitan transportation to go. Up *over* the streets and/or *underground*. London had already constructed an underground railroad in 1863, but an attempt to dig a New York subway by a Hugh B. Wilson—he raised $500,000 for the project—was vetoed by the Tweed gang, which controlled surface transit lines and wished to fend off any rival system.

In 1867 the state approved an idea by an inventor named Charles T. Harvey, who erected a section of elevated rail line on Greenwich Street from Dey Street to the Battery. It loomed thirty feet above the crowded streets. Harvey himself, in full formal attire, drove the first engine (steam), which wound up a cable as it moved to propel itself.

By 1871 self-propelled engines—not cable systems—were running on the Ninth Avenue El and tracks were being built from south to north on Second, Third, and Sixth avenues.

Not everybody cheered this progress. Often the El tracks were built over sidewalks, and the trains ran cheek by jowl past open windows, filling apartment and tenement rooms with dust and dirt, and live steam.

THE GREENWICH STREET EL, 1867
Charles T. Harvey making a test run on his Patent Railway System. The car ran by winding up a cable. This sample span never got much further. (Ross Collection)

Usually the four-car green-painted trains ran from dawn until midnight. During rush hours the fare was a nickel, the rest of the day a dime. There were no turnstiles. A conductor punched tickets and the ride was rough and noisy, with ashes and cinders flying all over the place.

In the great blizzard of 1888 in New York, 15,000 passengers were trapped in elevated trains by bad weather, which resulted in snow piling up in huge drifts on the tracks. Passengers began to feel the cold, and enterprising people—the city had a lot of them—came with ladders and charged up to a dollar to get anyone down to the street. One train that no ladder could reach was snowbound with its passengers for nearly sixteen hours. But some kind person got the idea of hoisting up potent drinks by the bucket with the help of ropes.

At this period the El trains were carrying a million people each day, very few of them finding seats. In this atmosphere the celebrated straphanger was born, and the dip (pickpocket) flourished.

WHEN THE ELEVATED LINES HAD CLASS
A hundred years ago this parlor car was "for city travel on the Third Avenue Line." (Author's collection)

John Sloan painted elevated trains and tracks. Reginald Marsh did genre pictures of the life of the moochers, rummies, grifters, and flop-house dropouts under the Bowery El pillars. But to a growing city the elevated lines after World War II were relics. Even before Pearl Harbor some of the structures had already been pulled down; much of the steel "sold to Japan to come back as shells and bomb shapes fired against American forces in the Pacific" (Dorothy Thompson). Soon almost all the elevated tracks in the borough of Manhattan were down (though several lines continued to thrust their ugly, paint-peeled steel structures along the streets of Brooklyn, Queens, and the Bronx).

Reginald Marsh, a New York genre artist of genius, also painted the dank, catacombs atmosphere of life in the subways. Subway proponents had at first experienced a more difficult time than that suffered by the El supporters in battling the surface transit owners, who wanted no rivals moving passengers under their trolley tracks.

In 1868 an inventor named Alfred Ely Beach, who also was half owner of the New York *Sun*, dug a block-long tunnel under Broadway from Murray to Warren streets, just to prove it could be done.

Tammany, to protect its above-surface tracks, killed a state bill to extend the tunnel. It was not until 1888 that the city asked for the legal right to build its own subways. But it took until 1891 to get a proper bid out to build the first line. "Nobody bid. Tammany was blamed [rightly] for this—threatening the contractors with work problems if they bid, and no more fat city contracts" (B.R. Memoirs).

It took the twentieth century to get the digging actually started. In February 1900 a contractor, John B. McDonald, "a Tammany boyo who knew how to divvy" (B.R. Memoirs), signed up to build, equip, and run the subway for fifty years—costs to be $35 million. The Tammany boys would divide the subcontracts among themselves. At the same time Tammany promised the slum voters thousands of jobs in the monumental construction task that was involved.

Of course, neither the city nor Tammany was putting up the cash to begin working on the subway. Investors were invited to back the project. August Belmont & Co., a firm well connected with the great Rothschild banking houses, was interested. They agreed to form the Rapid Transit Subway Construction Company, with Belmont II as president.

Manhattan is solid rock. To blast and dig into it requires power tools, explosives, and mostly, in those early days, muscle. Twelve thousand workers began to hack at the stone floor under the streets. Twenty cents an hour pay for a ten-hour day. Carry your own lunch. Though most of the workers were Irish, Italians, and Poles from tenement areas, there were some exceptions. One was Edwin Arlington Robinson, a New Englander and Harvard man, who was hired to check stone weighing during the removal of debris and rock. He was later to become a gloomy and great poet ("Like dead remembered footsteps on old floors"). John Masefield, another poet, tended bar and filled the growler (beer can) for thirsty subway workers. By 1904, after much sweat and many injuries, the first line was ready to go into operation.

BOOK SEVEN

The World
of
Jimmy Walker

24
Did the Twenties
Really Roar?

New York City certainly grew harder, more cynical in the postwar world of the 1920s. F. Scott Fitzgerald somehow became the prophet of the Jazz Age and the "jazz babies" without having much knowledge of the real jazz out of New Orleans, Chicago, and Harlem.

His flappers and sheiks, mostly produced for the *Saturday Evening Post*, and his over-romantic Princeton students in his amazingly successful novel *This Side of Paradise* have too often been pointed out as the true pictures of what the drinking, sexing young people took themselves to be.

But there were more sensational writings—Percy Mark's *The Plastic Age* and Michael Arlen's *The Green Hat*—to set a pattern for the full and wild life, usually blamed on Freud, postwar disillusionment, and alcohol. Ernest Hemingway, before the end of the decade, was to immortalize the refugees—the expatriates from the Village, the Eastern colleges, and newspaper offices who went to Paris—in *The Sun Also Rises*.

There were some losses in the 1920s that the city mourned. If the New Yorker believed in anything, it was the now gone well-kept saloon.

An unidentified news clipping stated the case for the male pleasure bar before Prohibition.

> The saloon . . . appeals first to man's sense of the beautiful. . . . In flashing crystalline, glass polished wood, hammered brass, beautiful frescoes, brilliant lights, warmth and cheer, he is bidden welcome . . . the free lunch counter . . . loaded with the most tempting food cooked by master hands.

There was now mockery in Bouguereau's *Nymphs and the Satyr*, still at the Hoffman House, only rivaled by Maxfield Parrish's *Old King Cole*, at the Knickerbocker Hotel. Both places dry—at least legally. Gourmets' hangouts began to give up early. In May 1919 Louis Sherry had closed the doors of his Fifth Avenue restaurant, blaming "Prohibition and warborn Bolshevism."

In May 1923 the orchestra at Delmonico's went into the somber notes of "Auld Lang Syne" to sob at the end of its own existence.

But did the twenties—after the deadly Spanish flu epidemic of 1919 —really roar? Was there a Speakeasy Age in New York—remembered as Leon and Eddie's, 21, Barney Gallant's, where the majority of the adult population spent so much time drinking bathtub gin and needled beer?

Many of the plays, the movies, the gossip columns, the popular novelists seemed to suggest a time of turning to the speakeasy as a national forum and water hole.

Katherine Brush's *Young Man of Manhattan*, Dorothy Parker's *Big Blonde*, the first stories of John O'Hara and Dos Passos' *Manhattan Transfer, USA* gave it all during those cataclysmic years a color and kind of ratty, shabby glamor.

Actually the New York of the hurdy-gurdy man grinding out "Santa Lucia" and "Funiculi Funicula," the leisurely dining at Mouquin's on 27th Street, was gone. The new sound of jazz in Harlem signaled different times. The first vipers (as pot smokers and sellers were originally called) made the gossip columns. The posh eating and gathering place soon was to be the Casino in Central Park, with its two bands, Leo Reisman and Eddie Duchin ("In dreams I kiss your hand, madam . . .").

Prohibition had come in on the night of January 1, 1920, and the Casino, a white mansion in Central Park with candlelit tables, wide verandas, and Joseph Urban décor, began to attract the first "café society" set (not yet called that) among the wisteria vines of the place. Jimmy Walker—the rising young songwriter and Tammany politician to become mayor in 1926—gave it color. He was a man of the 1920s; sleek and with a head of oiled black hair out of a John Held, Jr., drawing.

Jimmy Walker was a charmer, a far cry from the paunch-heavy Tweed Gang, the walrus-moustached, derby-hatted Tammany leaders of the prewar era. The crimes of William Marcy Tweed were remembered only by historians. The new Tammany still held control of the ward system, but Jimmy Walker was a new breed—polished, witty, cosmopolitan. The political corruption was just as thick—payoffs, bribes, dishonest inspectors, shakedowns, all remained, but rivaled in the 1920s in their take by the bootleggers and their gangs turning to the protection rackets.

On the surface, the 1920s in New York presented a city that Henry James and O. Henry would never have dreamed of in the shadows cast by the Ninth, Third, and Second Avenue Els. Of the older generation of writers, only Edith Wharton, back for a visit from Paris, tried to understand and picture the changing New York in her fiction.

The spokesmen of the people were certainly grotesquely new. The tabloid newspaper had appeared. The *Daily News*, an offspring of the Chicago *Tribune*, gone east and vulgar, was a small, handy-sized publication "given to large photographs of dead gangsters' funerals, show girls, gossip, love nests, and very short texts that could be read without moving the lips" (Harrison Smith).

One other tabloid was an even gamier object, usually with a pink front page—the New York *Graphic*. It brought Walter Winchell, a vaudeville hoofer, into public view as a razzle-dazzle gossip columnist. He was the first to reveal private lingerie in public since the blackmailing days, some years before, of a magazine called *Town Topics*. The *Graphic* also created "photo dramas"—pasting up many photographs and posed models to re-enact the love life and scandals of the period.

In show business Winchell had been an indifferent dancer, but as a journalist he was a shrill and gaudy performer. He gave the New York of the twenties new expressions like *pffft* for partners in marriage parting, *Renovating* for divorcing, *handcuffed* for marriage. But he was a remarkable success when he was taken over by Hearst for the third tabloid to appear, the New York *Mirror*.

Going on radio with his sharp, staccato voice, Winchell was immensely popular, and later he branched into national and international politics with rather strange items, and often not fully factual stories.

Another voice that the twenties felt was "the real McCoy" (1920s slang) was that of a sportswriter turned short-story writer, Damon Runyon. His guys and dolls of a mythical Broadway and the underworld, sentimental and stylized, with Lindy's as their watering hole, were praised as a new O. Henry world.

Runyon's characters and world were completely invented and artificial; his tough but softhearted hoods, his soiled but loyal broads, his hardshell but tenderized gamblers were a kind of dream existing in a New York that was limited to a few blocks around a legendary Times Square, "The Great White Way," and some rows of speakeasies along 52nd Street.

A truer picture of New York and its hustlers, prizefighters, phonies, Tin Pan Alley songwriters, theater promoters, agents, and their women was being drawn in somber colors by a man with a remarkable ear for the language of the times, a one-time sportswriter, Ring Lardner.

He had done a great deal toward exposing the rigging of the World Series of 1919, when the New York gambler Arnold Rothstein promised bribes (most of which he never paid) to eight Chicago White Sox ball players to throw the series. Lardner had written of this professional baseball world in a series of stories, *You Know Me, Al,* that exposed the low intellect of baseball "ivory" and the "World Serious," as he called it.

Certainly Fitzgerald, Winchell, Dorothy Parker, Runyon, and Lardner had as much to do with creating the public image of New York City of the twenties as the more important events of the town.

❦

The Casino crowd, dominated by Jimmy Walker and his official city greeter, Grover Whalen, "the last man who knew how to properly wear a top hat," entertained the Harrimans, a few Pinchots, The Honorable Daisy Fellows, Miriam Hopkins and Ethel Barrymore, various Oelrichs, Kahns, Lehmans, and Guggenheims. They were "items" in the gossip columns of Winchell, Mark Hellinger, and Louis Sobel, but of no great interest to the intellectuals playing out a charade of their own at the Hotel Algonquin's Round Table. They were a collection of self-styled wits who quoted each other frequently and log rolled each other's books.

There was FPA (a columnist named Franklin Pierce Adams actually), who once wrote a play, *Lo the Poor Indian,* with O. Henry and ran a column in the *World,* mostly made up of contributions from readers; Alexander Woollcott ("Alex has delusions of gender"[Anon.]), a snapping turtle of a mean spirit with a marshmallow style; Robert Benchley, not yet the Hollywood actor, a poker-faced funny fellow with a smudge of moustache, then writing for the old *Life* humor magazine; George Kaufman, who always collaborated on his popular plays ("Satire is what closes out of town Saturday").

Sometimes Heywood Broun was present (ten people were to claim they had first described him as "looking like an unmade bed"). Dorothy Parker was usually included as being a member of the Algonquin Round Table group. A tragic alcoholic, unfortunate in love, she had the sharpest wit, with the killing line that struck quickly, like lightning.

The great stars—Al Jolson, Bert Williams, Will Rogers, Eddie Cantor, W. C. Fields, the Barrymores, Ann Pennington—were often actually surviving figures of an earlier decade. After a Broadway opening, the people didn't all crowd into the Casino. There was the Claremont Inn on the Hudson, where one could feel more private with one's date *if* a married man or woman.

Midnight sailings for Europe were also social events. As expatriates or visitors Harold Stearns, Malcolm Cowley, Matthew Josephson, e. e. cummings, Edmund Wilson, Elliot Paul, Alexander Calder, and Hart Crane were moving across "the big pond." Their destination was usually Paris, whence they hoped to bring back tidings from such people as Sylvia Beach, Gertrude Stein, Ernest Hemingway, soon to be joined by names like Cole Porter, Zelda and Scotty, Virgil Thompson, Josephine Baker, and hundreds of thousands of Americans "unkown to fame."

The most fashionable sailings were those of the French Line's *La France*. One attended with baskets of Sherry's or Park and Tilford's goodies and bootleg bottles, usually in formal evening attire, including top hat and cane.

So many took that escape from Main Street and what was called, by people who didn't understand jazz at all, "The Jazz Age." It became a symbol more than just a sound, as Fitzgerald saw it: "The word jazz in its progress toward respectability has meant first sex, then dancing, then music. It is associated with a state of nervous stimulation."

However, jazz never really became respectable as music. The professors took it up and wrote erudite, pedantic texts about it. But the daughter of Scott and Zelda, Scottie Fitzgerald Lanahan Smith, writing in 1973, saw that the word "jazz" was really a way of explaining the atmosphere of a period: "My father and mother were not interesting just because they jumped into a fountain in front of the Plaza or even because they happened to write well, but because they were products of the complete and unique American experience."

In my youth I once spent a delightful day with the late Lucius Beebe, during which he spoke of the glory of the Cunard liner: "The only way to cross the ocean—the French line is fine, but the British sense of the proper thing is much more worthy of a gentleman."

In the twenties there was the *Aquitania*, known to the press as "an ocean greyhound." The staterooms, I remember, were done in a fine décor that did not shout at one. The true *viveur* preferred the English boats because of the tailoring of the first-class passengers "and the seamanship; the Frenchies aren't really sailors, you know."

A Cunarder at sea stocked nearly fifty kinds of fine cigars: shapes of Coronas, Panatelas, Perfectos by Gonzales, Upmann, Romeo y Julieta, Belinda. As for those gourmets who preferred English dainties, there were pickled walnuts and spring lamb, deviled beef bones, Yarmouth bloaters.

One can study old passenger lists, photographs of the *Berengaria, Olympia*, the first *France*. Here for posterity are members of society: Yale graduates, New Orleans debutantes, officers of Farmers Loan and Trust and Kidder, Peabody & Co., J. P. Morgan, an author from Harper's or Scribner's, a Carolina horse show rider, a Tuxedo Park dog fancier (also rubber-check passers, blackmailers, false titles, cardsharps). Men surrounding Connie Bennett (in cloche hat) or Grace Moore, bowing to Willa Cather, Mary Garden.

The essentials for permanence seemed to be there. That it was to pass after a hundred years of luxury travel by steam seemed outrageous to suggest. "Just as well to expect," said one old party on the *Queen Mary's* maiden trip, "the wonderful trains like the Twentieth Century Limited, the grand Pullman coaches, the Harvey diners with their crisp linen and shiny silverware were to pass, become crumby and run-down. Fiddle-faddle!"

Someone has said, "History teaches us that history teaches us nothing." Certainly the traveler enjoying roomy luxury is impervious to ideas of change. It is repugnant to one's vanity to think so much leisured ease and service would not be around for one's grandsons.

It all really began to go downhill when "Picasso and Braque destroyed formal grace in art"; yet people still talked of the great Melba and the greater Escoffier, and one could order a magnum of Moet & Chandon, but not with a credit card. World War I had turned the Cunarders into troopships—the great *Lusitania* took its hundreds, going to Paris and London, down to a watery grave. . . . The day of flying the ocean would come and comfort would go.

25
Inside Greenwich Village

One of the best pictures we have of the Village in the first half of the 1920s is found in W. W. Windstaff's privately printed memoirs: *

> After my first three years in Paris, I came back to America for a spell—that is, I got to New York. Which is not like the rest of America, but has a flavor all its own. It was a wilder New York—spinning in a different pattern than when I had last seen it as a seventeen-year-old kid.
>
> You were not supposed to like New York. The Paris crowd all said it was crass and commercial, materialistic, greedy, and ruled by rum runners and bootleggers. I have to confess I rather liked the city in the mid-twenties, at least from the Village where I settled in to wait for the family lawyers, those Daumier sharks' heads in their Wall Street offices milking family trusts, to allow me more money. . . .
>
> Everybody, after the war, was telling me the Village wasn't what it had been. I heard how it had been when the arty crowd of before the

* To be published by the Southern Illinois University Press, these quotes are used with the publisher's permission.

war—Carl Van Vechten and others—found it "creative"—a word I connect with fancy talk and bad breath. I had a letter of hello to Carl from Gertrude Stein, and I could see very soon, watching him shake down his ruby cuff links, he wasn't my kind. I didn't give a damn about high art or causes. And after having some stinking hooch with him and Robert Edmund Jones, I went down to Washington Square South and found myself a room near Romany Marie's tearoom.

While I waited . . . to get some money from a family trust, so I could get back to Paris. Then and later, I horsed around with a fine girl named Olga I met through "Jimmie" Criswall [Eliza Helen Criswall], who ran the Mad Hatter for some time. I was getting to know the Village. Going from a speakeasy to a tearoom, to some club meeting, I got to say hello to the same faces, and I'd chivy the changing uptown crowd come to look at the freaks. The girl Olga liked joints—the Crumperis and the Vermilion Hound, the Pollywoggie, the Kricket, Steps Down, the Jumble Shop.

Olga—I was living with her—painted lamp shades on fake parchment, and I'd help her carry them to Wanamakers and certain Madison Avenue shops where she took orders for shades picturing snow scenes and pirate ships and birds. She'd paint them in her one-room studio with a closet kitchen, and I'd color the backgrounds. When we figured we'd made enough for a night of it, we'd wash up, go find Bobby Edwards who ran a magazine, *The Quill,* or go to Jimmie's Mad Hatter and sit under the wall sign Olga had painted: WE'RE ALL MAD HERE . . . I'M MAD, YOU'RE MAD . . . YOU MUST BE OR YOU WOULDN'T BE HERE. . . .

Jimmie was being courted by this fat Dutchman, Hendrik Willem Van Loon, I had known in Paris, who practically lived in the joint. Always talking up a hurricane. There wasn't anything he didn't know about in detail, even if he was often wrong, and making miserable drawings on everything, even marking up the walls. . . .

Romany Marie explained to Olga and me, "The Dutchie is a bag of wind, and when I was born in a forest of Moldavia, my people knew how to tell if a man was real."

Olga put a fresh cigarette in her long holder, "Come off it, Marie. You were born in a pushcart shed on Delancey Street."

So there would start a slanging match between the two and if we had sold enough lamp shades, we went across 6th Avenue to Christopher Street, Sheridan Square, to Don Dickerman, who ran this really Toyland night club, the Pirates Den. . . .

Olga was very much a mind type—ideas smoked in her head. She was given to moving around among the intelligentsia of the downtown brain types—she painting scenery for little theater groups like the followers of the Provincetown Players. And there everyone talked about Gene, who turned out to be Eugene O'Neill, a serious horse-faced young booze fighter. But not soft and weepy like some drunks. Just full of ass-dragging dark thought; a sad feeling "life is a bucket of shit," to quote Gene.

I got along fine with him. I had his itch to drink, in fact at times I had it bad, but I didn't have the problem Gene had; I could hold it better and it didn't get me down. We'd be bellying the bar in some speak, or squatting in some dusty studio, and I remember him looking the true Black Mick he was, and saying things. One time: "Better not to be born. Better to have been nothing." But in a whisper that didn't carry.

I said, "Come off it, Gene. That's pretty easy poetry." He was well established as a playwright by then. Uptown was playing his dramas, but he liked to come down to the Village. . . .

For all his success, I thought Gene's plays humorless and deadly bores. Except for the sailor things, the one-acters he did. *The Emperor Jones* was just a great big show-off part for an actor. I saw Paul Robeson play the hell out of it and it worked. *The Hairy Ape* and *Beyond the Horizon* I thought college boy Gloomy Gus stuff, but the Downtown and Uptown ate it. I think he won a Pulitzer for one of them.

The character who had the village figured just right, was a Latvian, a little sawed-off fellow named Barney, who ran the Greenwich Village Inn. The college boys and stockbrokers, ad copy writers, could pick up girls from the *Greenwich Village Follies* or a show called *Hobohemia*. Barney got arrested for selling liquor after the Big Dry Up. Olga said arrest wasn't enough, "He should be shot, selling that stuff." . . .

Soon everybody was making and selling wine and what passed for whiskey and gin, and New York kidneys proved to be heroes. Beer was needled with ether to make it give you a jolt. Truth was, it was not art, music or theatre or literature that brought people with fat wallets to the Village. It was to drink and get laid.

Life in the Village in the late 1920s prospered in its own fashion; there was more demand for Bohemian love nests, the speaks and night clubs brought parties of uptown people downtown, the "geniuses" came at a faster pace, from Nebraska and Ohio and all points west and south. Rents skyrocketed and more stables in alleys became studios. The genuine creators—always a minority—began to drift out to Long Island, to Woodstock, Taos, Santa Fe, and to stay longer at Cape Cod. Even Hollywood lured its quota of those who had once dedicated themselves to Proust, Joyce, and Eliot, and now wrote for Clara Bow and Rudolf Valentino.

But there remained the landmarks of the Village—the poet Maxwell Bodenheim, Baroness Olga, the native socialists, vegetarians, Marxists, unsuccessful painters. Also teachers drifting in from nearby New York University. One of the freaks was six feet, seven inches tall—Thomas Wolfe, trying to write the great American novel and lurching, with the aid of a great editor, Maxwell Perkins, toward what would soon be *Look Homeward, Angel*.

As the 1920s advanced, the Village was in menopause—sliding into a change of life. The rich or the very successful were moving in, pushing out some of the flea-bitten and cold-water studio people. The smart parties were in MacDougal Alley, the studio of Gertrude Vanderbilt Whitney, the studio of Jo Davidson, who was making busts of all the millionaires. There was still the Boni bookshop, where you might run into Waldo Frank, Lewis Galantiere, Lewis Mumford, Deems Taylor.

The Village was visited by excitement seekers when midtown jaded its writers, actors, producers, gamblers, advertising agency hustlers. Bennett Cerf led parties to the Village; so did the escorts of Neysa McMein, a lovely painter of magazine covers who shared her studio with live mice.

Herbert Bayard Swope ran the *World*, the most entertaining newspaper in the nation, or so it was claimed by George Gershwin, another Village visitor. It was not Picasso, Matisse, and Braque who were the popular avant-garde artists, but Lyendecker (no first name), who painted the Arrow Collar ads and many *Saturday Evening Post* covers; Maxfield Parrish, who made the sky too blue; and Rose O'Neill, with her Kewpie doll drawings. Outstanding was John Held, Jr., who immortalized the long-legged flapper and her jelly-bean escort with larded-down hair and an enveloping raccoon coat. Milt Gross was a satirical genius, had the town reciting his ethnic humor of *"Nize Baby*, eat up all the Spinoza."

Serious graphic art was in the hands of the powerful radical artists William Gropper, Boardman Robinson, and Robert Minor. Roland Kirby worked for the *World*. The *Times* disdained to use editorial cartoons, and certainly *not* comic strips, called "funny papers" at first.

The most famous and popular comic strips are long gone: *Andy Gump* ("he wears no man's collar"), the brilliant cubistic patterns of *Polly and Her Pals*, and George Herriman's *Krazy Kat*, the Fitzgerald-type youth *Harold Teen*, the uncouth *Moon Mullins*, and Fox's *Toonerville Trolley*. Gone, too, the brilliant folk artist, the John O'Hara of the sporting world, who signed himself just "Tad."

Their fame was fleeting, yet they added a vital folk color and new language: "banana oil" and "horse feathers" as terms of nonbelief; "bee's knees," "cat's pajamas," "snazzy," and "ritzy" as terms of class. A bit more interesting than today's already fading "Yeah, man," and "Right on."

There was a kind of hovering connection between the city's pleasure seekers, from the "Blackbirds" chorus of Harlem down to the rooms of the Village where the gin was served in cups. Also part of it all were the great rococo *Art Moderne* film palaces, where even the demented luxury of the mad Ludwig of the true Bohemia was outbuilt. Among those were Roxy's, the Times Square Paramount, and Radio City Music Hall, just emerging from a huge hole in the Rockefeller ground.

There was never any thought of muggings, of prowling drug pushers trailed by narcs. You could get rolled if you flashed big bills, and got sexually serviced, even clipped, in some of the notorious mangy midtown hotels. The tabloids featured Homeric gang wars, bootlegger feuds.

26
Flappers, Bombers, and Other Citizens

Postwar New York was not to be the city of society's "400" or Stanford White's naked girls on a swing. There was a new kind of hurry and bustle in the old town, with only memory connecting it with the past of the Edwardian polished brass doorknobs, the genteel Washington Square houses, the placid walks in Central Park, the manly sanctuaries of the Hoffman House and the Ritz Bar. The saloon of the middle class was gone. Prohibition was a tradition, not a law to the city.

The flapper was in. A New York girl no one had seen before. Slimmer, hair bobbed or shingled, spit curls à la Clara Bow, the IT girl of silent films.

The city was harder, faster, the five-cent fare still took one underground in the subway at ear-shattering speed. Roseland Ballroom at ten cents a dance was not patronized just by degenerates.

The city's black population had jumped during the war, as sharecroppers and pushed-down Negroes came north for boom-time pay. There were now 150,000 in Harlem scuffling for jobs, and their wives or girl friends, known as the *swartzah* in the Bronx, were doing housework.

THE RADIO BLUES

The early 1920s produced the radio age—and strange-looking machines. The flappers listening show the bobbed hair and the marcelled wave of the period. (RCA photo)

Meanwhile, a number of radicals were picked up by police and questioned about their possible involvement in the great Wall Street explosion.

What happened on Wall Street that 16th day of September in 1920 has never been fully solved. Wall Street was its usual hustle and bustle, bearer bonds were delivered by messengers, the stock market was doing splendidly, and on the corner of Wall Street and Broadway the House of Morgan basked in the millions it had made in war loans to the Allies.

Diagonally across the street from Morgan & Company was the New York Stock Exchange, busy enlarging its space. The other two corners held the Subtreasury Building and the tall (forty stories) Bankers Trust. If anyone wanted to strike a blow against American capitalism, "Dis mus' be de place" (popular comic line in a Minsky's burlesque routine).

And someone did think it was the place. And the time. Near lunchtime. Down Wall Street came a small wagon, brown in color, with a canvas cover over it. It was pulled by a dark-brown horse, and the driver had it draw up to the curb at Wall and Nassau. The driver got down and walked away. No one later reported any suspicious action.

The Trinity Church clock at the top of Wall Street began its respectful donging out of the hour—twelve noon. Suddenly a tremendous explosion erupted from the vicinity of the horse and wagon. Then a rising cloud of bluish-white smoke, tinged with yellow flame, rose into the air, shattering whatever was caught in the force of its concussion.

Brown and black plumes of smoke followed the first white cloud as fragments of iron and stone began to fly through the air. Glass started to spill like sharp, lethal knives, and people began to fall, or run and scream with mashed limbs, bloody, lacerated faces, broken bones. Many victims suffered crushed skulls. Within an area of half a mile, in a vast circle of fury, glass was falling from windows, plate-glass shop windows became gleaming shards, and other spears of glass hurtled to the sidewalk.

The shock after the first blast left only the smoke, the torn façades, and then a loud screaming as the wounded began to realize they had been hurt. Young girls fell as life drained from them. Inside buildings fire was spreading—some office workers found their hair in flames.

A millionaire named Edward Sweet was killed; but he himself was never found, only a finger with his ring on it. J. P. Morgan's grandson Julius Spenser took a minor cut on his hand; otherwise, reported the *Times*, "no other important Wall Street figure was hurt." Total casualties were 35 people killed and 150 injured.

No one was ever arrested and charged with the crime. No one ever proved it was a radical, or a nut, or some personal plan of revenge against the House of Morgan.

◦§◦

Meanwhile, the federal government was busy trying to put teeth in the Prohibition Act, which had become law in January 1920. The act forbade the making, transporting, and selling of alcoholic beverages. The word "scofflaw" was coined for those who didn't respect the act.

The intellectuals led at first in breaking the law. Everybody who disliked the law and had a thirst did what he could to break it. Some made their own fearful beer, often with explosive results. Others distilled hair tonics and various scents for the "alki" content. Italians on Mulberry Street made wine, then gin.

Actually "bathtub gin," a popular expression, was usually a product of portable stills controlled by the Italian gangsters, survivors or heirs of the old Black Hand blackmailers and white slavers of prewar times. They were becoming dealers in hooch, beer, and soon in bullets.

Leaders were often called Moustache Petes—old-timers in crime. The Italians and some Jews—Little Augie (Jacob Orgen), Dutch Schultz, Legs Diamond—and lots of good clean old WASP stock were trying to seize power in New York, first as bootleggers, then in the rackets.

The rum boats operated outside the three-mile limit, carrying cargo from the West Indies and down from Canada. The New York under-world weaned by Kid Dropper, Monk Eastman, and Owney Madden saw no reason not to control the stuff. There had been about 15,000 bars and saloons in New York before the Prohibition Act came in. Illegal drinking was crowding the speaks, blind pigs, Bowery joints, and dives, and turn-ing exclusive clubs and private mansions into watering holes.

The federal government made some attempts to enforce the law, but guards, agents, police, the courts, and judges were happily open to bribes. Senators and congressmen, city and state officials all had their own favorite bootleggers.

Soon the demand for alcohol was so great that New Yorkers began to find dead bodies of hijackers, or their victims, lying on the streets. The Thompson submachine gun, a deadly light hand weapon, and the sawed-off shotgun (just right to fit under a topcoat) became identifying weap-ons of underworld bosses enforcing their rights. Trucks ran into the city at night in convoy—down from Canada, up from Florida—hoods riding shotgun. Sometimes they were escorted by local police as protection from hijackers or rival mobs.

One hero of the Prohibition enforcers was Izzy Einstein, a former post office worker. He got a job with the Southern District of New York sniffing out booze sellers. Izzy was about 230 pounds, had attained five feet, three inches in height. He had a comic bald head and claimed to know nine languages. He would order a drink in some speakeasy and then when served pour it into a hot-water bottle hidden in his pants. He had a friend, Moe Smith, who ran a closet-sized cigar store, and Izzy got Moe to become a rum cop too. Moe weighed even more than Izzy and stood only a few inches higher.

They were unique because they were the rare honest enforcers. Izzy and Moe loved to dress up—put on blackface, carry on like mugs, look like waterfront characters. They worked with the press, for both men knew the value of publicity. Yet the records show they achieved amazing results in their raids. It is estimated that Izzy and Moe had grabbed $15 million worth of alcohol in five million bottles during their raids. In addition, they put hundreds of stills and brewery joints out of business—equipment the mob often bought back later at auction or under the table in a private deal. Izzy and Moe claimed nearly 5,000 arrests and 95 percent convictions.

Perhaps Izzy and Moe were too good. Or their clowning hurt the sense of dignity of the federal people in Washington. In 1925 Moe and Izzy "were booted out as Federal Agents for the good of the service. Better-class people wanted to drink, eat, smoke, dance, get their ashes hauled in safety from raids by two Jews in comic getup" (Frank Fay).

Night clubs of all kinds flourished in New York, and it was a thrill to sit in a crowded room in stale air, the piano player noodling "Livery Stable Blues," among real gangsters in evening dress.

He (and she) turned to drink (Tiger Piss, King Kong) and to snow sniffing (cocaine). Also the first marijuana—called a reefer at the time, and sold by people known as vipers (there was no law against its use in the 1920s) appeared during this period.

Marijuana was also called mezz (after Milt Mezzrow, a white jazz man), muta, golden gauge, muggles, grefa, musta, the hemp, roach (a short butt). The 1970s terms—pot and grass—were not yet in use.

The heart of Harlem was 135th Street and Seventh Avenue—the walk between 131st and 132nd being known as The Stroll—and what remained of the Tree of Hope for the voodoo and juju believers. It was a mixture of misery and pink Caddys, whores and randy store-front preachers, hominy grits, murder, Bert Williams and Bessie Smith records.

It was quite safe then for the ofays (whites), at least during daytime hours and at night in the places that catered with music and food and sexual adventures to the "downtown trade." One could wander from rib joints (delicious food) to the Savoy Ballroom. The big lure was jazz.

By 1923 the early Dixieland bands like the Original Hot Five were there, and one could hear Jim Moynahan (clarinet) and Brad Gowans (trombone) taking the solos. Names that are now only footnotes were the Daniel Boones of Harlem music: the Goofus Five, Little Ramblers, Cotton Pickers, Ladd's Black Acres. Then came the Memphis Five, before swing softened the real beat. Later you could see George Gershwin listening with a party of smart friends, and soon what he heard was to echo in his "A Rhapsody in Blue," which astonished New Yorkers in a concert arranged by Paul Whiteman.

Harlem smelled busy and a bit decayed, yet the old buildings were teeming with life being lived at a fast pace. The small fry in the poverty-stricken area were always in evidence, on battered, broken roller skates sucking colored ices, jigging in front of the Performers and Entertainers Club, Connie's Inn, the cellar of the Hoofers Club, Tabbs' Restaurant, begging pennies from the downtown visitors who had come to hear Erskine Hawkins, Jimmy Lunceford, and Cab Calloway (a sensation with "Minnie the Moocher").

The smell of ribs and grits, chitlin's, Brunswick stew—all these were part of the scene, as were the cold-water flats, yard toilets, six to a bed in the tenement rooms, lots of rickets, and the horn man with his music in a brown paper bag looking for a gig.

The thing that was so surprising in the Harlem of before the Black Revolution and "Black is beautiful" was the acceptance of a way of life that was degrading, soul-shattering—the destruction of the minds of people who might have become writers and painters, businessmen, or public officials. There was crime, of course, and a dislike of the police. But disrespect and rebellious gestures were kept under control.

One had to know the old Harlem to see how much today's black world in New York has changed. Seeing the brisk, alert, even sassy black in his better clothes, and mixed with the white help in great offices and tall buildings, speaking with an accent as good as any in the city, one has a hard time remembering the older black pattern—when there was no black élite among the whites, no mass of college-attending blacks.

If Harlem is now speaking out, and raising its voice, it is also aware that only the advance guard has penetrated into Whitey's special world of the city.

◄§§►

Meanwhile, defying the law by making and drinking bad alcohol became a sport, a dangerous one, almost like hunting bear. Bootleggers courted excitement in going against the law-enforcement agents, who, it must be admitted, gave them a sporting chance, often by taking bribes to stand on the sidelines and merely observe.

Bribes were costly—according to a sworn statement the average New York City speakeasy paid off about $1,370 a month, $400 of it in graft to federal Prohibition agents; in addition there were the police department and the district attorneys, all good Tammany Hall men. The policeman on the beat got a meager $40 a month to insure that the neighborhood was kept in order and to help with the beer deliveries.

Most speakeasies passed themselves off as exclusive clubs and issued membership cards—"Cards," the late Robert Benchley once said, "which are about as hard to get as lion dung in Africa." The 5 O'clock Club card announced FREE LUNCH EVERY NOON; the card for Hoyle's Homelike Club read "There's a Difference." The best-known places plugged by columnists feeding and drinking on the cuff just listed their names, Leon and Eddie's, The Club, and Perroquet.

It was estimated—by whom surviving records do not show—that by 1925 there were 100,000 speakeasies in New York City. Prohibition agents said, "The wettest street in America is 45th Street." But the classiest, ritziest hooch joints were on 52nd Street between Fifth and Sixth avenues. "You could buy a drink in *any* building on the block."

To dry up the country and keep it dry there were 1,550 agents, some honest, some not. A lot of the wet goods they impounded got away from them and back to the gangsters. In 1925 agents seized one million gallons of hard liquor and six million gallons of beer.

The flapper and sheik, the people F. Scott Fitzgerald wrote of as the Jazz Age dancers, and those middle-aged hedonists of Peter Arno's cartoons in the *New Yorker*—all expressing their libidos—led to John O'Hara's rather secondhand lace-curtain Irish look at the rage to live of

FIFTH AVENUE IN THE 1920s
Before the cars were streamlined, the double-deck buses still reigned, as did the bronze traffic towers (and clocks), and traffic was not yet curb to curb. Note B. Altman & Co. department store, where buses are picking up and discharging passengers. (Museum of the City of New York)

the sporting rich in a world salted with country-club infidelity and youths from Skull and Bones at Yale and the Princeton eating clubs.

Somehow it all centered upon the objection of serious drinkers to Prohibition, and found its most lively focus in the night clubs, the speakeasies—a few years' whirl that was to lead to the final Wall Street Crash of 1929. The gay rich life for most would then go into a decline from which it has not yet recovered.

Seekers of the good fast life in the 1920s were often to be found at El Fay, 300 Club, Argonaut, Rendezvous, Club Richmond, Century, Salon Royal, Helen Morgan's, or the Club Intime.

The inexpensive dives were mostly cellars with fake paper grape leaves on the ceiling and the Bay of Naples painted on a grimy back wall. The vilest kind of whisky and needle beer was served, and the Capone-era Italian, who looked as if he needed a shave every hour, was the owner or front for Dutch Schultz or Legs Diamond.

College boys in raccoon coats carried Harvard or Rutgers banners, flat-chested girls in rolled stockings and shingled hair were there trying to look like John Held, Jr., drawings, attracting Wall Street brokers, the sporting squire from East Orange, New Jersey, the editors of *Vanity Fair, College Humor, American Mercury.*

All were to be found in the speaks, along with Polly Adler's girls, Packard dealers, publishers, and stone-age Madison Avenue types. Sporty dressers in spats, bowlers, snap brims; racketeers, auto racers, Texans ("already a plague") with their loot, and up from Washington were the exploiters of Harding, Coolidge, Hoover, stealing Teapot Dome or swindling the buyers of hot Florida lots.

The home-brew goddess of the clubs was Texas Guinan (born Mary Louise Cecilia Guinan on a ranch near Waco, Texas), once a cowgirl rider in a circus and a not very impressive actress in Western films. She realized that in 1922 her special talents—if not virtues—might best be exploited in New York, where she hit what was called by half-illiterate columnists "The Great White Way."

She was thirty-eight and looked older. Her first job was singing at the Café des Beaux Arts, where she caused no excitement among the sports and the big spenders. Texas changed her act, and as a glib mistress of ceremonies who was fast with the funny line, she was able to hold the customers' attention between the drinks of alcohol served in teacups.

The mob boss and hoodlum racketeer Larry Fay ran the El Fay night club, and he eventually lured Texas away. The two became a team that trimmed a lot of sports in town for a big night or weekend.

In time Texas Guinan night clubs appeared and vanished like aces from Houdini's sleeves. If one was closed another club opened. The federal men took bribes, but now and then they had to knock over and padlock a club selling hooch to show there was a law against selling the suff, whatever it was.

People liked to see Texas sitting on a piano, howling "Hello, Sucker." To the customers, most of them in evening clothes, her police whistle and a noisemaker called a "clacker," held high, and her line of chatter (called wisecracks) insulting to the rich and the powerful or famous were all grand fun.

Texas' red-orange-yellow hair, her big nude back—"acres of woman" —and all those teeth in that big-mouthed grin became famous. Everything in the clubs was costly, from the setups to the price for ice water. (Her big income came from fifths of what was mockingly labeled Scotch or Bourbon, sold at $25 each, and a champagne that was mostly doctored cider to which vile acids had been added.)

She also kept a lot of show girls—dancers and singers—around. Some *could* sing and some *could* dance, but none of them very well.

When they took their bows, Texas would open her big mouth and howl, "Give the little girl a great big hand!"

Texas Guinan, a densely textured roughneck, lasted out the dry era in more or less fair shape. In one year alone she is said to have banked nearly $1 million. She died in 1933, just a month before Prohibition was repealed. For all her years of loot-taking at the expense of suckers, legally she left only $38,000, three ex-husbands, and nearly a hundred girls for whom she had acted as mother hen, adviser, and agent.

The best-remembered night-club figure—perhaps the only one of all the night-club ladies (referred to on Broadway as "broads") who entered folklore—was Helen Morgan. She had a sad history of exploitation by the wrong kind of men, was battered by life, and always carried a flask of brandy in her handbag. She had a gentle, mournful face and hurt eyes. In her club she, too, sat on a piano, gowned in what looked like a soiled black peignoir, fingering a long, thin scarf as she looked blankly over the smoke-filled room. The customers became very still, some near tears, as she sang in her dark, husky, never scurrilous voice "Can't Help Loving that Man," and her other melancholy though sanguine number, "Bill."

While it was called The Jazz Age by historians who weren't there, who didn't know much of the real jazz, in most places it was never the true, pure New Orleans music, pure Dixieland, even if you'd find Jelly Roll Morton, Louis Armstrong, Bessie Smith, or even Bix Beiderbecke in some small club, or at Connie's Inn, the Cotton Club, the Alhambra Ballroom, the Savoy, or on the stage of the Paramount. Mostly it was Cab Calloway's cornball stunts, and the very talented Duke Ellington trying for concert status, Paul Whiteman—who never understood the true jazz —and clowns like Ted Lewis.

Prosperity and optimism marked this phase of the sporting life; George F. Babbitt, Edna St. Vincent Millay, Rudy Vallee, and a book called *The Green Hat* all mixed. And there was Rodolfo Alfonzo Raffael Pierre Filibert di Valentina d'Antonguolla, as he claimed he was named, but who called himself a modest Rudolf Valentino and carried off female hearts to secret complaisant dream rapes.

His funeral services in New York attracted the largest street turnout on record for an event of that kind.

27
The Nightclub Mayor

New York at the time of its most frenzied change is best remembered as the era of one man. As a teenage art student, I got to know the slim, elegant, and showy figure of James J. Walker, Mayor of New York City. We didn't, of course, move in the same circles, but as I began to sell little black and white drawings to the *New Yorker*, cartoons to the old *Life* humorous magazine, and did very minor journalism, I would attend some official cornerstone laying or perhaps a public greeting by the city of a flier or channel swimmer, even a Queen of Rumania. Any event where the freedom of the city or a mock-up of a key would be offered to some stuffed-shirt VIP. My conversations with the mayor were of no news value, but he had a politician's memory for names and faces and he'd sometimes greet me—for I had done some sketches of him. "Keep it up," he once said.

Jimmy had the charismatic charm of other Irish in public office; and his was virtually as strong as the Kennedys'.

Walker was born in 1881, on Leroy Street in the Village, "and born to Tammany, for my father was an alderman, you know, and assemblyman, too." Jimmy—hardly anyone ever called him Walker—had only Catholic elementary and high school education, and did not attend college. He claimed to have played pro baseball. He had an actor's flair and grace—a bit overripe, perhaps—but with enough skill to appear on stage in nonprofessional productions.

He also had a knack for making sentimental music, popular ragtime —what was to become Tin Pan Alley. Fingering the piano keys rather well, he set his musical sights on the popular song. Like Irving Berlin, Paul Dressler, and other composers of hit sheet music, vaudeville material, and early recordings, he hoped for success. But of all his songs, only the early lyrics he did for "Will You Love Me in December as You Do in May?" (1908) ever amounted to much.

It soon became apparent that Jimmy wasn't another Irving Berlin. The family decided to put him into politics, and in 1912 he was elected to the Assembly in Albany, becoming in time the Democratic floor leader to protect the city against the upstate Republican farmers.

Jimmy spent fourteen years in Albany performing all the tasks a Tammany man usually looked after there. It must be remembered that although Tammany had many schemes to boost the incomes of its members, it also backed a lot of bills that did aid social reform and helped the poor, which, at the same time, enabled Tammany to maintain a firm grip on political power and did no harm to their patronage. Walker had married a show girl, and while he remained on good terms with another Tammany faithful, Alfred E. Smith, the older man, a reasonably pious Catholic, frowned on Jimmy's fast and loose life.

Smith has been made the folk hero of "The Sidewalks of New York" by later historians, but he was actually a solid and cunning party man, a Tammany faithful, and he ran with the rich. He fronted for the building of the Empire State Building, and made a lot of money in real estate and the trucking industry. But though he took favors and made deals, he was honest and kept his word.

Jimmy lacked Al's stern backbone, but he had drive. In 1925 he felt that being mayor of New York City was within his reach now that bumbling Mayor "Red Mike" Hylan was out of favor with Tammany. Red Mike had listened too much to Publisher William Randolph Hearst, pulling strings in New York from his retreat at San Simeon on the West Coast. Smith closed his eyes to Jimmy's sinful living.

Jimmy was elected mayor and assumed office in January 1926, and proved that his loyalty to Tammany came first. No gleam of reform or idea of saving the city from its greed was seriously considered. He used with skill that new form of mass communication and popular entertainment—radio. (The Happiness Boys, Jones and Hare, Amos and Andy were early audience favorites.)

THE MAYOR SALUTES HIMSELF

The magazine *Vanity Fair* made the comment that Mayor James Walker—who spent so much time away from New York—could greet himself as a guest on his return. (Ross Collection)

It was the journalists and the city's publishers who built Jimmy into a glamor figure, a wit, a man for all classes. Six million New Yorkers knew his face and wiry dancer's figure, and he had a wisecrack or two reported nearly every day in the press from the *Times* to the *News*.

◆§◈◈

Jimmy Walker seemed to live to the sound of nightclub jazz. The saxophone was as much his symbol as his top hat and hip flask. Jazz had taken hold almost from the day he first impressed the city. While New Orleans saw its birth, and Kansas City and Chicago gave it scuff and elbow room, it was not until the jazz men began to gig in New York that public interest in the form really mushroomed.

The first New York applause occurred in those loud years, when Paul Whiteman, hardly an expert on the subject, gave a "Jazz Concert," and George Gershwin wrote his "Rhapsody in Blue," which to some jazz critics was a rather sleek misuse of jazz terms. But the music began to gather its followers, while Jimmy flourished and declined.

No matter where the jazz men (and women) came from, it was New York, the Big Apple, where the notice of press and public and jam session cults meant something. So over the years the city saw and heard Jelly Roll Morton (who modestly, and wrongly, claimed to have invented jazz), Bessie Smith, King Oliver, Louis Armstrong, Earl Hines, Fletcher Henderson, Benny Goodman and Coleman Hawkins, Fats Waller, and Billie Holiday. Others were to come too, much later—Ella Fitzgerald, Count Basie, Duke Ellington, Dizzy Gillespie, Charlie "Bird" Parker, Miles Davis, and Thelonious Monk.

Vanity Fair, cartoonists, and the Cotton Club, all had made Harlem a fashionable place for society to cut loose and have fun. There was the Savoy on Lenox Avenue, a ballroom like none other, and the beginning of the dances that were to be the steps of the era. The Shuffle, Black Bottom, and what was called the Charleston.

123rd Street between Lenox and Seventh avenues was Jungle Alley for the black sporting life, where bad likker and hog jowls and chitlings, fried chicken, and catfish (not yet called soul food) were to be had. The Clam House and Tillie's Inn were places where one could meet black writers, artists, actors, and dancers . . . talk knowingly with Bessie Smith and Clara Smith. In the minds of aging hedonists I talked to, memories remain of Walker applauding Florence Jones at The Nest, Connie's Inn, or Small's Paradise and listening to early Duke (Ellington), Satchmo (Armstrong), or Scat Cat (Calloway) playing "Shake That Thing," "Stormy Weather," and "St. James Infirmary."

NEW YORK SPORTS AT THE RACES
Watching the finish of a horse race at Sheepshead Bay. The wide-brimmed straw hat, or "skimmer," was made popular by George M. Cohan. (Author's collection)

Boss Tweed would have approved of how Tammany now began to loot the city, while the mayor paid little attention to what was going on. He had his quips, his womanizing, his nightclub and speakeasy life.

Protection was sold on threats of bombing by racketeers, gangs flourished, gangsters killed each other in public places for control of districts in the beer, whisky, milk, and dry-cleaning rackets.

Typical of political control of judges was the inability of an outstanding judge, David C. Lewis, to win re-election despite the unanimous endorsement of the newspapers, citizen unions, and city organizations; there was just no bucking the powerful Tammany machine.

Jimmy even outrivaled the late mayor of Los Angeles, Sam Yorty, for travel, and Sam had jet planes at his disposal. Jimmy traveled by ship across the seas, and by train to European capitals and the Florida resorts.

Besides the loot he was getting (the graft later to be exposed), his salary in that crucial year 1929 went from $25,000 to $40,000 (money that had five times or more the value it has today).

No one who did not live in New York City through the Walker era can fully comprehend the essence of a huge city in corruption.

Jimmy shared the celebrity limelight with Larry Fay, mob boss, taxi king, owner of night clubs, clip joints, organizer of the payoffs in the milk suppliers' racket. Then there was Owney Madden, the protégé of a Tammany sachem. Madden was a hijacker, alcohol smuggler, and had his tentacles in nightclubs, union racketeering, and breweries. His hobbies were raising pigeons, vast lofts of them, and promoting Primo Carnera, his pet monster, whom he pushed into the world heavyweight championship. Frank Costello, a link between Tammany and crime, ran the Unione Siciliane—later to be labeled by some as the Mafia.

The most dreaded gangster was Dutch Schultz (real name Arthur Flegenheimer). Schultz was homicidal, a paranoiac who, by some estimates, killed nearly 150 people. He was the most feared of the mob rulers in Jimmy's city. When at last he was shot down by rivals, he took a long time dying—out of his mind—muttering words that would have made Gertrude Stein proud. She never bettered his raving prose, of which "a boy has never wept nor dashed a thousand kim" is just a short sample.

William Vincent O'Dwyer was the real ruler of the city—he controlled the alcohol business of New York. No one could feel safe moving likker, buying it from rum boats, selling to speaks, unless O'Dwyer gave the nod.

One city clerk during Jimmy's best years piled up nearly $390,000 in boodle and had over two dozen bank accounts. A top public official socked away $400,000 while earning $8,000 a year in office. Mayor James Walker kept much of his fortune in metal boxes in safety-deposit vaults.

A group of prominent respectable lawyers ("A minority group, of course" [Wilson Mizner]) asked the Governor of New York, Franklin D. Roosevelt, to appoint men to investigate conditions in the New York courts. FDR wasn't too happy about the request. He needed the Tammany machine and its splendid talent for piling up Democratic votes in his move to become president of the United States. The New York delegates could become a major voice in his carrying the nomination at the next Democratic convention.

In September 1930 Samuel Seabury began an official probing of facts. He was a well-respected lawyer and a former associate justice of the State Court of Appeals. In 1916 running as a Democrat, he had been defeated for the governor's seat. Seabury began by closely questioning a number of the city's magistrates in chambers about their honesty and ethics. Many resigned suddenly because of "bad health," others abruptly formulated plans to "settle in Florida" far from the "burdens of office." Seabury called the conditions of the city's courts "a scandal . . . disgrace . . . a menace to the city."

He was already aiming at Jimmy, who was still referred to as "our dapper mayor" in the tabloid columns. He was drinking more and was involved in an affair with a show girl, Betty Compton.

Seabury's investigation was being soft-pedaled by FDR, who wanted no serious break with Tammany. But when Seabury put an informer on the witness stand, it was like an early Warner Brothers' melodrama bust-ing into headlines. The informer worked with the police vice squads in framing innocent girls and women as whores. His favorite gambit was to visit a doctor's office, scatter some money around, then strip naked before the shocked nurse—at which point the vice cops would enter on the run to arrest the staff for running a brothel. Usually there would be payoffs by the victims to the police involved in the raids.

The informer fingered twenty-eight New York patrolmen for whom he had worked his dirty striptease tricks. They were dismissed, but that hardly cleaned up the whole department.

Religious leaders formed the City Affairs Committee and presented a detailed paper directly to Franklin Roosevelt charging Jimmy Walker with a whole list of crimes and mismanagement of the city and noting the boodle and graft extracted by his appointments to public office and city jobs. FDR in person, in that cold, patrician manner he had, crisply told off the committee and their ten charges against Jimmy. FDR was beginning to taste a future in the White House. He sent the report directly to Jimmy with a well-this-is-what-they-are-saying-about-you note.

Jimmy wrote back to Albany that the committee was part of "the Socialist Party," and its leaders were "agitators and Soviet sympathizers."

However, FDR had a problem he couldn't shake. He would have liked to bury the attacks on Jimmy. But the legislature was dominated by upstate, hard-nosed Republicans. As one of them told me years later, "We had FDR over a barrel there and we rolled it over him. . . . In March [1931] we insisted on a hard-boiled committee to dig deep for rottenness in all the departments—the Tammany scum—that ran New York City. So the Hyde Park gentleman had to say yes to $250,000 in funds for the committee chairman, Sam Hofstadter, one of ours. And we kept Sam Seabury as the legal eagle to keep kicking their ass."

It all came out as the hunt went on—Jimmy's hidden graft, all the twists and turns of his Wall Street dealings. A probe of his tax files took place. But it didn't seem to prove anything wrong until a bank clerk told Seabury to keep looking for letters of credit. A quick subpoena got a full record of these letter transactions. It showed that big business and political fat cats, grafters, contractors, and taxi fleet owners had set up special funds for Jimmy, in return for which he gave them whatever they wanted in the courts, in city contracts, in protection for their illegal rackets.

One taxi fleet manipulator had delivered to Jimmy at City Hall nearly $27,000, "his share of a deal in oil stocks into which he never put a red cent." When the day of the trolley car seemed over, some eager groups set up the Equitable Coach Company to grab bus franchises, and for this favor he got a vacation in Rome and London with Betty Compton.

Officially, Jimmy lived on St. Lukes Place with a wife—but actually

HEAVY TRAFFIC ON THE BOSTON POST ROAD
The time of the Model T and solid truck tires. (Library of Congress)

FREE AIR
A sales point in this primitive gas station of the early 1920s. Gas cost 17 cents
a gallon and was pumped from a handcart. (Standard Oil photo)

he had rooms at the Ritz-Carlton, and later he transferred to the Park Avenue Mayfair Hotel.

His favorite hangout was Billy La Hiff's Tavern on West 48th Street, where the fancy newspaper crowd gathered—sportswriters with by-lines and columnists who wrote of a mythical New York of glamor and high living that they insisted was just like Main Street back home, "but with more electric signs." Damon Runyon, O. O. McIntyre, Mark Hellinger, and others, all forgotten now except for Runyon.

Jimmy's old hit of 1908, "Will You Love Me in December as You Did in May?" was being revived as his theme song, and over the years he collected $10,000 in ASCAP royalties on it. As a second office he had the old city-owned Casino on the Central Park Mall done over (at a cost to the city of $400,000) as a nightclub and posh eating place.

A high-living publisher of a chain of newspapers reaped a fortune from producing the tiles for the New York subway systems. Jimmy and the publisher opened a joint account with a Wall Street stockbroker. Again Jimmy had not one cent of his own money in this account, yet he pulled out nearly $250,000 from it. With another stockbroker Jimmy had a secret account of $1 million, two-thirds of which had come in from someplace as cash. This money could not be banked, for New York banks, unlike those in Switzerland, were not taking in numbered accounts without names, and Jimmy couldn't explain where the money came from.

Loaded with this kind of information, Seabury called all this exposure "the fatal blow to Tammany Hall." He added that it was "the first time in the history of New York that a mayor has been caught taking money with his actual receipts of the bribe."

So in May 1932 many of the people of the city of New York felt that a final dawn of reform would come about as Jimmy obeyed orders to appear before the committee.

At 8:30 A.M. all seats in the hearing room in the State Office Building on Foley Square had been filled, although the hearing would not open until near noon. Five thousand well-wishers stood on the sidewalks outside the building to cheer Jimmy, fedora brim tipped at a sharp angle, as his limousine came to a stop.

"Hi, Jimmy!"

"You tell 'em, Jimmy!"

Jimmy did a Jack Dempsey self-handshake high over his head and went in, a champion of the streets, to defend himself.

The committee room held enough of his admirers to again elicit a cheer. Senator Hofstadter made the usual threat to clear the place if that happened once more. He recovered, to turn to Samuel Seabury and say, "The committee is ready, if you are?"

Seabury said he was ready, and he asked Jimmy, "Mr. Mayor, will you be good enough to take the stand."

Guilty public men had often boldly proclaimed their innocence; Jimmy tried to do it with wit. Seabury was well prepared and he hammered away at Jimmy, avoiding the arrows of his projected charm by not staring at him directly. As Seabury began to list the mayor's odd ways of making fortunes item by item, Jimmy tried to use his humor, his comic answers, and then was stung to acid jabs. But Seabury remained calm.

Jimmy's cool began to melt, and no matter how he turned and twisted, Seabury kept holding him close, demanding detailed answers.

Jimmy began to wander in his replies, then to make certain admissions. Like most people in a bad corner, he said more than was wise.

FDR was in acute discomfort when Seabury handed to him fifteen major charges of crimes against the city by Mayor James J. Walker. The Democratic National Convention was too close, only some weeks away. Roosevelt knew he badly needed that mass of lemming-like delegates from Tammany. To dump a Democratic mayor of such a big city controlled by a powerful vote-getting machine like Tammany was madness.

Roosevelt is said to have asked one close adviser (Raymond Moley), "How would it be if I let the little mayor off with a hell of a reprimand . . . ?" No. That would be weak.

Actually, FDR was too canny a political genius to fool himself for long that after what had been proved against Jimmy Walker he could just shake a finger at him. Roosevelt, exercising his right as governor to ascertain the facts, attended a dozen sessions, sitting as an informal judge on the Walker case.

Back in New York to attend a family burial, Jimmy was meeting with the Tammany policy makers in the Hotel Plaza on September 1, 1932. Jimmy realized he was being tossed over the side. Al Smith gave it to him. "Jim, you have to resign for the good of the party."

What else was said? Not all that was discussed was fully reported. Jimmy knew this was the end of his career. He tried to keep up an ironic front, but he did not jest much. That night he sent down to City Hall a short, terse message: "I hereby resign as mayor of the City of New York, the same to take effect immediately."

BOOK EIGHT

The Depression Thirties

28
Wall Street Blues

The stock market crash of 1929 saw New York sink into despair and apathy. Life became grim and gray and hopeless, even for the middle class. Yet, at the same time, the gay life went on; there was money in misery. The gangs became more deadly in trying to grab what was left of any business. A kind of cynical nastiness overtook many of the rich.

At first few believed the Great Bull Market was dead. New York, Wall Street, the Stock Exchange had become all through the 1920s the Golden City of easy money as the common ordinary citizen—janitor, shoe clerk, plumber, housewife, auto mechanic—read and heard of something called the stock market, and the reports of how you put down a little— something called margin—to play the game. Say 10 percent of the value of the stock you bought. It was sure to go up; it always had risen, and fast. And it did, for the most part, until late in 1929.

Most of the New Yorkers my family knew were deeply involved in buying things by installment payments (the credit card and charge plates did not yet exist). Every household owned a radio set of sorts—usually with a big morning-glory horn, often battery powered, with too many tuning dials to line up to trap a station. The Model A had replaced the Model T flivver, and parking was becoming a problem in the city.

A good car cost almost a thousand dollars, but you could see in the future a Dusenberg with gold-plated fittings if your holdings in stocks kept going up. Rent for a cold-water flat began at $25 per month, but on Park and Fifth avenues there were people paying $50,000 to $60,000 a year for the kind of penthouses you saw in Metro-Goldwyn-Mayer movies.

It had been too easy; shopkeepers, actresses, waiters, taxi drivers, bankers were making paper fortunes through symbols—Wall Street letters for steel, oil, cars, chemicals—never the products themselves.

※

What had happened on October 24, 1929, to kill American faith in prosperity for investors without working for it? That fateful day the market opened in what appeared to be its usual good shape. Then a drop occurred, and brokers began to dump margin accounts that their customers weren't covering. There was a flood of selling orders.

Anything done to raise panic at the strategic wrong moment can start a cattle stampede. By noon fear and horror had set in. The ticker tape was running half an hour behind, and the board boys chalking up figures were out of step. A man standing on a New York roof doing some repairs was seen as a would-be suicide. On the basis of this slim mistake, a rumor quickly circulated that a dozen ruined stock speculators had leaped to death, or blown out their brains.

As usual, the stricken money men turned to the House of Morgan. The surviving Morgan was reported to be in Paris, in London, in Rome. Holding the bomb-scarred fort was the senior partner, Thomas Lamont. He confronted the gray-faced bankers who had secretly come to a special meeting at the House of Morgan. Lamont's plan to stop the decline seemed simple and direct: "Your banks hold six billion dollars in reserves. Gentlemen, form a pool of millions and begin to restore confidence in the stock market by buying, *buying*. Acting for you will be Morgan's floor manager, Richard Whitney."

The visitor's section of the Stock Exchange was closed, and after a good lunch, Mr. Whitney worked his way through a steaming, sweating mess of brokers, agents, clerks, and runners up to U.S. Steel's post #2. Paper millionaires of Broadway, like the Marx Brothers and Eddie Cantor, were trying to raise margin money, as were thousands of other people.

Whitney waved an offer for ten thousand shares, "205 for Steel." Since Steel was selling at 193½, the stock market floor men believed the tide was turning. Moving cheerfully about, distributing his orders, Whitney made offers for about $30 million worth of stocks. This seemed to stop the market panic.

When the bell ended the day's trading, U.S. Steel had risen to 206. Nearly thirteen million shares of various other stocks had been bought and sold. It was not until after eight o'clock in the evening that the stock tickers caught up with the day's dealings. Brokers worked through the evening and late hours phoning clients for more margin to protect themselves.

Customers began to put up cash and sell assets to meet margin calls. But as second and third calls for margin came in, and still their stocks fell, the mirage faded. Many people, having added thousands of dollars to their stock losses, dropped out or were sold out, financially ruined.

In the ensuing troubled days as more and more drops in stock prices occurred, the last margin calls went out. Even a financial newspaper had to admit it was "the greatest stock market catastrophe of all times." Someone added, "Well, we like records in America, don't we?" Millions of dollars in savings were wiped out, nearly one thousand business firms went bankrupt, and an alarming number of banks began to foreclose.

With the stock market collapse tormenting the times, and the Depression descending like a curtain of gloom, New York became a different city than it had been in the wild-living 1920s. Gone was the gloss and tinsel of fancy speakeasies, gone the Great Gatsby crowd rushing into town for night clubbing and parties in suites at the Waldorf.

It didn't all turn to dust, however. Some people still had money and didn't believe that a new, sadder city was in the making. But they were wary about spending it. On Park Avenue some of the tenants were not paying their rent (or servants).

Physically the city was in decay. Great weathered girders of unfinished luxury apartments and hotels bled rust along Central Park South. Long lines of unemployed men stood outside the soup kitchens and flophouses, many with cord-tied packs or bundles under their arms, others wearing broken shoes and worn jackets, with no shirt underneath. The entire city was rimmed, as if by besieging armies, by settlements and squatters' communities called Hoovervilles.

I remember apple sellers beating cold feet on frosty sidewalks and the first public works under FDR. Among these was the Federal Arts Project, designed to foster the pleasure of creating that came to thousands of artists, writers, actors, dancers, and unemployed journalists. The program offered a ray of hope of eating better, paying back rent, and providing assistance to down-at-heel professors, lawyers without briefs, and mechanics with no tools.

I supported three people by selling little drawings to the *New Yorker* at $9 a shot. Occasionally a cartoon of mine was accepted by *Colliers* and other popular magazines, usually at a fee of $35 for all rights. I'd do a poster for R. H. Macy's, some men's fashion drawings for Wanamaker's.

So we lived in a Depression-dominated New York. If I averaged $35 a week, we felt we were better off than the Oakies drifting west in their jalopies, blown out of the Dust Bowl and hunting a new and better destiny in a California that didn't want them.

The Federal Theater Project and the Federal Writers Project came to the city, but I didn't join them. I wasn't writing at the time and I was selling enough graphic art to get by.

We bought no new clothes and were careful of shoe leather. I drew for several faltering magazines, and filled some space as a film and music critic (!). This was paid for, not in cash, but by something called "due bills." Advertisers in New York often paid for their ads with slips of paper that could be exchanged for their products—food if you were lucky.

We would park the baby with an in-law and go off—me as film critic—to see at least three movies a day. Evenings we'd have a sixty-five-cent chicken salad at Schrafft's and go to the opera, to concerts, now as a music critic for *Golfer and Sportsman*, which never published the reviews, only the drawings that accompanied them.

The WPA in New York set men to work, if only to lean on shovels. The Group Theatre, the Federal Theater projects did amazing work ("The Living Newspaper," early Orson Welles). The Theatre Guild was active. All through the bad years the theater of Odets, O'Neill, Rice, Sherwood flourished or at least survived.

Harlem held rent parties of dancers, jazz men, and Negro intellectuals. The Village also gave parties and you brought your own bottles and cold cuts. Tammany supplied bags of coal to loyal party workers.

How did New York survive without major rioting, burning, looting of warehouses? The blacks, the slum minorities, the muscle workers, the shop girls, all the unskilled, or the skilled who had worked in factories whose chimneys no longer smoked—they all remained amazingly placid.

The blacks suffered no more than the poor whites, although legend has said they did. The Negro population had grown and would grow still more. In 1910 there had been 90,000 blacks in New York (2 percent of the population). By 1920 the war years had increased this figure to 150,000; by the end of the decade it had leaped to 330,000. No Social Security existed during the Depression.

Meanwhile, immigrant generations still lived in New York in enclaves where English was rarely spoken and where rituals—criminal, gypsy, or Talmudic—ruled. Rabbis issued divorces (getts), voodoo rites were performed in Harlem, and store-front gypsies inspected a bride for virginity.

The Jews and the Italians and other non-Wasps suffered resentment, but less than the blacks. While the Jews might not get into the better country clubs (a Westchester restricted club's board: "Well, maybe *one* Gimbel"), throughout the Depression in New York, Jews remained dedicated to charity, to taking care of one's own. But the anti-Semitic claims of the Klan and of some America Firsters that Jews were all international bankers or Communists was not proved in any of the surveys.

Among some of the young and the older Socialist sweatshop workers during this period there was a radical dream that for the thinking Jew, the agnostic, the atheist, Lenin and Stalin had the one true answer in Soviet Communism. There were, of course, Trotskyites in New York raising a fuss, the Lovestone opposition, much debating and painting of posters of a Marxist Heaven and a bestial America.

This lasted until 1939, when Hitler and Stalin signed their nonaggression pact. Many New York radicals still remained loyal to the party line, and they cheered the rigged Moscow trials, and refused to acknowledge the firing-squad executions of millions of innocent pepole.

Every New York minority group had its overseas hero. In Chinatown it was Chiang Kai-shek. Among the Irish, there was Parnell and the dead of "The Trouble." The Italians had Mussolini. His jowled cannon-ball head often hung beside the tinted wedding picture.

New York City's Italians were busy producing lawyers and doctors, composers and designers. But the city's media paid most attention to the Italian mobs. With the repeal of Prohibition the rising power of the Mafia in bootlegging became a thing of the past, so they went into waterfront racketeering, union controls, trucking, protection blackmailing schemes, whorehouses, and the pioneering of the big-time hard drugs industry.

"Italians are musical like the Negroes, have natural rhythm" (Jimmy Walker). The school kids, often hired, were mobbing Frank Sinatra at the stage doors of the Paramount, and there would be howls of delight over Perry Como, Russ Columbo, and Guy Lombardo.

The Irish managed to hang on to the city's money trees and direct its politics and contracts until a short, square Italian named Fiorello La Guardia became mayor of New York. And then they went into hibernation, as Tammany usually did when out of power, planning for their next trip on the gravy train.

❧

Nothing so pointed up the battle of the times—the have-nots against the haves—as that 1933 war between the billions of dollars of the Rockefellers and the art images of the Mexican radical Diego Rivera. It concerned the fresco painting facing the main entrance of the RCA Building in the new Rockefeller Center of New York City. The Rockefellers had decided on the overall theme for the painting in October 1932. It was to be Man at the Crossroads Looking with Hope and High Vision in the Choosing of a New and Better Future.

It's hard to believe anyone would seriously offer such windy banality to an artist as a subject in the height of a great national Depression.

ROCKEFELLER CENTER: THE PROSPEROUS BOXES

Begun in the Depression year of 1931 and finished in 1939, Rockefeller Center is now assessed at more than $260 million and pays a yearly real estate tax of more than $12 million. As David Loth, an admirer, put it, ". . . in the words of the founder, a maximum of income . . . but as beautiful as possible, too." (Rockefeller Center photo)

Radio City, in the name of the Rockefellers, offered walls to Picasso, Matisse, and Rivera. They announced it was to be a contest. The three men were to submit sketches of their ideas for the wall.

Picasso refused to see the agent who came to make him the offer, and had him thrown out. Matisse also said no; it was not his size (although he had done fine huge murals for the Barnes Collection in Philadelphia).

So the Rockefellers changed the rules. Rivera was asked to design a sketch, and *not* in competition. However, the Rockefellers, having been snubbed by Picasso and Matisse, brought in two décor makers, Frank Brangwyn and Jose Maria Sert, for the two walls adjoining the Mexican's. This didn't sit well with Rivera. Also, he wanted to work in fresco, on wet plaster, not in oils on canvas. In the end he got his way.

The artist submitted a sketch that could only be read as a revolutionary Socialistic poster mural. It showed lightning (symbolizing science) blasting a Greek god (organized religion), the execution of a Roman emperor (the end of mass-enslaving dictators), and lots of armed marching workers, a brotherhood of men at machinery producing a new world of workers, farmers, and soldiers—all surging on together to some Marxist never-never land of greener pastures. There were also slanted images showing moneymen and the wars they produced. Included were the plight of the jobless and signs of their rebelling.

Back came word on inspection of the sketch, "Sketch approved by Mr. Rockefeller."

Were they all blind at Radio City? Did they think a mural genius, a great modern artist would later make changes at their suggestion? How could anyone have missed the attempt to place a Marxist wall in a citadel of the greatest master capitalist?

By March 1933 Diego Rivera and his crew of assistants, plasterers, paint mixers, and brush cleaners (one was Ben Shahn) were in the RCA building ready to cover more than a thousand square feet of wall space for $21,000. All costs, hired hands, were to be paid for by the artist.

It was an amazing mural that went up on the wall. There was a scene of the unemployed being beaten by the police. There was a section devoted to a New York night club, showing rich socialites dancing and having a gay time. Touching this was the world as seen through the microscope—revealing, among other things, a field of syphilis germs.

Doubt had begun to appear on the faces of the directors of building in Radio City. It was not a restful mural. There was too much realism, animation. Nelson Rockefeller still had faith, and sent a note to Rivera:

> I saw your picture [in a newspaper] of you working on the mural . . . an extremely good photograph . . . it will be tremendously effective to have your mural there to greet the people as they come in for the opening.

In April the New York *World-Telegram* attacked the artist's work:
RIVERA PAINTS SCENES OF COMMUNIST ACTIVITY AND J.D., JR., FOOTS BILL.

By May 1 the artist had finished his mural, paying little attention to rumors. Four days later came a letter from Nelson Rockefeller:

> I noticed you had included a portrait of Lenin. . . . I am afraid we must ask you to substitute the face of some unknown man. . . .

Rivera was advised by some admirers to remove Lenin's head from the mural. But his staff, staunch radicals all, stated, "If you remove the head of Lenin, we will go on strike."

Rivera thought things over; he had the attention of the nation. He wrote that he would remove the dancing couples so near the VD germs and in their place show some solid American heroes such as Nat Turner, John Brown, and the inventor of the McCormick reaper, these to balance the head of Lenin, so the mural would now become a symbol of "fundamental feelings of human love and solidarity."

Who was conning whom? Nat Turner? The painting was a magnificent mural by a master wall painter. But it was also radical propaganda.

The Rockefellers acted quickly when Rivera didn't remove Lenin. Police and detectives converged on the painter and his crew as they were applying the finishing touches. Rivera was ordered off the scaffold and a bulletproof curtain was set up in front of the building. The painting itself was boarded up by carpenters, and armed guards stood before it.

Mounted police began to gather in front of the now locked-up building. The radicals of New York were alerted. In half an hour there were shouting, sign-carrying protesters in front of the RCA Building, accusing the Rockefellers of being vandals, Philistines, bastards.

Rivera was backed by John Sloan, Walter Pach, Lewis Mumford, Alfred Stieglitz, Van Wyck Brooks, George Biddle, and many others—but not by the president of the National Academy of Design, who declared the Lenin head "unsuitable," and some other conservative art groups that were delighted to see "the death knell [of] the pseudo superiority of foreign artists." Ultimately the brouhaha ruined the artist in the U.S.

A Rockefeller statement appeared—a solid guarantee about the mural's survival—in the New York press on May 12, 1933: "The . . . fresco of Diego Rivera will not be destroyed, nor in any way mutilated."

The art world and left-wing political clubs protested this was a lie. Offers were made to remove the mural from the wall without harming it. Soon after that, one calm night at the stroke of midnight, wrecking crews moved into the RCA Building with tools and power hammers and smashed the mural to dust and powder.

The Rockefellers, feeling their oats as art critics and patrons, now rejected the bland mural of Brangwyn because he had, with respect, included in it the figure of Jesus Christ.

However, Brangwyn and the Rockefellers could play ball together. The artist moved the Christ figure deeper into the shadows, and he also had him turn his back "upon the temple of the money changers."

29
New York Picks a Flower

Fiorello ("Little Flower") La Guardia, born in New York City, was also known as "Butch." Since he often favored a black headgear he was also called "The Hat."

His grandfather had been one of the Italian Red Shirts who followed Garibaldi, and saw the sellout of their hero's hopes to the set of dwarf kings. This grandfather had married a Jewish girl—one ·of those whose forefathers had been driven out of Spain by the brutal Inquisition of the Church. Fiorello's father had played as piano accompanist for the great singer Adelina Patti on her tours, and when he arrived in the United States, he stayed. And, like his father, he sought military adventure. He became the bandmaster of the 11th Infantry Regiment, U.S. Army.

In 1898 he was on his way to a small war in Cuba. In Tampa he was joined by his sixteen-year-old son, Fiorello, acting as war correspondent for the St. Louis *Post-Dispatch*. Both came down with food poisoning from the "embalmed" beef sold to the army by the big American meat packers. (It killed many more Americans than did Spanish bullets.) But father and son managed to survive. Discharged, the father moved his family to New York City, but the remaining effects of the poison killed him in 1901. Fiorello decided to study law.

By 1912, through the auspices of New York University's night law school, *F. H. La Guardia* was painted on a door over the words ATTORNEY AT LAW. In 1916 he was elected to Congress, but The Great War was straining to involve the United States and Fiorello took lessons on how to pilot a plane.

A year later he was captain of a squadron of American planes based in Italy. He flew for two years on the Austrian-Italian front, bravely fighting red tape. At war's end he was a major and had to get used to being a civilian once more. He again won the right to be called Congressman. In Washington he fought the lost cause of the League of Nations and the policies of a very sick man, Woodrow Wilson.

Fiorello despised the Prohibition Act and, as many still do, he warned and condemned the Soviet Union for its persecution of its Jews.

"New York is my home town," he insisted, and he was elected President of the Board of Aldermen of his home town.

In 1921 the Republicans knew the city was expecting them to run La Guardia for Mayor of New York, but they wanted no part of his "bleeding-heart views." It was a bad time for Fiorello—for his wife and also his small daughter were dying. The party felt all he was entitled to was the offer that he could run for Congress from the 20th District (which included a large part of Harlem). The Tammany candidate at once pulled the old ploy—accuse your rival of something racial. He insisted La Guardia was a Jew-hater, a closet anti-Semite.

La Guardia grinned at this turn of events. He offered to debate his rival, the Tammany nominee—a Jew—and in Yiddish. *Only* in Yiddish, and in every Jewish section of the city. It was a marvelous bit of one-upmanship, for he knew the Tammany candidate did not understand or speak Yiddish.

Elected to Congress, Fiorello fought those things New Yorkers disliked—the Ku Klux Klan and Mr. Andrew Mellon's tax bills, which favored the rich and created tax loopholes for them.

The 1932 Democratic victory of Roosevelt and Herbert Lehman (as Governor of New York) helped defeat Republican Fiorello La Guardia. Hoover had given the term Republican a tainted sound while New Yorkers stood in bread lines, slept on piers, froze in heatless rooms.

But FDR liked the "Little Flower," knew good stuff when he saw it. He got La Guardia, as a lame duck congressman, to sponsor many of the New Deal ideals. La Guardia did, and then retired to a cottage in Westport, Connecticut.

La Guardia saw his chance to return to New York politics as a candidate for mayor by supporting Judge Samuel Seabury in uncovering the Tammany scandals of graft and injustice under Jimmy Walker. La Guardia made such an impression that the party, again not too happy about having him on their side, nominated him for the post of mayor against the man who was finishing Walker's term after Jimmy resigned.

The Tammany Tiger growled in a dark corner of its cage while His Honor Fiorello La Guardia became the best of all of New York's mayors. He served twelve years as the city's head, being elected for three successive four-year terms. He was honest and always kept his word, and the city was run more expertly than it ever had been before. He went after the gamblers who were protected by police payoffs, he hammered at gangsters in the protection rackets, and he brought the New York City Police Department nearly back to honesty and respectability.

La Guardia put good men, nonpartisan executives, into the city system to get it back on its feet. Soon the city was again on a working, paying basis. Because it was growing shabby he hired Robert Moses as Park Commissioner. Slum clearance and low-rent housing became realities in some sections of the city. Unhappily, however, they became near slums again in a few years.

As one of Fiorello La Guardia's closest advisers told me, "The poor—they hate each other and are slobs at times. I'll say this for the 'Little Flower' on the poverty question in New York. He used to quote Bernard Shaw, 'The only thing to do with the poor is abolish them.' Fiorello did keep the subway fare at a nickel for the citizens. But his mistake was having the city buy the transit lines. Whoever came after him had the city raise the fare and today it's up, up. While you could keep a corporation from raising fares, go fight City Hall.

"My kids liked him reading the *Katzenjammer Kids* Sundays over the radio when there was a newspaper strike. He was a great Popeye."

In 1945, after three terms as mayor La Guardia announced he would not run again. Disliking the candidates of his own and the New Deal Party, he supported the Tammany man, William O'Dwyer, who later left office under a cloud, accused of friendship with some shady individuals.

The Little Flower expected some important office on the national scene—a job, perhaps, in Europe. While Harry Truman was loyal to the Prendergast gang—he pardoned the boss out of a federal prison—he turned his back on Fiorello.

La Guardia wrote a column for *Liberty*, did milk commercials on radio. But he discovered that few people really care very much after you've had your turn at bat and are sitting on the sidelines. He was seriously ill at the end. When Fiorello died in his sleep, in September 1947, people came forward to say he was the greatest, the longest-running reform mayor in office New York ever had.

❧

As I turned the pages of old newspaper files for the 1930s, I was amazed to see how many of the events that had seemed so important at the time now were merely sad past history forming a background to the years I had spent in New York. The headlines were large in October 1931 when Al Capone was sentenced to prison for income tax fraud. But I had forgotten the Japanese Empire had moved in that same year to occupy Manchuria, and my friends in protest had refused to join me at a Japanese eating place on Third Avenue.

And was it in the summer of the next year that I had gone over to New Jersey to sketch the turmoil resulting from the kidnapping of the Lindberghs' baby? New York had tossed nearly every reporter and picture taker into the story, trying to satisfy readers' interest. Yet all the time the kidnapper and killer was living in the Bronx.

By 1933 New York Jews by the thousands were beginning to fill out legal papers to bring people out of Germany, where Hitler had just been made chancellor. I was personally touched by world change when FDR proclaimed a bank holiday; I had ninety-six dollars—all my wealth—on deposit in a closed New York bank, and it was years before I got back at least eighty dollars of it.

The night of December 5, 1933, I was with a group of artists, writers, theater and advertising people as well as college couples. We were helping to close our favorite speakeasy on East 52nd Street, for Prohibition was over. It died by law that night.

There was the death of Will Rogers in a plane crash in Alaska, and the Italian invasion of Ethiopia. So I sold a drawing I had made of Rogers during an interview, and United Press, just for a moment, thought of sending me to cover a war. It was in July 1936 that Franco began to destroy the Spanish Republic, and I was to sketch a war.

When I came back in 1938, New York had changed. The hangdog look of grim survival of the last memories of the Depression virus was gone. All the unfinished buildings were finished and rented. There was a briskness and a new pattern to women's styles in the city. Everyone on the editorial pages expected war in Europe as Hitler proclaimed *Anschluss* with Austria. I also arrived in time to be caught in one of the major catastrophes to hit the New York metropolitan area.

Leaving out street battles, like the 1863 Draft Riots or the Harlem Street uprisings, the three biggest disasters to hit New York were the Great Blizzard of 1888, which isolated the city; the Black Tom Explosion during World War I, which did a lot of shattering of windows and overturning of plates in the city; *and* the September 1938 hurricane.

I was staying in a rented waterfront cottage at Blue Point, Long Island, working on a novel, when the air went dead and someone in the household felt in the atmosphere "a sense of doom" (it was that kind of a household). The point was made that we should pack and get back to New York—which we did as the wind came up and trees and poles began to fall. The sea broke through Fire Island that night and all the cottages we had lived among were destroyed and the people drowned.

By the time we reached Brooklyn ancient trees were blocking many streets and telephone and power lines were down. I remember seeing huge signs and billboards sailing by. We continued into Manhattan, where the roar of the wind was fierce and frightening. Ash cans and loose timbers were moving like projectiles, and signs of all kinds were soaring through the air like rigged sails.

Subsequently I became aware of New York as a journalistic center of the world. Wire services, radio news, daily newspapers, and news magazines were briskly informative. I was soon to go to work for *Time* as an editor. New York was a city of impressive gossip and rumor. One read, listened to Edward R. Murrow, H. V. Kaltenborn, Gabriel Heatter, Lowell Thomas, and others. Hanson Baldwin was a military expert.

The news magazines were rising in importance, and for many people *Time* had become, with its "March of Time" on radio and on film, the voice of wisdom mixed with a hint of doom. But nothing was as popular as Amos and Andy, Lum and Abner, Vic and Sade.

It was the last decades of a New York with at least half a dozen major daily newspapers of merit, plus high-circulation magazines in power—magazines that were doomed, in time, to succumb to television.

Close up, as warnings of the coming war emblazoned the horizon, the publishing world of New York was never the romantic, interesting news area it appeared to the outlanders beyond the Hudson.

I was hired to "help change *Time* style," which had been mocked by many, best by Wolcott Gibbs in the *New Yorker* with some famous last lines: "Backward ran sentences until reeled the mind. . . . Where it will all end, knows God!"

Unlike most *Time* people who left angry and bruised, I enjoyed my stint with that fascinating chunk of fast-paced journalism Luce had produced. The pay was good, the demands slim, the company stylish, almost foppish. Its air of snide rancor, I felt was the proper way to impress its type of reader. Its projection of a philosophy that had all the answers seemed to me to be a marvelous snow job, expertly carried out.

In W. A. Swanberg's *Luce and His Empire*, I am quoted as saying of Henry Luce, "He was not at all the evil man most people thought him. He was, as he saw it, God's classmate, and any slanting or twisting of journalism was for God and Yale."

Luce's great problem was that he lacked the ability to relate with the common people. It was a fault he shared with Adlai Stevenson.

I rather liked Henry Luce. He had the same quality that Churchill had (without the Churchill wit or hedonism). It was a boy's view of the world—simple, direct, built on homegrown generalities.

～§§～

"This is a valley of ashes—a fantastic farm where ashes grow like wheat in ridges." So wrote F. Scott Fitzgerald in his 1925 novel, *The Great Gatsby*, about the depressing desolation of the Flushing Meadows. Here one "Fishhooks" McCarthy, a deserving Tammany man, and his Brooklyn Ash Removal Company had been creating the largest ash dump in the world for thirty years. The town of Flushing on Long Island Sound, first settled in 1645, was just outside Manhattan. By the 1920s the ash desert was a smelly, dusty, smoldering version of one of Dante's Hells.

Long-range plans called for covering the mess with topsoil and converting the area into a public park. And to meet the cost of the conversion it was decided to hold a World's Fair on Flushing Meadows' ash heaps in 1939. Mayor La Guardia was sold on the idea.

Even for those days the costs were heavy. Robert Moses, the Fair's major planner, was a man whose parks and bridges projects had helped make New York fairly well marked as to exits and entrances.

Moses' work crews began leveling the huge ash heaps; two lakes were dug; Flushing Bay's waterfront was rebuilt and a boat harbor was created. Topsoil, trees, shrubs, and grass appeared like stage sets. And "the fairyland of fair buildings" gradually became a reality.

The theme was The World of Tomorrow, a rather apprehensive, ironic concept, for Hitler was on the move in Europe, the Blitz was due to fall on London, and as for France, said a returning journalist, "it would hold behind the Maginot Line." The fair opened in the fall of 1939. Soon the panzers would move in their blitzkrieg into the Low Countries.

Thirty-five million people attended the New York World's Fair, which ran into 1940. The World of Tomorrow was mostly commercials for America's big advertisers and those nations who bought space and sold everything from Wiener schnitzel to toy tom-toms. I attended with my daughter Joan, then five years old. I was living nearby, in Great Neck, Long Island. I still have some of my notes on visits to the fair:

> This is not the first NYC World's Fair. New York held one in 1853, copied the Crystal Palace Victorian, a fair in England, and inspired, some felt, too many new-fangled ideas in the use of glass and cast iron.
>
> Today at the WF Joan found the Borden's milk display, with a live Elsie the Cow lying in a real bed. We spent most of the day there between snacks. When I could get away, I saw exhibits that hint The World of Tomorrow will be an H. G. Wells inhuman collection of shapes that are created to photograph but are not very livable.

A Time of Splendor
Air view of the 1939–1940 New York World's Fair, showing Trylon and Perisphere as the theme center. (Wide World Photos)

The food is only fair, mostly bad. Some few posh eating places, but overpriced and service lousy, hot food usually cold. Jewel show great. Soviet exhibit large, depressing, their machines on show shoddy. Girls, girls, tired feet, yelping kids, long lines waiting to enter free exhibits.

In 1946 the United Nations took over the surviving Assembly Hall at Flushing Meadows, and the nations sat and talked and did very little else until 1952, when the UN moved to its present site on the East River.

In 1960, with peace more or less official on the planet, it was decided that New York needed a second World's Fair, 1964–1965, on the same spot as the first.

The Fair theme this time was a little fearful of making too many promises about a greater tomorrow. What was picked "had a poor sound," Henry Luce told us over a very good lunch. The theme was Man's Achievements on a Shrinking Globe in an Expanding Universe, and as a tail to that there was added the objective of the Fair, Peace Through Understanding. Truman had thrown two atom bombs on Japanese civilians, the dreadful Korean War had petered out into Koreans slaughtering other gooks (GI term for natives), and the disaster of our Vietnam "police action" with "American advisors" was being brought to a furious boil. Peace was finding it difficult to find a perch.

The Fair was impressive as I toured it with some of New York's avant-garde painters, even if U.S. Steel's armillary sphere, the Unisphere, didn't please the abstract school of New York artists rallying around Jackson Pollock's spillage, the Chinese-laundry-ticket art of Kline and de Kooning's disemboweled women. A whole new school of art had appeared in the 1950s. Through clever dealers and publicity it had emerged to establish New York City as the new Paris of abstract, free-flow action painting. "However, it already was becoming passé as Pop and Op took over as the IN themes for the art freaks" (Helen Wurdemann).

While the artists sneered at the fountains and the splendid night lighting, the public enjoyed the New York World's Fair. From Madrid General Franco himself okayed the design of the Spanish Pavilion. The Vatican, under the great Pope John XXIII, sent over Michelangelo's revered *Pietà*, which, however, was so overlit that it was almost vulgarized.

There was no peace at the Fair either. There was picketing, attempted stall-outs of cars on the roads to the Fair, a stall-in for Civil Rights. Of the one hundred pickets, thirty were arrested. A Pinkerton guard, one of forty, was booked for kicking one of the pickets. As the cops and Pinkertons swarmed over them, the protesters chanted: "Moses must go, [Governor] Rockefeller must go! [Mayor] Wagner must go!"

THOUSANDS BID FAREWELL TO THE FAIR
Throngs of people mill about in the vicinity of the Unisphere and the fountains in this photo, taken from the air on October 17, 1963, the last day of the second New York World's Fair. Nearly half a million paid admissions were recorded at the gates of the Fair as it approached the end of its two-season run. (Wide World Photos)

THE UNITED NATIONS ON THE EAST RIVER
Called the world's biggest bookend, the United Nations remains a debating club without much clout. (United Nations photo)

Mayor Robert F. Wagner, Jr., was an earnest, well-meaning man. But the press and the public often presented him as a bumbling, butter-fingered son of a great father, the late Senator Robert F. Wagner, Sr. Actually New York City was becoming a problem no mayor, hard worker *or* fuddy-duddy, would ever again be able to handle properly.

Pope John XXIII died, and Pope Paul VI came to New York to address the United Nations and visited the Fair in October 1965. By then nearly fifty-two million people had paid to go through the gates. Robert Moses juggled words to find in the new Pope "the paterfamilias of the world, rather than the Holy Father."

No one has yet erected a statue to Robert Moses—a Yale man, '09; Oxford '11; Ph.D. Columbia—for his prose style. But as New York City Commissioner of Parks from 1934 to 1960, he created Jones Beach, one of the most magnificent park areas and waterfronts in the nation, in addition to seventeen miles of other beaches, 20,000 public acres, nearly 700 playgrounds, and fifteen swimming pools.

From 1954 to 1963 he was chairman of the State Power Authority and built both the $720-million Niagara Power Project and the $650-million St. Lawrence Power Project. As chairman of the Triborough Bridge and Tunnel Authority, he saw to the creation of seven beautiful, awe-inspiring bridges and two tunnels. To this add the East Side Airline Terminal, the Coliseum, and a raft of expressways, parkways, and highways, too many to count. He coordinated the erection of the waffle-thin UN building, and was one of the founders of Lincoln Center.

BOOK NINE

The War Years

30
Flags on Fifth Avenue

I was standing on a quiet street when someone said to me, "The Japanese are bombing Pearl Harbor." I should have been prepared, the city should have been prepared. But we weren't. In 1939 Poland had gone down to a blitz as swift as the Chopin "Minute Waltz." The French had sat in slippers (I remember the Times Square newsreels) in the Maginot Line, and the English went to digging up Hyde Park, sending their children into the country and celebrating Dunkirk as a victory.

It had become the phony war, as we wrote of it, and on Fifth Avenue and Park Avenue the best people were packing Bundles for Britain. Then in June 1940 the moving sign on the *Times* building read GERMANS IN PARIS. A year later Hitler attacked Russia.

Now, in December 1941, the U.S. Pacific Fleet was burning in Pearl Harbor and I began to write of the activities in Brooklyn Navy Yard. The army and navy uniforms, which had been seen in increasing numbers in Times Square and in Radio City Music Hall, seemed to flood toward embarkation points.

31

New York and the Atoms

During World War I, as already noted, a German zeppelin officer, Kapitan Peter Strasser, had planned to bomb New York. But his demands were filed away by Admiral Reinhard Scheer, marked *"Nein."* During 1917–1918 the German high command had other problems more urgent than flying the new gas bags—the super zeppelins—across the Atlantic to bomb an American city. But in World War II Hermann Goering, director of German air power, began to dream the old dream of attacking the city from the air. He gave orders for research on planes able to cross the ocean and drop five-ton blockbusters on "the arrogant folk over there."

Serious study was given to the project. Maps were drawn and targets marked out on Manhattan's heartland. Air Defense Command of the Eastern coast line took very seriously any rumors about bombing New York. At midday, December 9, 1941, Mitchell Field was alerted by an air-raid alarm reporting unidentified planes approaching from the east.

Bombers and Air Cobras—these last with cannon in their noses—roared into the air to protect New York, some of the planes fanning out to hunt the sea. Whatever it was that had caused the alert—Canadian

258

geese or odd cloud formations (radar was still *very* primitive)—no Nazi *Jagdstaffel* of bombers ever showed their crooked crosses over New York.

Meanwhile, the wartime city still had its best mayor. La Guardia, forceful, honest, with an active personality, had the voice of a Disney toy and a desire to make the wartime city truly noble. As German U-boats prowled off the Eastern coast and dead men in life jackets coated with fuel oil were cast up on the Jersey coast from torpedoed ships, the mayor worked harder.

When some of the city's politicians insisted the mayor have an official home worthy of the city, he turned down the Charles M. Schwab seventy-five-room French palace, with all its gold and marble and grand staircase, picking instead Gracie Mansion as a mayor's abode. It was a good colonial house on the East River at East 88th Street, with pleasant porches and fireplaces. There had once been a fort of sorts on the place, until a rich Dutch merchant named Gracie built the present wooden federal-styled house in 1799. The city somehow became the owner of Gracie Mansion in the late 1890s, and used it for various purposes until it became the official home for New York mayors.

As World War II progressed, the city became more crowded and desperate in its hunt for pleasure. Rationing came, and with it the dealing in ration coupons. Black marketing, profiteering took over; from the grocery clerk to the Mafia boss, it was "What's in it for me?" Soldiers and sailors on leave made New York the Mecca for what could be their last days on earth.

Meanwhile, the Dr. Strangeloves were busy at Columbia University. John R. Dunning and Enrico Fermi were blasting uranium with neutrons to split the atom, the idea being that once they did that a great deal of energy would be let loose. And energy could be turned into horrendous explosive force never before seen by man.

Then on January 25, 1938, "a sad day for our earth" (Carl Sandburg), the scientists started their final experiment, using the cyclotron in the cellar of the Pupin Physics lab at Columbia University. Setting their devil's brew together, their material in position, they switched on and stared at the oscilloscope. Then it happened. Great strong fruit-green lines shot out as they split uranium, releasing atomic energy through two hundred million electric volts. Thus the Age of the Doomsday Bomb was born.

At the New York Public Library—a library serene behind its slumbering stone lions on Fifth Avenue—another impressive event was taking place. A hunt was going on for an old Mexico City directory. National intelligence had been at work trying to break the Japanese Navy Code. The code, they discovered, was keyed by this out-of-date Mexico City directory. The library found the book in its files—the only surviving copy, it was said, in the Western world (Mexico had none)—and with its aid the Japanese code was broken.

A whole group of specialists invaded New York, to live in the city, often to come and go on hush-hush missions. The Signal Corps was making army and navy films. Movies about how to be a proper killer, how to survive, how to face capture. And who the enemy was. Scores of authors, screenwriters, cameramen, and directors congregated in New York, drank, made love, fought each other, went to operas and dives, got drunk, yet managed to process thousands of miles of film.

Much of it was helpful, some of it worthless and unneeded. I remember working on a film about a new-type tank and special tank gun, long after it was proved in battle in North Africa that the tank and the gun were ineffective and would not be produced in any great number.

New York was riddled with home shop inventors. In the cellar of his home on Third Avenue, George Hyde produced for the armed forces of the United States the light and tactical M-3 machine gun. I remember talk that the invasion of Europe was held up until eight million M-3s could be made and sent overseas.

Meanwhile, up at Columbia, now that the professors had split the atom, the problem was how to get the nation to accept this new hope of a superkiller and to make use of it. Albert Einstein was recruited to contact President Roosevelt about turning the deadly package into an atom bomb. Einstein wrote a letter that was delivered to FDR by a partner of Lehman Corporation, a Wall Street firm.

FDR read it and agreed further action should be taken. At Columbia the professors were "busy as Santa's helpers at Christmas" (a fellow professor), building an atomic furnace to make the atom bomb possible. Money began to flow into the "Manhattan Engineering District" (later shortened to "Manhattan Project").

By 1941 the professors had more space and tons of graphite and uranium oxide were being stockpiled on the college grounds.

Soon, with progress made, the Manhattan Project was on its way to a safer inland site. The first self-promoting nuclear chain reaction took place on a squash court at a Midwestern university.

"The scientists were a little late. The war in Europe had ground down in May. All the Nazis were now claiming to be innocent Germans" (Elliot Paul). But the bomb could still be tried out on living subjects. On August 6, 1945, a bundle was dropped on Hiroshima, followed later by a drop on Nagasaki. *The New York Times'* crawling news sign was announcing that President Truman was making it official; the full surrender of Japan had taken place.

◈

New York and Mayor La Guardia both came out of the war sick. He would not run for mayor again. He had done a great deal for the city, but he was now faltering and would soon die. La Guardia was supporting a fusion ticket headed by William O'Dwyer.

Some felt that O'Dwyer—lawyer, politician, and lover of good times —was too much in the Jimmy Walker mold, "cursed with Irish charm." He had been a district attorney, a solid Tammany man filling positions, as was only proper in victory, with the party faithful. O'Dwyer had connections with the wrong people, uniting them on occasion with other Tammany chiefs. Yet the New Yorkers elected him. To celebrate, the sixty-year-old mayor-elect and a young fashion model were married in Florida. O'Dwyer soon had a scandal involving his police department invading horse betting organizations that were being protected and left the mayor's office through the medium of President Truman making him our Ambassador to Mexico.

Before leaving, O'Dwyer took care of the boys, handing out $125,000 in salary raises. Among the recipients was a fire commissioner later jailed for blackmail and extortion in the matter of fire department permits.

Harry Gross, who ran a $20-million bookie ring in New York, testified that he and all the big city bookies had been forced to shell out "campaign expenses" and that the fire commissioner was the collector.

New York had come out of World War II a different city. One of its more significant changes was the fact that it now had a bigger welfare load, with more and more blacks and Puerto Ricans taking over sections of the city. Its streets were becoming more unsafe.

The Police Commissioner and his staff resigned. They didn't want to go but they went. Two hundred policemen were caught with their hands out. One hundred sent in their resignations. Others were fired. Only a handful were convicted of taking bribes. If city justice seemed ineffectual, would the federal government do better?

In 1951 the Kefauver Committee began its sittings in New York in the Federal Building. There was television coverage to record the parade of hoodlums, informers, killers, drug peddlers, pimps, and Mafia big shots brought before the cameras. Senator Estes Kefauver, a lanky Daniel Boone type who had hopes of the White House, put on a grand show.

Frank Costello, the boss of the city's crime syndicates, appeared. He blandly stated he knew of no crime syndicate, and that he wasn't head of one. What if someone testified, "Costello reached the heights of his power in New York politics. . . . [He had] complete domination over Tammany Hall." Where was the proof? Of course it was true Tammany now was headed by Carmine de Sapio, the first non-Irish head of the organization. (He would soon go to prison for a city shakedown scheme.)

Costello admitted he and de Sapio and the Tammany leaders knew each other. "I knew them, know them well." Friendship was no crime.

O'Dwyer flew up from Mexico to answer the committee's questions. Yes, he testified, Costello was a sinister power in Tammany Hall. Yes, he had thought the police department was clean and had called the investigation of it a witch hunt. Yes, bookmaking was all over the city when he was mayor. Yes, he had visited Costello in his home. Yes, there had been top men of Tammany there too.

O'Dwyer resigned as Ambassador to Mexico in 1952, stayed away from New York until 1961. When he returned to the city, he joined a large law firm. He never again ran for public office. At times he would defend himself, "I've never been charged with a crime, or been convicted."

True. But he was a stranger in the changing city he no longer knew. The streets were given over to sounds of Spanish, and the odor of red beans and rice filled the air. The gay liberation, the black revolution were making it a different city.

BOOK TEN

Into the Sixties and Seventies

32
Local Color and Genes

One who took the sixties seriously was Sidney Hook, well-known philosopher and educator:

> There have been periods in the past where life in the cities was unsafe, but I don't recall in my own comparatively long life any period in which people living in the cities felt as if they were in a state of siege as soon as night fell. In New York a woman will very rarely go out at night without an escort.

While the black revolution has been written about in great detail, much of its background—its growth from the Harlem and Brooklyn ghettos—has not been fully presented to the average citizen. Black writers like James Baldwin and LeRoi Jones have given sharp, acid pictures of the Negro individual as involved in a major change. But often there is a sour resentment, a hatred in their writing that lacks balance.

They have become addicted to the idea of the modern city as the incubator of intolerance, producing not healthy citizens, but victims, as described by the glum German historian Oswald Spengler. In his *Decline of the West,* he, too, doesn't like "the stone colossus of the cosmopolitan city." For to him it is the sure sign that such a city comes only at the end of "the life span of each great culture." And the city dweller is taken over by what he had himself created, the city, and becomes "finally its victim."

The black resentment against the city's whites keeping "them in their place" began with the lynchings and murders of New York Negroes in the Draft Riots of the Civil War. But it did not become really vocal with certain extremists like Marcus Garvey until the 1920s. It grew all during that decade, when going to Harlem for fun and sex was the "in thing" with café society and thrill hunters.

What brought New York to facing, in the 1960s, the true facts, was a rioting city and much burning and vandalism. Also the rise of Black Muslims (The Nation of Islam), Malcolm X, the Black Panthers, and revolutionaries and fanatics, some of whom were dedicated to cop killing.

It was not only grinding poverty that made the tragedy of the blacks a problem in the city; there were drugs—from pot pushing to deadly heroin. Those addicted found themselves chained by habits that, with inflation, could cost $100 a day, and could only be paid for by breaking and entering, mugging, prostitution, and the rackets.

Not much attention was paid to the fact that not only was the city infected with crime but that most of the black outlaws and criminals directed their crimes against decent, law-abiding Negroes.

Nor has this been helped, a retired New York judge told me, "by the fact that you can't get most juries with even one black juror present to bring in a conviction in even the most solid case of murder or violence. Either they fear retaliation, or their attitude is that anything for a black soul brother or sister is against Whitey.

"This badgering of Whitey has carried as far as trying to remove all white members from the National Urban League, the NAACP, and CORE. If Adam Clayton Powell, the Harlem preacher and playboy congressman, did nothing else, one must admit he did give the Negro the idea that black could be fun if you were bold enough."

Now, near the middle of the 1970s, New York City is one-seventh black, and the percentage is rising fast. The black population has a progressive minority of its own—the working wage earner, the civil service employee, the growing number of black doctors, dentists, and professional people in insurance, banking, and publishing. But, in the main, the slums are welfare enclaves accepting the rackets, the black pimps and their stables of prostitutes, the drug pushers.

Nevertheless, black progress has been made. One reads the reports of blacks in the once closed unions of hard hats, involving tough, hard-bitten construction workers in the building trades. And most big corporations and industrial giants have well-organized hiring programs that include concentrated efforts to hire people from minority groups. Black actors and models are given places in television commercials and advertising. Black sales personnel appear in all the better shops.

To penetrate into the Harlem of today is almost impossible for the white man. The writing by the blacks on the subject—even if good—is prejudiced, as one would expect. James R., a Negro student in one of the writing classes I taught at a college, had showed great promise but gave up writing to join the Black Panther movement. He helped me with the background of a novel I was writing that needed some black ghetto details. Several times he took me up to the fringes of Harlem. I have the notes of a trip to meet one of the black leaders.

James R. was delighted he could show me "a real proud ass black Lenin. Going to take you to meet one of the black revolutionaries. Calls himself Yobbo now. Yobbo says you'll be safe if you want to go with me."

We took a taxi with a black driver up past 125th Street. A light rain fell, and I regretted the insistent feeling that I was entering an enemy camp. I couldn't think why they should be my enemy; I wasn't a bleeding-heart liberal or a hard-nut reactionary. I considered myself an observer.

The taxi soon brought us into the black belt. The people all seemed to know James. They greeted him with, "Hi, what you doing away from the white shucks scene and with us badass loose folk?"

Harlem was certainly active, even in the damp, rainy weather, as we passed porno shops, wino alleys, soul food stores, populated by standing or strolling studs, rock pimps, chicks in A-1 racing pants and dashikis.

After a row of barbecue shops, beauty salons, and bars, we reached a house front painted birthday-cake pink with windows featuring Che Guevara, Flip Wilson, and Al Fatah posters. We went into a narrow hallway where blacks of both sexes, in belled herringbone or blue denim trousers slowly made way for us.

A young man came over, "Hi, Jamo. Mah bird been makin' round with stray studs, so I put the muscle to her—and I come up Wednesday for a shucks scene. What you think?"

"Thirty days if you didn't use a knife."

"Naw, I just give it to her on her smart-cattin' smile with my fists." He leaned over and whispered, pointed a thumb ceilingward.

As we climbed the rickety stairs, I could smell pot, okra, pinto beans, doggie odors, yams, and fish frying. James knocked on a brown door.

The door opened and a white girl with huge blue eyes, naked except for a set of beads, blinked at us, shook her uncombed blond hair.

"Wing it."

"We're expected."

She blinked again. There was no calculated insolence in her stare. "Oh, it's you. I'm real stoned, Jano. Come on in. I gotta sack out."

The flat was long and narrow, a series of rooms attached one to the other with no hallway—all full of cots and mattresses on the floor, but no occupants. The rooms smelled of grass, bug powder, and decay.

We came to a figure in the front room seated in a bay window on a white contour chair beside a color TV set. He was a short, plump man, stained the color of an overripe lemon, dressed in a red and gold dashiki, a beret, Black Watch plaid pants, and cordovan brogues. He wore dark shades, which he lifted off his eyes. James introduced me to Yobbo.

He did not rise but held out a hand with a blue-stoned ring on it.

"James, you still riding that Honda-riding crotch-spreader?"

I said, "You're a lawyer?"

"Nobody black cares to talk in the Man's fink courtroom. No Fili-pino, no true black brother is alive inside the Establishment—catch? We go for face-offs."

"It seems to work."

"You station-wagon suburban rape-fantasy folk, you got all the wrong ideas about us. You need us." He laughed. "The spectacle of evil is a reassurance to the good. Black is nasty. White is good."

"I've got no preconceived ideas."

"Sure, sure. How about your society folk, the limousine liberals? Oh, they let us do a mau-mau face-off in some big fancy pad. A real badass rubble. We bring along some Maoist revolutionaries, do the slant-eyed Marxists' sexy stunt with pendants, lots of beads, Yoruba-Afro hairdos . . . Show is a big shakedown."

The little plump man moved his contour chair way back.

"We can't stay satisfied. We must always ask for more from Whitey."

I heard a lot more—a half-hour of things I had heard before. We parted with a handshake. Yobbo shot back the chair until he was lying on his back, pulled down his Cuban shades and closed his eyes. I had not penetrated far into black revolution.

Down in the street some children were kicking around empty cartons of Dash and Whiz. The young studs still stood around kidding some hard-looking chicks, who, James indicated, were street prostitutes.

"Yobbo is sure clever," said James, stepping round some refuse. "One of the best law students they had at Columbia. Got involved with some—well, never mind what—the police busted him. He's been out of jail a year now. The revolution couldn't get along out here without him. He keeps the ghettos in tune—but not exploding. Just mad."

"Is he any help to these people?"

"He keeps them excited. So they're living at high speed, man."

Later I heard that during the time of the Knapp Commission reports Yobbo had been murdered. It was all confusing. The drug pushers had done it, or the Panthers, the Muslims, Federal Narcs, or New York police on the take. As James said, "He sassed them all, and he knew too much about their ways."

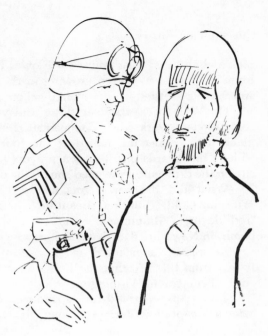

33
The Wars of Signs and Slogans

As the 1960s slid into the 1970s, there was a kind of reversing of roles. Walter Lippman, the house pet of liberals in 1968, had come out for all to "Vote for Nixon." And the women's liberation feminist movement began to develop howls from strange organizations that were pure chauvinism, such as SCUM (Society for Cutting Up Men).

The right wing, too, went in for acronyms, but without much lightness or shock. The Birch Society produced such bumper stickers as SYLP (Support Your Local Police), MOTOREDE (Movement to Restore Decency), and TRAIN (To Restore American Independence Now).

The late 1960s brought a mocking, raucous version of the city. The "Stop the War" peace marchers were active, and the reaction of the hard hats to their presence in the streets was bloody. The blue-collar workers, always disliking educated people, saw a chance to strike a blow against freedom of speech.

In April 1967 Central Park was the rallying point of the Flower Children, carrying pots of blooms to exchange, a crowd of smiles, a lot of Day-Glo clothing, jump suits, and peace symbols. The bands played rock and all lifted their voices for Flower Power. Public exposure to new forms of protest had been growing in the city, and to the older citizen and the more settled-in apartment dwellers, it was public madness.

On Wall Street the war stocks did well, and bankers and brokers commuted to work from Connecticut, Long Island, by yacht and sea-plane with connecting ramps at the foot of Wall Street. In the East Village the beards and the Zen prayers made news, and to the senior citizen the drug culture seemed something out of science-fiction.

What did the new terms mean? Like "teeniebopper," "balling," "Yucatan Gold," "Black Is Beautiful," "narcs," "uppers," "downers" and "red devils," "Minutemen." And even nice family girls were making bombs in New York flats that sometimes went off too soon.

An antiwar sign asked, LYNDON, HOW MANY KIDS YOU KILL TODAY? It was from the city that the buses were loaded to go down to march on the Pentagon in Washington.

Twenty-five-year-old Kay, spending a few months on a fashion magazine as a caption writer, went along. She wrote to me as follows:

> Marchers from the loft studio and the Third Avenue bars entered political folk art. When the November Moratorium was really giving us all a high, I marched with natives of New York, like Norman Mailer, coy in reporting of it, all in third-person prose. Then came mass illegal arrests by the fuzz—thousands of us, and a concentration camp set up in Washington Ball Park. I didn't know it but already the powder train was laid for Watergate. Some of the New Yorkers who did march saw it as a test between God or the President for top billing.

In the opinion of some people New York City was under siege from then on, by hippies, muggers, carriers of Viet Cong flags at meetings behind the New York Public Library. Kay went on:

> But what busted everything wide open for my family, was the city in the grip of "them" in public view—the march in June 1970 of the big Gay Liberation parade out in the streets—thousands moving up Sixth Avenue, hands or fists lifted high, demanding to be treated as equals, and cheering for *Gay Power! Gay Power! Less Population! More Deviation.* My father said the city was going to Hell in a basket.

I know Kay's family. Their shock at any change in city life was traumatic. Their city of the well-off middle class and the proper middle-aged "seemed to have melted like a snowflake" (Kay's father). There had been the New York of 1920 of the grandparents, so well embalmed in the gangster epics and speakeasy sagas of Helen Morgan, Harry Richmond, Edward G. Robinson, and James Cagney. The Roaring Twenties, was it?

And then the Depression and "that sonofabitch FDR." But everybody rallied and got together to Beat the Japs and Nix the Nazis.

"Crusades, really," Kay's father told me over his best Scotch. "It had been bad enough, the coming of the Puerto Ricans and the Panthers spoiling it for the good Negroes, the civil service ones. But the homosexual thing right out in the open and in Times Square. I mean, I'm no saint, but what has New York come to?"

Kay had made it early as one of the Beautiful People around the Jackie Onassis gang. Kay's mother had been a café society doll, and her grandmother had actually seen Zelda Fitzgerald jump into the fountain in front of the Plaza. Kay, bright, wary, a city-child "Eloise" grown up, was in direct line—the end product of generations of New Yorkers, all by birthright topping the mode of the period.

Later, in a meeting I had with Kay she elaborated on her feelings.

"Three different New York cities are still alive and snapping fingers. Grandma, Mother, me. This gay thing, of Underground movies by Warhol, or the tatty Zen of Allen Ginsberg never shocked us women. It only lasts for a time, grandma says. How right she is. Take Norman Mailer. He's an old man, right for New York TV talk shows. But let's face it. A lot starts here—any kind of new ideal, a game, black humor—both kinds. I mean, look at the way reading to jazz records came on, the Beatles, the Free University, and the best gauge, the Golden Red from Mexico, and blasting grass never did go away. But the Peppermint Lounge with Chubby Checker, and the *Telegram, Tribune, Sun*—they're all gone.

"My aunts and uncles shake their heads about the gays—often one of their best friends—Yale, Union League, America Firsters—coming out of the closets and the women's libbers in ugly Charles Adams' hairdos and owl glasses. Really! What can my family find to do? Free clinics, milk funds? It's not what it was in Jimmy Walker's days.

"Art? Don't you believe it. Art, painting, exhibitions in New York are not for the really smart people anymore. It's for collectors who need social status."

Seeing New York at the beginning of the 1970s, to see it through Kay's young eyes, is to miss the young poor, the welfare young, the liberal college student, and the short-haired William Buckley crowd.

I interviewed a number of upper-middle-class people—trying to achieve a balance of opinion—to get a feeling of the city from their viewpoint. Several had been John Lindsay workers—stamp lickers, envelope folders, and mailers—during election campaigns. To a few he seemed to be the living, breathing twin to the Kennedy boys.

Now he's gone and his supporters think New York likes thick, short Irishmen, Jewish family men, or flashy Italians. It's not bigotry, they contend, merely a holding on to values. Lindsay looked good on the

Johnny Carson show and he was décor the city needed with all the mean-mouthing that was going on. However, many agreed that the high-class charmer had frequently disappointed his followers.

These upper-middle-class New Yorkers are remarkably able men and women—a board member of a mutual fund, an executive editor of a publishing house, a head buyer of women's clothes at a posh department store, a commercial bank vice-president.

They are still enthralled by the excitement of the city, the ease of getting to the theater, the opera, the ballet, the first-run movie. Though Central Park isn't safe to walk through at night, it's still a place to go during the day. There is Lincoln Center, Rockefeller Center, the United Nations, the great museums, the magnificent churches and cathedrals, and Madison Square Garden for big sporting events.

Of course, there are things that concern them: crime and violence in the streets, traffic and congestion in midtown and downtown areas, the decline of West 42nd Street into a row of porno movie houses and peep show parlors, street repairs that never catch up with the potholes, belated and inefficient removal of snow in winter (particularly in the boroughs of Brooklyn and Queens), the proliferation of sleazy stores and abandoned and stripped cars, graffiti on buildings and subway cars.

A banker friend of mine told me, "The whole world seems to be going down the drain. People are shocked at the graft in the city, payoffs to cops, payola as if it is something new. However, it's been going on a long time."

To many individuals with whom I've talked New York is still a great city. The Empire City it used to be called when I was young. But there's no denying the place has changed. So what can you do but put the whole place on an alert, double locks on your doors, buy two police dogs, and never protest when some street waif asks for your wallet and watch.

Affluent residents still live the good life. They may worry about conditions in the city and the world, but they sense they belong to some special order of New Yorker. To them New York is the only place to live.

The Melting Pot theory and Lady Bountiful charity of their fathers and grandfathers, in the days when it seemed that all races would become obedient to their betters, and live in accord, have gone out the window. The past was a mirage. Reality is school kids smoking, getting sex wisdom at an age when they once played with a teddy bear.

The middle-class New Yorker has to face drugs in his children's lockers and the unwashed smell of his sons, often dropouts with long hair, quoting Mick Jagger, Tim Leary, or some newer guru and listening to rock sounds on tape recorders given to them by parents who dug Irving Berlin and Cole Porter and Morton Downey.

❧

The city likes its legends. There are those who swear that under its major streets huge alligators thrive and multiply on the muck the city flushes into its vast network of sewer lines. 'Gators grown from pets sent up in the mails from Florida, and then flushed, either by accident or on purpose, through the outlets into the city's jungle.

A major myth—more easy to swallow—is that of the aftermath of the power blackout of November 1965. (NOBODY DIGS POWER FLOP [New York *Daily News* headline].) Did it produce a huge crop of babies just nine months later? Was this fertility caused by people caught without electric power, who were able to face a world without radio, television, or a trip to a neighborhood movie only if copulation was handy?

The story of the birth increase, reported by all the city newspapers as fact, was carried all over the world. There was some jesting discussion of it on the late-night talk shows. It was agreed *that* night was Liberty Hall—everybody who could, made out.

34

. . . and the Puerto Ricans

If New York's whites were bigoted about the blacks being in the majority, anti-Semitic, and pro-Arab, slum blacks in turn resented the Puerto Ricans—the *jíbaros*—immigrants who seemed, at first, hardly the minority to take over so much of the city, because of the language barrier and foreign styles of life, from food to music.

Nevertheless, the opposite has been true. Puerto Rico, an island under U.S. administration since the Spanish-American War, was a disgrace—a nest of disease and poverty. Named "Rich Port" by Ponce de Léon, it had not prospered. Nearly two million in population by 1940, it had the highest birth rate in the world. There was no industry, and the island's crops—sugar, mango, tamarind, and papaya—were all in the hands of American exploiters and native whites. No one had enough to eat, and the population presented a textbook of diseases.

The right of migration to New York City had, by 1930, brought 45,000 Puerto Ricans to the city, mostly to East Harlem—from 97th to 125th streets and from Fifth to Third Avenue—with a growing colony in Brooklyn. They packed the old-law tenements, got out the oil and the rice and red beans, and prepared to stay. One report observed: "The American Negro is inclined to resent all the people from the West Indies because of their competition in the labor market."

Disliked or not, by 1940 70,000 of them were settled in the city. As air travel made it cheap and simple to come from San Juan to the city, 40,000 a year were coming north by 1946. Four years later there were 250,000 Puerto Ricans and their children in New York.

If the men found it hard to get employment, the women became sewing machine operators and houseworkers. In World War II 65,000 Puerto Ricans went into the army and fought well. During the Korean conflict 43,500 served in the army, almost all volunteers.

The Latin calm, the taste for *Pescado Gursada*, the old family ties with the island and the church are breaking up. Conflicts are developing between parents and the children as the latter grow up. The new generation seeks rock and roll, a wider part of the larger culture; the young Puerto Rican resents the accent with which he is tainted and feels stuck between the blacks, who dislike him, and the whites, who still think of him as a kind of tropical semi-ape.

The younger generation is moving out slowly from the bind of a minority. And the older? In an average year 30,000 return to the island.

The Spanish-speaking poor, like the ghetto blacks, live, for the most part, in a welfare world. Some of the young are resorting to prostitution, pimping, robbery, and drugs. One can read cheerful predictions of the future in reports, but the present is grim, and the decaying districts in which the poor live shame the high-rise towers they can see from the rotting windowsills of their crowded tenements.

Unlike the black, the Puerto Rican is not sure who he is racially. Today, officially, one-fifth of Puerto Ricans can be listed as Negroes. As for the rest, I have been unable to find any text that can sort out with certainty the percentages of people with pure Spanish genes, those with a black or Indian strain, and those with a mixture of all three.

⋖§≥

In the early 1970s it was apparent, even to the casual visitor, that New York and the nation were changing.

It was more than a loss of innocence (an innocence that has never really existed in New York anyway—only legend and the Old Nostalgia could think of the city as ever having a sense of trust in its politicians, fat cats in city government).

Peter Schrag, a well-known British journalist, recently pointed out that by the 1970s the blinders were off. There was an admission of the problems, a feeling of fear, and a sense that the country could not, if these conditions continued, change for the better.

35
Mayoral Musical Chairs

One of the singular facets of our contemporary world is the radical alteration in life styles and the marked changes in public attitudes. A recent article in the *New Yorker* pinpoints the phenomenon quite clearly:

> Louis Harris concludes that the change in American life and thought has been all but revolutionary, and he thinks that a failure to recognize this accounts for the failure of our political leaders to command respect or have much effect on events. Before the last world war, there were a number of institutions and professions—the church, the federal government, education and educators, and so on—that commanded the respect of a majority of Americans. Today, there is not a single one that holds the esteem of fifty per cent. . . .

A top politician who agreed with the change in public attitudes was Mayor John Lindsay, speaking in 1972: "I ran for President at the wrong time. But I have no regrets at having done it. Absolutely none . . . it was a very interesting experience to see if another political approach was workable. And it clearly was not workable."

For a likable, honest mayor, lots of things didn't seem to work. During his terms in office there were always those news items of major wrongdoings. For instance, eleven present and former city narcotics detectives were indicted on charges of selling narcotics they had seized during arrests of large-scale narcotics dealers, from December 1969 through the fall of 1970, and dividing among themselves the proceeds.

That is how it was during Lindsay's two terms as Mayor of New York. John Vliet Lindsay came to the mayor's office as a forty-four-year-old former congressman from the Silk Stocking district of Manhattan.

Lindsay said his years as mayor were "The best . . . I've ever had. It's been a really glorious period. Even the bad parts . . . It's really been an unbelievable experience, uplifting. Being a six-foot, four-inch WASP has its advantages. But it sure has distinct disadvantages, too."

There is a lot of truth in the self-appraisal. Lindsay's first meeting with old labor leader Mike Quill had been a bit raspy.

"Mr. Mayor," the head of the Transport Workers said, "why don't you grow up? You're a Boy Scout in knee pants." And the strikes came and went for eight years.

Lindsay tried to improve the city. He created 29 new police stations, a police headquarters building, and 140 schools. Facilities were modernized, 2,300 miles of streets got high-intensity lighting, and police teams on the beat were equipped with walkie-talkies. But even computer modernization of the sanitation department couldn't get the streets clean. The Lindsay administration was plagued by crime and scandals—the conviction of Water Commissioner James Marcus; the bribery indictment of Youth Services Commissioner Ted Gross; revelations by the Knapp Commission of corruption within the New York City Police Department.

Was Lindsay aware of the scope of police corruption? Certainly he shied away from it. Like Willie Loman, he "wanted to be well liked."

◆§§◆

Early in 1974 while ex-mayor John Lindsay, a sometime star on the Johnny Carson talk show, was sailing to the West Indies, Abraham Beame, mayor-elect, was in City Hall thinking of new drapes for his office. Beame, a bit over five feet tall, sometimes stood on a chair while addressing reporters or being photographed for television.

A serious, hard-working, lifetime politician, he had once been a high-school teacher of accounting, later became Budget Director under Mayor Vincent Impellitteri, and then was elected City Comptroller twice in the 1960s. He had steered a budget that at times came to nearly $10.5 billion per year. He also looked after the $6-billion city pensions funds.

In November 1973, running against four opponents—Norman Mailer and Jimmy Breslin played street-jester candidates—Beame captured 57 percent of the votes cast. Among the spoils of victory he had the power to appoint four deputy mayors, a process that resulted in some of the most comic pratfall shambles ever seen in City Hall.

Beame promised no appointments would be made until the candidates had been screened and found fit for office "by a committee of distinguished citizens" and the city's Commissioner of Investigation. It turned out to be just eyewash.

The first signs of confusion and trouble appeared as soon as the new mayor mentioned the name of a certain man as being qualified to be a deputy mayor, a man who ran a small insurance business and was a close early buddy of the mayor's son, Bernard "Buddy" Beame.

There were immediate protests. Then the mayor announced that another deputy mayor he wanted was a former Commissioner of Buildings. So far, all nominees had been white party workers. There were approximately 1.7 million blacks in New York City, most of them vocal and skilled in harassment tactics against Whitey. They now asked, *where* is the Negro deputy mayor for us?

The mayor nodded and mentioned the name of a man who had led the black voters toward Beame. The candidate was labeled "a sheer genius" by one of his political friends, with no qualifying detail about his special talents. Some black power people also wondered—and made it clear to the mayor that to them the party worker was "a man who's not known to anybody." Again a hunt went on for a proper black man, and the next name put up for consideration as the first black deputy mayor of New York was that of a one-time member of the Board of Elections and "a main wheel in a big law firm."

It was time for the Spanish-speaking people—nearly one million of them in the city—to demand one of *their* own as a deputy mayor.

The early buddy candidate, the insurance man, would settle for being Director of Special Programs, so the mayor expected no trouble there. But in the meantime someone had sent out letters to 600 customers of his company—nothing illegal in that—cheerfully explaining how he was now on the mayor's staff, adding, "My circumstances will no doubt enable you to get even greater benefits from your association with —— Brokerage Company."

The resulting outcry over this promotion letter was shrugged off as "nit-picking . . . a question of semantics . . . poor sentence structure." Certainly grammar had never before figured just this way in politics. Mayor Beame, cornered about the candidate's letter, said, "He is not with us anymore."

Additional difficulties developed when the man to be appointed the first black deputy mayor suddenly withdrew from the honor, muttering that he had "unsolved tax matters," which turned out to be four years of undeclared, unfiled city, state, and federal tax returns. He had paid up at the last moment, explaining that he hadn't "committed a crime. What I did was fail to comply with the law."

The cry out of Harlem and all over the city where the black belt was expanding was, *where* is our Negro D.M.? Mayor Beame pored over lists and came up with the name of a state senator. The mayor assured the city that the black senator had passed with "flying colors all the tests"— tests for honesty, integrity, and no hands in anybody's pockets.

The senator announced he would resign his post at once. However, he didn't follow through on the promise. As he prepared to come to City Hall to be sworn in at a mass public ceremony, the senator may have been aware that a journalist was investigating his rather loose reporting of certain money in funds raised for him for political campaigning. It seemed that $2,050 in collected funds was unreported and most likely illegally collected and disposed of. The senator explained in haste that there was "a special campaign committee" that got all that money, made up of his wife, daughter, and son-in-law.

When Mayor Beame heard about this development, he decided *not* to swear in the senator on the morrow, and the candidate was told of the mayor's adverse reaction. The senator stated that whatever he was guilty of, it was "only maybe bad accounting." He said the mayor had promised him the job and the black brothers wouldn't like it if he wasn't sworn in. He'd raise a real ruction. But when a district attorney began to dig up the details, the mayor reported that the senator had decided to bow out.

So the problem still remained of finding a stainless man to be the first black deputy mayor of the city. It wasn't that there weren't thousands of honest Negroes in the city, but the appointed individual also had to have political muscle, be a loyal party man, and possess the savvy to perform in office for the party's good.

So one morning all the brothers and sisters, the important political blacks of the city and the ward bosses, were there in City Hall to see the first black deputy mayor being sworn in—Paul Gibson.

The mayor was one of those loyal men who liked to put old friends into public positions—creating almost a wall of defense around himself. He appointed a lawyer friend—an honest man—to run the Taxi and Limousine Commission (an important job in an overburdened city where the streets can't hold the traffic, and the taxis crawl crosstown slower than a glacier). Since the days of Mayor Jimmy Walker, the taxi business had often been run by racketeers. The lawyer appointed by Mayor Beame had been the legal representative for medallion (hereditary rights to hack) taxi owners, most of whom were white—Jewish or Italian. The lawyer's appointment did not sit well with the gypsy black and Puerto Rican taxi drivers—they didn't want to be controlled by a man who had represented the medallion crowd. (The so-called "gypsy" cab was usually a car-for-hire that could be mistaken for a taxi. It did not have to have a meter and could charge whatever it liked.)

The mayor was caught in turmoil. It was not only the blacks, the Spanish-speaking, and the Jews of the city who were making demands, screaming unfair, and talking of taking to the streets. The Italians also wanted something. There were nearly two million of them in the city, and an Italian-American Committee was set up to put pressure on the mayor and ask *why* was there no Italian-American deputy mayor?

The problem in dealing with Italian-American groups in New York was that no matter what the front was called, someplace there could be Mafia leadership, backing, money, and guns. During Lindsay's mayorship there was a mass meeting of Italian-Americans in Columbus Circle to demand that they no longer be portrayed as mob men and godfathers in films and radio and to protest against discrimination. This rally had ended with the founder-backer, a head of an important Mafia family, being shot down by a black gunman, who himself was at once assassinated—by, it was suspected, the mob that fingered the killing.

Ex-mayor Lindsay, who was fishing in West Indian waters, during the deputy mayors shambles and comedy routines, said he didn't think he'd run for public office for a year or so. Lindsay admitted that he had always felt the lure of show business. He might, he said, give television a try. Pinned down, he confessed, "I'd love to do one or more documentaries on what cities are all about. . . ."

36
Summing Up

One's first view of the city, from plane, ship, or bridge, is still breathtaking. From its solid-stone foundation rise skyscrapers, crowded more closely now than ever, dominated by the twin towers of the new World Trade Center. It is a vertical city on a magnificent harbor and busy rivers—a natural setting for great achievements, as first recognized by European explorers. Once an island hunted over by well-satisfied barbarians who produced neither gunpowder nor machines, the city is now so tightly packed—laced together by its bridges and tunnels—that it seems nothing else can be added. It is a city bizarre, monolithic, and perhaps doomed.

Here still are the money markets of the nation and much of the world: the Stock Exchange and the powerful, secretive private banks of the Morgans, the Rockefellers, the Lehmans, and others. And in this city once noted for its journalism, one solid, full-sized newspaper survives. New York remains the center for the publishing of trade books and the creating of best sellers, book clubs, and bland reviewing. There is a garment industry that has always outproduced Paris and now is often outdesigning it, too.

The great stores—Bergdorf Goodman, Lord & Taylor, Saks—are not the bastions of merchandising and style they once were. Now they are branching out into the suburbs, cutting down their dependence on their original settings. As for the more mass-appeal stores—Macy's, Gimbel's, Bloomingdale's—they have leveled off to compete with the standards of Sears, Ward's, J. C. Penney's, Grant's and the discount centers.

The fabulous eating places where disciples of great chefs worked with the best butter and crêpes soaked in orange brandy have come down to overcharging for ordinary food and fancy settings. As a gourmet friend wrote me after a tour of the most touted New York eating places:

> Even what should have been top cuisine by price and reputation is second, even third rate. Too much frozen, dried food prepared ahead of time. Careless cooking, even the service in places claiming *cuisine française*, Continental, is many times slovenly. The more the cost of the meal, *ristorante ultimo*, the more you often are getting inferior food.
>
> You can find some good regional Greek, Indian, Italian, some Chinese eating places where the food is decent. Luchow's, Romeo Salta, Monsignore, Mercurio's are satisfying if no longer reasonable in price.

New York flourishes as an international art and junk market. Sotheby Parke-Bernet makes history with the prices it gets for pictures, ceramics, and furniture. But a canny Parisian art dealer I've known for years is not impressed by New York auction prices.

"It's status buying by people without too much taste but a great deal of money. They buy names, periods, to acquire class they themselves lack. In New York everything older than last week is an 'antique,' and prints, etchings, and lithographs, which are, of course, nothing more than reproductions on paper, go for costs people will some day regret.

"Meanwhile, since the masterworks of solid value are rare on the art market, New York has developed a kind of Emperor's New Clothes Syndrome; make your own instant geniuses, have them paint a board blue, copy a beer can, pull a plaster cast of someone seated on a real toilet or motorbike, raise up a twenty-foot enema bag, draw a line down a canvas and 'voilà!' New York galleries have the stuff to feed the foolish rich, the endowed loafers of your museums, which are social status clubs."

The theater of ideas and genius does not flourish in New York, and the great film palaces have gone down before the wrecker's ball, or have been changed over to other uses. Yet New York reviews can make or break a play—and often a film. New York critics' awards are taken seriously, unlike Hollywood's senile, oddly selected Academy Awards.

The city does remain active, vital. On certain days it is beautiful, exciting, invigorating. Its girls are magnificently lush, its fashions marvelously imaginative, and its citizens—from the dispatch-case-and-furled-umbrella-carrying broker to the East Village dropout in already outmoded long hair, beard, and soiled feet—give the city a many-sided flavor. The winos and flophouse bums know they are characters. The hired hands move Seventh Avenue's dress carts, and the police continue to write thousands of traffic tickets as double-parking spreads to triple-parking.

The great avenues of New York still provide magnificent vistas, and the people step along with a sense of going someplace. They are, perhaps, a bit too fish-belly white, often jumpy, usually in a hurry. But New Yorkers are lively, pert, and to some just a bit too loud and not given to manners, either in Times Square or Lincoln Center.

If there is health in movement, in doing, being, creating, husking, trading, buying, selling, New York is alive and kicking. "At Dracula time—sundown"—everyone seems to be aware of the coming of darkness. There is a pattern of talk of the grabber, the mugger, the flasher, the stud for sale, the drug addict on the prowl to make the daily cost of his habit, and the booted whore on duty.

~§§~

On November 7, 1974, Mayor Abraham Beame had to remind the city that, besides its acceptance of its everyday crime problems as normal, there could emerge something bigger than grabbing purses or lifting a TV set from an apartment to pay for a drug habit. Commissioner Nicholas Scoppetta had just handed him the results of a two-year investigation of the habitual long-standing and widespread graft and corruption among the top department heads, down to the inspectors, among the city's 750 employees in the Building Department.

The mayor said at a City Hall news conference: "I cannot recall any scandal as pervasive as the one shown in this report. I am outraged, shocked, and damned angry . . . I am determined to use the full power of the law to see to it that bribe-takers and bribe-givers are prosecuted and punished."

The cold print of bribe-taking and corruption in the Scoppetta inquiry included systematic payoffs to some ninety-five Building Department employees, including nine top executives, fifteen supervisors, forty-three inspectors, and twenty-eight office employees and plans examiners. Involved in the corruption were people in the building trades, landlords, real-state agents, and managers.

The preliminary report of the two-year investigation covering the five boroughs charged that bribes to employees of the city's Housing and Development Administration ranged from $5 to $5,000. In some cases inspectors were on monthly "pads" to receive payments ranging from $100 to $300. The average corrupt inspector, the report said, could double his salary of $11,000 to $18,950 a year. Aggressive inspectors made $20,000 to $30,000 a year in graft.

The mayor announced the creation of a special review board "to come up with specific recommendations to insure reliable, safe construction free of the yoke of corruption."

I talked about the Scoppetta Report to a man, now retired and living on the West Coast, who once ran night spots in New York City.

"Don't make me laugh," he said. "Another commission? Another report? Then the same old cycle of graft and payoffs starts again. Let me tell you it can take about forty thousand in handouts to open a top eating place, a posh club in New York. There's the cash laid out to be permitted to knock down walls, to okay new blueprints, the graft to get your wiring passed, the handout for the plumbing inspection. How many crappers, how many urinals does the law say? And how many do you really need? Then there's the fire inspection; for that, not just a case or two of Scotch, but solid moola.

"There's the bar permit, the liquor license—it's a *long* way from New York to Albany. The Health Department has to give you the nod for the kitchen layout, and they can find a hundred little things to make you tear out your refrigerators, dishwashers, gas stoves, grease traps, flues, meat safes, unless you come up with the long green.

"I'm not saying they all take in the Building Department, or that you can't open a restaurant or club without city payoffs. I accept miracles. Never saw any, but they're there. So I just paid. Sure, I'm guilty as hell. But, like a hundred thousand other business people in the city, I never had any place to go to demand honest inspecting."

If one studies the last census figures—1970—one wonders where it will all come together in change and what that change will be. The city racks up $12 billion in retail sales a year. The average family income of those not on welfare is a bit over $10,000, but that's average, and no one seems to be average.

Since the days of the Dutch the population of the city has always been on the move, and some of those who move never come back. In the last ten years more than one million whites have left New York City and 500,000 blacks have moved in. One does not have to be Archie Bunker to see how unhealthy this pattern is.

I have watched in the mornings a daily migration of managers and workers coming into the city from the suburbs—from Jersey, Long Island, the far reaches of Connecticut, Scarsdale, Tuxedo Park, Great Neck, Rye, and Yonkers—by car and bus, train and subway. They enter tall buildings, where photocopying machines live cheek by jowl with computers and IBM punch cards, to begin the daily round of ordering cities, nations, and much of the world, doing its business in hog bellies, mutual bonds, frozen and processed foods, chemicals, textiles, shapes in steel, and the newer plastics.

The airports surrounding the city are horror pits—Black Holes of Calcutta expanded into sweeping, meaningless modern forms. Flying into or out of New York is an ordeal: Planes from Canadian cities, from California, Florida, Chicago, Japan, and Latin America are stacked in layers over Brooklyn, Long Island, and parts of New Jersey, the passengers hoping they will not have to circle for too many hours.

Below, in the airports, gone is any trace of leisure, grace, or comfort in travel, no matter what one pays. There is no charm, no comfort in traveling by air. It is a modern version of nineteenth-century steerage passage. Getting one's baggage can be a nightmare of delay and lost or damaged luggage.

The city itself is shackled by traffic all day long. The taxis crawl, the sidewalks are booby-trapped with dog turds. Still, comes twilight and the lights go on—even if dimmed by an energy crisis—and the city becomes for a few hours to some of us—and I am among them—what it was after the turn of the century, when Flo Ziegfeld and George M. Cohan made its music and dance steps and when the best of foods was served by well-trained old waiters, what it was even in the age of Jimmy Walker, when O'Neill was at the Theatre Guild, Cab Calloway at the Cotton Club. Then New York is like no other city has ever been.

If the faces are now of many colors, the language basic ("Man, you know, like"), if the air is polluted and the headlines on the Times Building speak of a less placid, less proud world, New York City retains a sound, a greatness, a vital image—all set in a kind of patina that suggests that it had a hell of a past and that the surface is hard enough to attempt a risky future.

◄§►

It seems fitting to end this book at a time when New York faces another change. The city will go on, and its story will still be one of continual moving from one era into another, from one pattern of life that has slowed to a walk or lost its drive into a new one that promises, for a little while anyway, more color and action. But also a stirring of aspirations, a bolder dreaming, newer art forms, and bigger swindles.

What marks a New Yorker, born or adopted, lonely or gregarious, is the faculty of enjoying the city, even while griping about its arbitrariness and transiency.

If this book's theme could be put into a single line, it would be the words of Dylan Thomas, spoken as a tribute to the city one night in a Third Avenue saloon, "What does not kill me, makes me stronger."

Chronology of Events

1524   Giovanni da Verrazano sailed French *Dauphine* into New York Bay.

1526   Esteban Gomez sailed into New York harbor without landing.

1609   Henry Hudson, first European to land in New York, sailed *Half Moon* up the "great stream" to what is now Albany.

1610–1612   Trading begun between Holland and new American territory.

1621   Dutch West India Company formed to exploit and regulate trade.

1623   First permanent colonists arrived and settled on Governor's Island.

1626   Peter Minuit bought Manhattan Island from Indians and named site New Amsterdam.

1629   Dutch Government issued Charter of Privileges to Patroons to encourage settlement of colony.

1647   Peter Stuyvesant became director general of colony.

1654   Brooklyn sold to Dutch by Canarsie Indian tribe.

1654   First Jewish settler arrived in New Amsterdam.

1664   New Netherland captured by British and renamed New York, in honor of Duke of York.

1673   New York briefly recaptured by Dutch and renamed New Orange.

1674   New York ceded to British by Dutch for all time.

1682   Colony of New York divided into counties of New York (Manhattan), Kings (Brooklyn), Staten Island (Richmond), and Queens.

1689–1671   Jacob Leisler briefly seized New York from British, became boss and ruler, subsequently was tried for treason and hanged.

1700   Jesuits and other Catholic priests ordered out of New York.

1712   First slave uprising put down.

1725   The *Gazette*, New York's first newspaper, started by William Bradford.

1733   *The New York Weekly Journal* started by John Peter Zenger.

1735   In first recognition of freedom of the press, Zenger acquitted of libel charges.

1741   Slave rebellion put down, eighteen slaves hanged, fourteen burned, and seventy-one transported to West Indies.

1754   King's College (now Columbia University) chartered by George II.

1765   New Yorkers protest British Stamp Act by boycotting British goods.

1770   First American Revolutionary War fatality occurred when New Yorker was killed as mob fought British at Battle of Golden Hill.

1774   Cargo of British tea ship dumped into Hudson River by New Yorkers.

1776   George Washington entered New York to defend citizens from British, was repulsed at Harlem Heights and forced to retreat to White Plains. For balance of war, New York was held by British.

1776   Nathan Hale hanged as spy by General Howe.

1779   First St. Patrick's Day parade in New York presaged march of Irish to political power.

1783   British fled as American troops retook city.

1783   Washington said farewell to his officers at Fraunces Tavern.

1789   Washington inaugurated as President of the United States in New York, then the capital of the new nation.

1789   New York Tammany Society begun as a fraternal and patriotic organization of bankers and merchants.

1804   Right to vote for alderman granted to New York males paying $25 a year in rent.

1807   Master plan devised for numbering New York City streets and avenues.

1807–1809   U.S. Embargo Act forbidding trade with Britain created heavy suffering in New York shipping trade.

1812–1814   New York escaped invasion in War of 1812.

1815   First great wave of immigrants began through Port of New York.

1822   Epidemic of "Yellow Jack" fever raged in New York slums.

1825   Opening of Erie Canal made New York the nation's principal seaport and the gateway to the West.

1835   Native American Democratic Association formed to keep city government out of hands of foreign-born.

1836   Ancient Order of Hibernians, forerunner of Tammany Hall political machine, organized by Irish immigrants.

1837   Charles Tiffany opened dry goods and stationery store on Broadway, later to become today's Tiffany & Co. on Fifth Avenue.

1840   Tammany Society, changing original purpose, became political machine aimed at controlling votes of the masses, the state capital, the courts, and the judges.

1844   The Native Sons of America, the American Brotherhood, and The Native American Party, pro-American, antiforeigner groups, formed.

1849   Astor Place theater set afire as pro-American groups incited Irish to riot against performance of English actor, William Macready.

1850   William Marcy Tweed elected alderman of Seventh Ward.

1852   First dramatic version of *Uncle Tom's Cabin* played at Purdy's National Theater on the Bowery.

1852–1862   Ships out of New York harbor charged with being in the slave trade.

1853   First New York World's Fair opened.

1858   First Chinese settled in New York.

1860   Abraham Lincoln's speech at Cooper Union brought him national prominence, led to Republican nomination and his election to the presidency.

1863   Unjust Conscription Act created draft riots in New York. Two thousand were killed, and property damage exceeded five million dollars.

1863–1870   "Boss" Tweed held post of deputy street commissioner.

1866–1871   Tweed Ring dominated New York politics, dealing in patronage, controlling jobs, embezzling funds, and corrupting officeholders.

1868   The Benevolent and Protective Order of Elks formed. Originally for theater people, membership later opened to select males.

1868   Block-long tunnel dug under Broadway by Alfred Ely Beach, inventor and part owner of New York *Sun*, to prove subway feasible.

1868–1872   Abraham Oakey Hall, Tammany-elected mayor, fronted for the Tweed Ring, as it "stole the city blind."

1869   On "Black Friday," September 24, the bottom fell out of the gold market, ruined many stockbrokers, caused countrywide depression.

1870   New York City population came close to million mark.

1870   Boss Tweed failed to buy off *New York Times* and Thomas Nast, foremost attackers of Tweed Ring.

1870   Tweed Ring passed new city charter giving Tammany airtight control of New York City government.

1871   Ninth Avenue El trains began regular run; tracks were under construction on Second, Third, and Sixth Avenues.

1871   Criminal charges begun against Tweed Ring. "Committee of Seventy" accused Ring of unparalled villainy and subversion of free government.

1872   Railroad tycoon Jim Fisk shot by Edwin S. Stokes in love-triangle killing.

1872   Victoria Woodhull first woman to be nominated a candidate for president of the United States.

1873   Boss Tweed found guilty on 204 counts, sentenced to prison.

1875   The Reverend Henry Ward Beecher sued for alienation of affections in scandal that rocked New York.

1875   Tweed escaped while awaiting new trial, fled to Spain.

1876   Irishman Richard K. Fox became owner of notorious *National Police Gazette*, oldest weekly in America.

1876   Boss Tweed deported from Spain, returned to New York jail.

1882   John L. Sullivan became world heavyweight champion.

1882   Thomas A. Edison opened world's first central electric light power plant in New York.

1888   Great Blizzard paralyzed New York, trapped 15,000 in elevated trains.

1888–1891   Tammany rulers, who controlled surface transportation, defeated city's attempts to build subway.

1893   Emma Goldman sentenced to imprisonment for political agitation.

1893   Eleanora Duse in *Camille* and Sarah Bernhardt in *Phèdre* made New York debuts.

1897   Ulysses S. Grant buried in New York memorial tomb, built by public subscription.

1898   Counties of Brooklyn, Queens, and Richmond added to Greater New York.

1900   Twenty-five daily English-language papers, plus Italian and German dailies, and a Yiddish press flourished in New York.

1900   Fifty makers of "horseless carriages" exhibited models at Madison Square Garden.

1900   Easter Parade, begun in 1869, became annual New York event.

1900–1906   First Chinese tong wars erupted between rival clans.

1900–1915   Early Bohemia in Greenwich Village included such burgeoning writers as Sinclair Lewis, Lincoln Steffens, Theodore Dreiser, and Upton Sinclair.

1901   Flatiron Building opened at Broadway and 23rd Street.

1904   Excursion steamer *General Slocum* burned off Blackwells Island; over 1,000 lives were lost.

1904   Operation of New York's first subway line begun.

1905   Widespread investigations begun on management practices, following James Hazen Hyde's $200,000 society ball, openly charged to his insurance company. Charles Evans Hughes was chief investigator.

1906   Architect Stanford White shot and killed by millionaire Harry K. Thaw to avenge honor of Evelyn Nesbit, Thaw's wife.

1909–1910   Chinatown tong wars ended with aid of Chinese ambassador and Chinatown Committee of Forty.

1911   One hundred and forty-six lives lost in tragic Triangle Shirtwaist Factory fire.

1911   Main branch of The New York Public Library at Fifth Avenue and 42nd Street opened.

1911   Pujo Congressional Committee asserted "Money Trusts" concentrated financial power in hands of few, such as Morgan and Rockefeller interests.

1912   Racketeer payoffs to high-echelon police exposed by New York *World*.

1912   Over 200 New York lives lost in sinking of *Titanic*.

1912   Third Chinatown tong war suppressed when Chinese government threatened reprisals on relatives in China.

1912   IWW strikes at Patterson Mills and by New York waiters supported by socialite Mabel Dodge.

1913   "Robber Baron" J. P. Morgan died in Rome.

1913   New fashion in art started by avante-garde paintings exhibition at Seventh Regiment Armory.

1913   Vaudeville at its height featured Harry Lauder, Al Jolson, Irene and Vernon Castle, among many others.

1913   Woolworth Building, then the tallest in the world, opened.

1913   Grand Central Terminal opened.

1914   Bronx became a county of New York.

1914   German declaration of war against Allies supported by German-language newspaper *New Yorker Herald* and William Randolph Hearst's *Deutsches Journal*.

1914   John Purroy Mitchel became New York City's youngest mayor at age 34.

1916   Explosion at Black Tom, New Jersey munitions depot, which rocked New York, traced to German saboteurs.

1916   Charles Evans Hughes, Republican presidential nominee, defeated as Woodrow Wilson is reelected by last-minute California returns.

1917   Federal agents seized eighteen German ships, four anchored in Hudson, when war was declared on Germany.

1917   New York became port of embarkation for American Expeditionary Force en route to France.

1918–1919   International Spanish flu epidemic killed nearly 13,000 New Yorkers.

1918   Armistice signed as New York celebrated.

1919   Ring Lardner contributed to exposé of New York gambler's attempt to bribe Chicago White Sox players to throw the 1919 World Series.

1920   Old-time saloonkeepers mourned as Eighteenth Amendment ushered in the Speakeasy Age.

1920   Mysterious Wall Street explosion killed thirty-five people and injured over a hundred.

1922   Texas Guinan became most famous New York speakeasy hostess.

1922   First traffic-control standards erected on Fifth Avenue.

1923   Dixieland bands made Harlem the smart place for society to go.

1925   An estimated 100,000 speakeasies thrived in New York.

1925   *The Great Gatsby* written by F. Scott Fitzgerald, prophet of the Jazz Age of the twenties.

1926–1932   James J. Walker mayor of New York City.

1926   Death of Rudolf Valentino, motion picture idol.

1929   Wall Street crash ushered in Great Depression.

1930   Samuel Seabury, former associate justice of the State Court of Appeals, began official investigation of corruption in Mayor Walker's regime.

1931   Construction of Rockefeller Center begun; completed in 1939.

1932   Kidnapper of Charles Lindberg, Jr., hid out in Bronx.

1932   Jimmy Walker forced to resign as mayor "for the good of the party."

1933   New York banks closed when President Franklin D. Roosevelt declared national bank holiday.

1933   Rockefellers enraged by Diego Rivera's radical socialistic mural in RCA Building at Rockefeller Center. (Mural was later destroyed.)

1933	Prohibition repealed.
1934–1945	Fiorello H. La Guardia served as mayor, reformed New York City government.
1934–1960	Robert Moses, as New York commissioner of parks, created Jones Beach, miles of other beaches, acres of parks and playgrounds during his tenure.
1939–1940	New York World's Fair (World of Tomorrow) held on Flushing Meadows.
1938	Scientists at Columbia University split the atom.
1938	Disastrous hurricane struck New York and Eastern seaboard.
1939	Hitler-Stalin nonaggression pact signed as New York radicals cheered rigged Moscow trials.
1941	Two days after Pearl Harbor false air-raid alert reported unidentified planes approaching New York.
1942	Manhattan District, atomic bomb project, officially established.
1942–1945	New York was embarkation point for troops en route to war.
1946	William O'Dwyer elected mayor, but later police department scandal forced his resignation.
1951	Hearings opened in New York by Kefauver Committee to Investigate Organized Crime in Interstate Commerce.
1952	United Nations moved to present site on East River.
1954–1965	Robert F. Wagner, Jr., served as mayor of New York.
1957	Last trolley retired from New York streets.
1964–1965	Second World's Fair held on Flushing Meadows, dedicated to Peace Through Understanding. Michelangelo's Pietà loaned for exhibition by Vatican.
1965	Pope Paul VI, in New York to address United Nations, visits World's Fair.
1965–1973	John V. Lindsay served as mayor of New York.
1965	In November massive power failure blacked out New York and most of northeastern United States.
1967	Flower Children rallied in Central Park to protest Vietnam War and advocate peace and love among mankind.
1970	Gay Liberationists staged parade on Sixth Avenue.
1972	Mayor John Lindsay defeated in campaign for Democratic nomination for president.
1972	Knapp Commission reported mass corruption in New York City Police Department.
1973	Abraham Beame elected mayor, with 57 percent of votes cast.
1974	Paul Gibson sworn in as first black deputy mayor of New York.
1974	Graft payoffs by landlords to Housing and Development Administration employees revealed by Scopetta Commission.

Bibliography

Abbott, Lyman, *Henry Ward Beecher*. Boston: Houghton Mifflin, 1903.

Abels, Jules, *The Rockefeller Millions*. New York: Macmillan, 1965.

Ade, George, *The Old Time Saloon*. Chicago: Long & Smith, 1931.

Allen, Frederick Lewis, *Lords of Creation*. New York: Harper, 1935.

Amory, Cleveland, *The Last Resorts*. New York: Harper, 1941.

Andrew, Wayne, *The Vanderbilt Legend*. New York: Harcourt Brace, 1941.

Andrist, Ralph K., ed. *The Confident Years*. New York: Amer. Heritage, 1969.

Asbury, Herbert, *The Gangs of New York*. New York: Knopf, 1927.

Beebe, Lucius, *The Big Spenders*. New York: Doubleday, 1966.

Beecher, Henry Ward, *Lectures to a Young Man*. New York: 1860.

Beer, Thomas, *The Mauve Decade*. New York: Knopf, 1926.

Birmingham, Stephen, *Our Crowd*. New York: Harper, 1967.

Botkin, B. A., ed., *New York City Folklore*. New York: Random, 1956.

Browne, Julius Henri, *The Great Metropolis*. New York: 1869.

Callow, Alexander B., *The Tweed Ring*. New York: Oxford, 1966.

Churchill, Allen, *The Improper Bohemians*. New York: Crowell, 1957.

————, *The Year the World Went Mad*. New York: Crowell, 1961.

Colman, Elizabeth, *Chinatown, USA*. New York: Day, 1946.

Comstock, Anthony, *Traps for the Young*. New York: 1883.

Dickens, Charles, *American Notes*. London: (Date unknown).

Duffus, R. L., *Nostalgia, USA*. New York: Norton, 1963.

Einstein, Izzy, *Prohibition Agent No. 1*. New York: Stokes, 1932.

Ellis, Edward Robb, *The Epic of New York*. New York: Coward, 1966.

Ernst, Robert, *Immigrant Life in New York, 1825–1863*. New York: King Crown Press, 1949.

Farley, James A., *Jim Farley's Story*. New York: Whittlesey, 1948.

Fowler, Gene, *Beau James*. New York: Viking, 1949.

Genung, Abram Polhemus, *The Frauds of the New York City Government Exposed*. New York: 1871.

Ging, Eng Ying, and Grant, Bruce, *Tong War!* New York: N. L. Brown, 1924.

Glazer, Nathan, and Moynihan, Daniel, *Beyond the Melting Pot*. Cambridge, Mass.: M.I.T. Press, 1963.

Glick, Carl, and Hong, Sheng-Hwa, *Chinese Secret Societies*. New York: Whittlesey, 1947.

Greeley, Horace, *Recollections of a Busy Life*. New York: Ford & Co., 1868.

Hale, William Harian, *Horace Greeley*. New York: Colliers, 1961.

Hertford, Joseph, *Personals: or, Perils of the Period in New York*. New York: 1870.

Hibbin, Paxton, *Henry Ward Beecher*. New York: Doran, 1927.

Holbrook, Stewart, *The Age of the Moguls*. New York: Doubleday, 1953.

Horan, James, *The Desperate Years*. New York: Crown, 1962.

Hoyt, Edwin P., *Vanderbilts and Their Fortunes*. New York: Doubleday, 1962.

Johnson, Johanna, *Mrs. Satan.* New York: Putnam, 1967.

Josephson, Matthew, *The Robber Barons.* New York: Harcourt, 1934.

Keller, Morton, *The Art and Politics of Thomas Nast.* New York: Oxford, 1968.

Lehr, Elizabeth Drexel, *King Lehr and the Gilded Age.* New York: Blue Ribbon, 1938.

Lewis, Arthur, *The Day They Shook the Plum Tree.* New York: Harcourt, 1963.

Lippard, George, *The New York Upper Ten of the Lower Million.* 1854.

Lord, Walter, *The Good Years.* New York: Harper, 1960.

Luhan, Mabel Dodge, *Intimate Memories.* New York: Harcourt, 1933–1937.

Lundberg, Frederick, *Imperial Hearst.* New York: Equinox, 1936.

Lynch, Denis Tilden, *Boss Tweed.* New York: Boni, 1927.

Matz, Mary Jane, *The Many Lives of Otto Kahn.* New York: Macmillan, 1963.

McCabe, James D., Jr., *Lights and Shadows of New York Life.* Philadelphia: National Pub., 1872.

McCullough, David, *The Great Bridge.* New York: Simon & Schuster, 1972.

Meyer Berger's New York. New York: Random, 1960.

Meyers, Gustavus, *History of Bigotry in the U.S.* New York: Random, 1943.

————, *History of Great American Fortunes.* New York: Modern Library, 1936.

Mezzrow, Milton, and Wolf, Bernard, *Really the Blues.* New York: Random, 1946.

Millett, Kate, *Sexual Politics.* New York: Doubleday, 1970.

Minnigerode, Meade, *The Fabulous Forties, 1840–1850.* New York: Putnam, 1924.

Morrell, Parker, *Diamond Jim.* New York: Simon & Schuster, 1934.

Morris, Lloyd R., *Incredible New York.* New York: Random House, 1951.

Mumford, Lewis, *The Brown Decades, 1865–1895.* New York: Dover, 1955.

Narratives of New Netherland, 1609–1664. New York: Scribner, 1909.

New York Society for Suppression of Vice, *Reports,* 1874–1891.

O'Connor, Richard, *The Scandalous Mr. Bennett.* New York: Doubleday, 1962.

————, *Gould's Millions.* New York: Doubleday, 1962.

Paine, Albert Bigelow, *Thomas Nast.* New York: Harper, 1934.

Peel, Roy V., *Political Clubs of New York.* New York: Putnam, 1935.

Philip Hone, His Diary, 1828–1851. New York: Rinehart, 1957.

Phillips, Cabell, *From the Crash to the Blitz, 1929–1939. N.Y. Times,* 1965.

Pisani, Lawrence, *The Italian in America.* Jericho, N. Y.: Exposition Press, 1959.

Reid, Ed, *The Shame of New York.* New York: Random, 1953.

Reynolds, James Bronson, ed., *Civic Biography of Greater New York.* New York: 1911.

Sachs, Emanie, *Terrible Siren, Victoria Woodhull.* New York: Harper, 1928.

Sann, Paul, *The Lawless Decade.* New York: Crown, 1967.

Schlesinger, Arthur M., Jr., *The Crisis of the Old Order, 1919–1933.* New York: Houghton Mifflin, 1957.

Schriftgiesser, Karl, *Oscar of the Waldorf.* New York: Dutton, 1943.

Schwab, Arnold T., *James Gibbons Huneker.* Stanford: Stanford U. Pr., 1963.

Seitz, Don C., *The Dreadful Decade.* New York: Bobbs, 1926.

Seldes, George, *Lords of the Press.* New York: Blue Ribbon, 1938.

Shannon, William V., *The American Irish.* New York: Macmillan, 1963.

Singleton, Esther, *Social New York Under the Georges, 1714–1776*. New York: Appleton, 1902.

Smith, Alfred E., *Up to Now, An Autobiography*. New York: Viking, 1929.

Smith, Arthur D. Howden, *John Jacob Astor: Landlord of New York*. New York: Blue Ribbon, 1929.

Smith, Matthew Hale, *Sunshine and Shadow in New York*. Hartford, Conn.: Burr, 1868.

Sonders, Frederic, Jr., *Brotherhood of Evil: The Mafia*. New York: Farrar, Straus & Giroux, 1959.

Soule, George, *Prosperity Decade, 1917–1929*. New York: Rinehart, 1947.

Steffens, Lincoln, *The Autobiography of Lincoln Steffens*. New York: Harcourt, 1931.

Steinman, David B., *The Building of the Bridges: The Story of John Roebling and His Son*. New York: Harcourt, 1945.

Stevenson, Elizabeth, *Babbits and Bohemians*. New York: Macmillan, 1967.

Still, Bayrd, *Mirror for Gotham*. New York: NYU Pr., 1956.

Stokes, I. N. Phelps, ed., *Iconography of Manhattan Island*. New York: Dodd, 1928.

Stowe, Lyman Beecher, *Saints, Sinners and Beechers*. New York: Bobbs, 1934.

Strong, George Templeton, *The Diary*. 4 vols. New York: Macmillan, 1952.

Sullivan, Mark, *Our Times*. New York: Scribner, 1935.

Swanberg, W. A., *Citizen Hearst*. New York: Viking, 1961.

————, *Jim Fisk*. New York: Scribner, 1959.

————, *Luce*. New York: Scribner, 1972.

Sylvester, Robert, *No Cover Charge: A Backward Look at the Night Clubs*. New York: Dial, 1956.

Talese, Gay, *A Serendipiter's Journey*. New York: Knopf, 1961.

Tebbel, John, *The Life and Good Times of William Randolph Hearst*. New York: Dutton, 1952.

Van Every, Edward, *Sins of New York*. New York: Stokes, 1930.

Van Wyck, Frederick, *Recollections of an Old New Yorker*. New York: Liveright, 1932.

Walker, Stanley, *The Night Club Era*. New York: Stokes, 1933.

————, *Mrs. Astor's Horse*. New York: Stokes, 1935.

Wecter, Dixon, *The Saga of American Society*. New York: Scribner, 1937.

Werner, M. R., *Tammany Hall*. New York: Doubleday, 1928.

Wilson, Edmund, *American Earthquake*. New York: Doubleday, 1958.

Winkler, John, *Morgan the Magnificent*. New York: Star Books, 1932.

Young, Art, *On My Way*. New York: Viking, 1928.

Zangwill, Israel, *The Melting Pot*. New York: Macmillan, 1909.

Ziff, Larzer, *The American 1870s*. New York: Viking, 1966.

Index

Index

1977